# Research Methods
in **POLITICS &**
**INTERNATIONAL**
**RELATIONS**

# Research Methods
in **POLITICS &**
**INTERNATIONAL**
**RELATIONS**

Christopher Lamont
& Mieczysław P. Boduszyński

Los Angeles | London | New Delhi
Singapore | Washington DC | Melbourne

Los Angeles | London | New Delhi
Singapore | Washington DC | Melbourne

SAGE Publications Ltd
1 Oliver's Yard
55 City Road
London EC1Y 1SP

SAGE Publications Inc.
2455 Teller Road
Thousand Oaks, California 91320

SAGE Publications India Pvt Ltd
B 1/I 1 Mohan Cooperative Industrial Area
Mathura Road
New Delhi 110 044

SAGE Publications Asia-Pacific Pte Ltd
3 Church Street
#10-04 Samsung Hub
Singapore 049483

Editor: John Nightingale
Editorial Assistant: Eve Williams
Production Editor: Manmeet Kaur Tura
Copyeditor: Sarah Bury
Proofreader: Sharon Cawood
Indexer: David Rudeforth
Marketing Manager: Susheel Gokarakonda
Cover Design: Francis Kenney
Typeset by: C&M Digitals (P) Ltd, Chennai, India
Printed in the UK

**Library of Congress Control Number: 2019949073**

**British Library Cataloguing in Publication data**

A catalogue record for this book is available from the
British Library

ISBN 978-1-5264-1907-1
ISBN 978-1-5264-1908-8 (Pbk)

# CONTENTS

# LIST OF TABLES AND FIGURES

# ABOUT THE AUTHORS

**Christopher Lamont** is Assistant Dean of E-Track Programs and Associate Professor of International Relations at the Institute for International Strategy, Tokyo International University.

**Mieczysław P. Boduszyński** is Associate Professor of Politics and International Relations at Pomona College, California.

# ACKNOWLEDGMENTS

This book would not have been possible without the feedback of students who have enrolled in our classes, as well as that of students whose thesis projects we have supervised in recent years at the University of Groningen, Pomona College, and Tokyo International University. We would also like to thank Natalia Aguilera at Sage who started the conversation on writing a textbook with accessibility to students as its primary aim. Later, John Nightingale and Eve Williams played an instrumental role in pushing us to meet deadlines and deliver the final book. Their input also guided us to writing what we feel will be a very useful and accessible introductory-level methods book. We also wish to thank Erica Dobbs and Graham Odell for their advice and assistance.

# INTRODUCTION

As students of Politics and International Relations (PIR), you will aspire to do more than simply read about debates about politics and international affairs in the classroom. Hopefully, you will also want to contribute to these debates in your own voice. Research skills give us the ability to put forth observations and arguments that get noticed. This textbook on research methods provides you with a practical guide for doing your own research. The methodological and methods debates that you will encounter in the chapters of this book are presented primarily for the purpose of demonstrating how understanding these debates constitutes a prerequisite to understanding and defining your research purpose and situating it in PIR scholarship. As such, this is not a textbook on political theory or international relations theory, although you will notice that we draw upon debates informed by both.

Both of us have taught undergraduate and graduate students from a wide range of backgrounds over the years. We have taught at institutions in Europe, the United States, and Japan, and our students have hailed from almost every country in the world. We are aware that PIR are taught differently in various national contexts. At times, this reflects the idiosyncrasies of how these disciplines emerged. In the United States, politics is often taught as 'political science,' whereas in the United Kingdom, it is not labeled as such. In some European traditions, the study of politics takes place within faculties of law, while international relations has distinct roots in departments of history. By contrast, in the United States, international relations is often seen as a sub-field of political science, or is taught in the context of interdisciplinary international studies programs. As a result, many of you who enroll in classes that require you to write essays on PIR topics will have different kinds of exposure to research norms and expectations. In this textbook, we have included examples from research practice drawn from numerous research traditions and best practice guidelines from a number of different countries. Moreover, when surveying PIR scholarship, you will notice a broad diversity of debates, methods, and approaches used by scholars. As we will emphasize throughout this textbook, PIR is defined by diversity. We do not aim to bring homogeneity to research practice, but rather to emphasize the richness and plurality of research practice in our field while also highlighting certain characteristics of all good research.

Our aim in this textbook is to provide you with an accessible resource that will be relevant to the challenges you will face when undertaking your own research projects, regardless of where you might be studying. As such, our hope is that not only will this textbook provide you with the ability to independently carry out your own research, but also to gain a strong appreciation of diverse research practices and traditions in PIR.

# 1

# Getting Started

━━━━━━━━━━ Learning Objectives ━━━━━━━━━━

- To distinguish between methodology and methods;
- To understand how methodological debates shape research in PIR;
- To grasp why methodology and research methods can be seen as a framework for making research choices;
- To describe the choices you will make as part of the research process.

---

If you have picked up this book, you are likely on the cusp of beginning your very own research project. Whether it is a paper or an essay for a class, bachelor's thesis, or a post-graduate thesis, a core element of academic writing in Politics and International Relations (PIR) remains constant, and that is **methodology** and **methods**. While you may see learning methodology and mastering methods as a chore, it may help to consider that methodology and methods are simply expressions of what you want to know and how you aim to go about knowing it.

Because PIR **research** is a systematic activity in which we analyze or interpret the social world around us, we need to think critically about how we are going to go about trying to make sense of complex practices and processes that make up politics or international affairs. Our aim as researchers is to help resolve conflicts over different interpretations, understandings, and explanations of the reality which we inhabit. In order to do this, we must consider the ways in which we produce knowledge (how we do research) and the ways in which we evaluate knowledge claims (how we evaluate and make judgments about research). But what distinguishes research from other kinds of written work? What tools of the trade must one learn before engaging in the craft of research? Is all research of equal value? How can we tell good research from bad research?

For some, the answer to this last question is the **scientific method** (Van Evera 1997). According to Moses and Knutsen, the scientific method is 'a process that involves systematic observation, scrupulous note taking of things and patterns observed, and thoughtful efforts to make sense of it all' (2012, 19). The scientific method was first applied to making sense of the natural world, in the natural sciences. Biologists and chemists tested theories, or law-like propositions, through empirical observation or experimentation. Later, it was applied to the social world, or the social sciences. For some scholars of PIR, such as Stephen Van Evera, there is no reason that the standards of research should differ between the natural sciences and the social sciences. Van Evera argues, 'I remain unpersuaded by the view that the prime rules of scientific method should differ between "hard sciences" and the social sciences. Science is science' (1997, 3). Yet, other scholars argue that the standards and practices we use to learn about natural phenomena like the weather are ill-suited to furthering our understanding of complex social practices. In Chapter 2, we will delve deeper into this debate.

**Methodology** has been defined in a number of ways in social science literature. According to Gerring, methodology refers to the 'tasks, strategies, and criteria governing scientific inquiry, including all facets of the research enterprise' (2012, 6). Linda Tuhiwai Smith tells us that methodology is a 'theory of method' or, in other words, the reasoning that informs which methods we use in our research (2012, 1). Others, like Moses and Knutsen, argue more generally that methodology is a way of knowing or a way of making sense of the social world (2012, 4). What does this all mean in terms of doing our own research? Methodologies are the underlying assumptions about what is knowable and how we know about the social world around us. This social world we inhabit includes all facets of life, from major international crises and interstate wars to the mundane and everyday choices we make. Indeed, before we can go on to evaluate which particular approach you might find most useful for your own research, you will need to stake out a methodological position to justify your choice of those strategies.

While the aforementioned debates over the ways in which we know will inform our overall research strategies, what about the means by which we know? For example, what if you are interested in explaining voter behavior in the 2016 US presidential elections? If so, have you thought about what kinds of data might be most useful to respond to this question? How will you go about collecting this data? How will you analyze it? Methods are what we use in our research to collect and analyze data. They are, in a sense, the researcher's tools.[1]

This textbook is not just about research methods but also about research methodology. Teaching methods without methodology would be like trying to build a house with all the necessary tools and materials, but with no architectural plans. You could put together the individual components of the house, but you would not be able to organize these components into some form of coherent structure. But, as there are many schools of architectural design, there are also distinct methodological traditions in PIR. In order to make sense of this methodological plurality within our fields, we will provide you with a basic overview of methodological debates that have shaped research in PIR and also a guide to some common strategies for data collection and analysis.

**Table 1.1**  Key terms

| Methodology | Assumptions about what is knowable and how we know the social world around us |
|---|---|
| Methods | Techniques for data collection and strategies for data analysis |
| Scientific method | A standard of research that privileges causality and the testing of law-like propositions against observation and experimentation |

## Methodology, Methods, and Making Sense of Politics

In PIR research we seek facts. But what are facts? This question might seem simple at first, but there is much debate today about what is factual, and what is not, in politics at home and abroad. Old ways of knowing in politics, which were formerly dominated by well-established news agencies and political parties, have given way to what Persily (2017) describes as an unmediated media environment. Purveyors of fake news pump out more, and increasingly

---

[1] Moses and Knutsen use the analogy of research methodologies constituting a researcher's 'toolbox' and research methods being the researcher's 'tools' (2012, 2). We will discuss what this means in greater detail in Chapter 2.

outrageous, stories as a means to expand their bottom line or advance their ideological agendas. This has made the task of conducting 'good' social research that improves our understanding and helps structure policy responses to the complex challenges that we are faced with today more challenging.

Politics, from the time of Aristotle and Plato, has been about setting the rules by which we live our lives. There is conflict because there is significant disagreement about what these rules should look like and how best to achieve a community's goals, and even what these goals might be. Politics has therefore always been characterized by polarized debates, and it is not surprising that sometimes we might feel that looking for facts is an elusory endeavor.

In part, it is the debate over how we know, and how we evaluate knowledge claims, that makes finding consensus even more challenging. If we have different perspectives on what is important and what is not when it comes to evaluating claims in politics and international affairs, then we lack a shared framework for evaluating each other's positions on any given issue. We need to ask some fundamental questions about how we arrived at what we believe we know. Are all facts knowable? Can the same material fact have different meanings to different audiences that are both equally valid? How you answer these questions says something about how you make sense of politics. We will dive deeper into this question in our discussion of methodology in Chapter 2.

A second, but related, question is, how do we evaluate between two opposing and seemingly contradictory claims in scholarship or policy? Let's take a principal assumption in the study of electoral politics in democracies, that the state of the economy acts as a primary determinant of voter behavior (Lewis-Beck 1986, 315–346; Lewis-Beck and Stegmaier 2000, 183–219). As Lewis-Beck and Stegmaier argued:

> The powerful relationship between the economy and the electorate in democracies the world over comes from the economic responsiveness of the electors, the individual voters. Among the issues on the typical voter's agenda, none is more consistently present, nor generally has a strong impact, than the economy. (2000, 211)

Or, as the then US presidential candidate Bill Clinton put it more succinctly in his 1992 campaign for the presidency against a candidate who highlighted his foreign policy credentials, 'It's the economy stupid.' But if voter choice is determined by economic performance and not by other issues such as race or identity, how then do we account for the more recent rise of populist parties that play off these very anxieties? Indeed, when Sides, Tesler, and Vavreck looked at voter behavior in the 2016 US presidential election that resulted in the election of Donald J. Trump, they found that Trump's electoral victory was a result of voter behavior turning on 'largely issues related to racial, ethnic, and social identities' (Sides, Tesler, and Vavreck 2017, 41). With two opposing explanations of voter behavior, how can we evaluate which one of these arguments is more convincing? Here, your knowledge of methodology and methods will help you to be able to critically engage with such debates.

## Politics, Political Science, and International Relations

Why do we address methodologies and methods for politics *and* international relations in this textbook? Whether you are a student of Politics, Political Science, International

Relations, or International Studies, you will find the methodological debates and methods tools presented to you in this textbook helpful not just in evaluating 'truth claims' advanced by scholars, politicians, lobbyists, or the media, but they will also help you to answer questions you may have about how to go about researching your own topic. There is quite a bit of common ground covered in the aforementioned programs and fields of study. After all, as students of PIR, we all seek to explore questions of how power is exercised at the local, national, or international level of governance.

Recent decades have witnessed the globalization of world politics. This has made disentangling domestic and international politics research increasingly difficult to sustain. We see this in the classroom, as student research topics span a wide range of topics that challenge traditional barriers between the study of domestic and international politics. With politics and access to information becoming increasingly globalized, even traditional questions of domestic politics, such as political party competition, cannot be divorced from a transnational context. The 2016 election of Donald Trump to the US presidency and the vote of a majority of UK citizens to leave the European Union (Brexit) that same year are but two examples of political mobilization that cannot be understood without reference to transnational anxieties and debates that take place within an increasingly global public sphere. Taken together, these developments highlight why unpacking the ways in which we make sense of the world around us in a manner that allows for scholarly and policy debate is not only a prerequisite for good research, but also for making informed decisions about issues that will impact the world around us.

The breaking down of barriers between the study of the domestic and the international has been reflected in PIR curricula across the globe as more and more programs either add an international relations component to the study of politics or establish departments and taught programs under the label of PIR. What we see as politics 'at home' and politics 'abroad' are increasingly intertwined. Over the last three decades, the number of combined undergraduate programs in PIR has experienced a steady growth.[2] In sum, how we practice politics has changed, and so has how we study politics.

Nevertheless, despite these developments, boundaries still exist. If you are in a program with an American government, political science, or comparative politics focus, you might find International Relations-specific resources harder to find.[3] However, you might also want to write on US foreign policy or how domestic processes, such as democratization, can be shaped by foreign governments or non-governmental organizations. Conversely, curricula that focus on International Relations often do not directly address comparative politics research, even though many students will choose to write essays or theses on questions of comparative politics, such as democratization.

---

[2] Evidence for this includes the tendency for academic departments to group Politics and International Relations together within a single organizational unit, and external rankings, such as Times Higher Education, treating Politics and International Relations as a single subject area. See www.timeshighereducation.com/student/what-to-study/politics-international-studies-incl-development-studies

[3] While political science textbooks are too numerous to review here in full, examples include Van Evera (1997) and Kellstedt and Whitten (2009).

## Methodology and Methods: Research Choices

Despite the importance of understanding the logic of research and the tools you will need to collect and analyze data, research methodology and methods are often seen as somehow difficult to grasp. This is particularly the case for the student of PIR because our disciplines embrace **methodological pluralism**. While some scholars define methodological pluralism as simply an openness to using different kinds of methods, such as quantitative or qualitative methods, we see methodological pluralism as having a broader meaning that accounts for the diverse ways we make sense of the world. While this may sound vague at this point, what we mean will become clearer in Chapter 2. Methodological pluralism is in part what sets PIR apart from other disciplines that are defined by their method.

---

## Clifford Geertz on Research Methods and Research Disciplines

According to Clifford Geertz, in order to know what makes up a discipline in the social sciences, we should not first look to its theoretical propositions, or what it claims to tell us about the world around us. Instead, we must look at how scholars in that field 'do' their work. Or in other words, we should look at their research methods. It is these ways of doing research that, according to Geertz, define our disciplines.

For example, in anthropology, students and scholars have traditionally made use of ethnographic methods. However, for students of PIR, we cannot rely on any single method to define our discipline. Instead, one of the challenges of teaching and 'doing' methods in PIR is our acceptance of methodological plurality, which means that familiarity with only a single method limits our ability to understand scholarship in our diverse fields.

**Reference:** Geertz, Clifford. 1973. Thick Description: Toward an Interpretive Theory of Culture. In *The Interpretation of Cultures: Selected Essays*. New York: Basic Books, pp. 3-30.

---

Research methods and methodological debates are not the subject of obscure debates among scholars where passions are heated but the real-world implications are frigid; rather they are in themselves prerequisites to making sense of politics. When starting a class on research methods or when picking up a book on the topic (such as this one), you are probably thinking about methods as a chore. After all, you would probably rather be reading about your topic of interest. But a good research methods class or text will help you explore that topic. From the very beginning, it will demonstrate to you that research is about choices. And methodologies and methods inform our choices. Sometimes students make research choices without really questioning whether or not there are other ways of going about researching their topic, asking their research question, or gathering and analyzing information. This lack of awareness functions much like a set of blinders. You follow along a particular research path, while remaining oblivious to the other paths available. Here our aim is to take these blinders off and present to you the many different ways of going about research in PIR. With an open mind, and an awareness of methodological debates in PIR, you might discover new and exciting ways to examine your topic.

Research options are also more than just about an awareness of the choices that are out there. They can also be seen as a set of skills that will help you write a better research paper. In addition to this, they will equip you to better evaluate other scholarly works, and also to evaluate a wide range of policy-relevant claims that you will hear being presented in the media throughout your life. As noted earlier, assumptions we make about voter behavior as being motivated by economics or identity will inform how candidates and political parties will seek to appeal to voters in campaigns. And a better understanding of voter behavior may give one campaign an upper hand in a hotly contested election. In short, once you understand the choices you have made in your own research, you are in a better position to evaluate a wide range of causal claims that you will encounter in both social science research and the media.

Thinking about the *how* and the *why* you find your topic interesting is the first step in starting the process of making informed research choices (Lobo-Guerrero 2013, 25–28). Research methods are about how to find answers to those questions that arise from your own curiosity about issues or topics in PIR. When thinking about what interests you, often your starting point may very well be policy debates, such as electoral system reform, migration, or Brexit. All of the research we do within PIR says something about real-world policy debates. Some pundits reference scholarly or academic studies to support their own position on an issue. Thus, the impact of our research may very well go far beyond a narrow academic community.

Why do we value academic knowledge? How do we evaluate the claims put forward by scholars? How do we know whether or not we can generalize Sides, Tesler, and Vavreck's research findings about electoral behavior in one country, the United States, to other countries, such as the United Kingdom, France, Germany, or Japan? When making research choices, we explain why we have chosen our topic of study, we explicitly state what we hope to learn from our research, and we state how we will go about doing it. This process helps us to better reflect upon and design our own research project, and it allows our readers to evaluate our findings and retrace how we arrived at our findings. These are skills that will help to make us better researchers, whether the task before you is a thesis or a professional report for non-academic audiences.

In sum, research choices are embedded in our own understandings about how we make analytical judgments about major issues and debates both at home and abroad. The **Glossary** at the end of the book provides an easy-to-access overview of key terms in methodology and methods that can be consulted as you read the text and can also serve as a resource for future classes or research projects. As you read through the following chapters, you will see how these research choices constitute a practical guide that will help you through every stage of your research project, from beginning to end.

## Methodology and Methods: How they Matter

A basic grasp of methodology is essential in informing your research, because, as we have emphasized throughout this chapter, PIR is a field of study defined by a plurality in methodologies and research methods (Eun 2016). As will be examined in Chapter 2, there are different kinds of questions we can ask in PIR, but at the same time many introductory texts on research methods remain largely focused on just one particular kind of question, which may lead students to assume that PIR research projects must be done in a way that emphasizes the application of scientific methods (Kellstedt and Whitten 2009; Van Evera 1997). That is, many textbooks push students towards research designs and methods focused on **causal inference**, which will be discussed in greater detail in Chapters 2 and 6. In its most basic form, causal inference is about linking two variables by positing that a change in one variable causes a change in another. Do changes in electoral law affect electoral outcomes? Does age influence voting preferences? Does economic development strengthen democracy? All of these questions imply causality.

But how do we really know that there is a causal link between variables? What evidence do we need to find to demonstrate that this is the case? Is it because we have found that a change in one variable always coincides with a corresponding change in the other? Or is that not enough? How will we trace the process that brings about the change?

However, as you will see in the pages that follow, not every research question asked must be causal. Indeed, no issue is more contested among scholars of PIR than debates about the ability of the tools used to understand the natural sciences to explain the social world around us. Rather than taking a dogmatic position in such debates, we start from the assumption that you have an understanding of the full spectrum of the plurality of methodologies in PIR, and make choices based on your own research design. As such, we will provide you with the broadest possible overview of research practice within PIR. Moreover, the following pages are meant to be accessible for even the most novice undergraduate researcher. You can also read this book independently, or as an assigned text for a research methods class. Each chapter aims to present one of the core building blocks that you will need to understand both research methods and the research process.

## Methodology and Methods: A Practical Guide

In PIR research methods classes, the focus is sometimes more on learning how to use a certain tool for data collection and analysis, rather than on thinking critically about a research topic. As a result, you may feel left with little direction on how to formulate a research question, which is the first and, in many ways, the most critical step in the research process. Research paper assignments often assume you are able to come up with your own research question and collect and analyze data with little to no guidance. These skills are often only taught in passing, or, in some cases, not taught at all, leaving you with the challenging task of writing a research essay without having thought about the underlying questions of how a research question will influence your research design.

In addition to the hurdles that you will encounter as a student when faced with writing theoretically informed research papers for the first time, one of the challenges of *teaching* research methods is the perception that methods training is a self-contained end in itself rather than being integrated into the broader curriculum. As noted above, often research methods classes focus primarily on teaching you *how* to use methods for the purposes of data collection and analysis. Sometimes this is done without asking probing questions about why you are gathering the data that you seek to analyze, or what knowledge you hope to gain from using these particular approaches.

To remedy these shortcomings, each of the following chapters is written with two purposes in mind. First, they provide practical research guidance to both undergraduate and postgraduate students of PIR. You can therefore use this textbook as a roadmap for research. As such, the following chapters can be consulted as a handbook resource for essay, paper, thesis, or dissertation writing throughout your research career.

Our second purpose is to supplement this practical guide with a 'state of the field' overview through a broad survey of research agendas present in the discipline today. Whereas many textbooks that focus narrowly on research methods adopt a singular understanding of research methodology focused on causality, we also examine research agendas that do not see a focus on causal inference as the only type of knowledge of value to scholarship. We do this by focusing on practices that unite all good research, such as asking good questions and gathering valid data.

## A Brief Chapter Overview: The Research and Writing Process from Start to Finish

The chapter sequence described below closely follows the stages of the research process and the challenges you are likely to encounter as you carry it out from start to finish. Yet, we should also emphasize that academic writing, whether for a research essay or a PhD thesis, is not a linear process. For example, after having better familiarized yourself with the literature on your topic, you might go back and revise your research question. Or, while analyzing the data you have gathered, you might find that you are missing something and return to data collection. Thus, while the chapters in this book follow a basic trajectory of the research process – from start to finish – you might find yourself moving about the various stages of that process.

The textbook is divided into four parts. Part I (Chapters 1–3) covers the the logic of research practice and the ethical standards associated with it, while Part II (Chapters 4–6) is a practical guide to setting up your research. Part III (Chapter 7–10) covers qualitative and quantitative methods and Part IV (Chapters 11–12) examines how to write up and share your research.

### Framing the Debate

In **Chapter 2**, we introduce you to methodological debates in the context of the historical development of Political Science and International Relations. In order to describe such debates while highlighting the diversity of research methods and methodologies within PIR, we focus especially on the divide between positivism and interpretivism, terms which we will define in Chapter 2. We do this not to present positivism and interpretivism as a rigid dichotomy, but rather to illustrate that much of our research, and the questions we ask, can be seen as falling along a spectrum that ranges from questions about causality to questions of understanding and interpretation. Chapter 2 thus presents you with a balanced overview of competing research agendas within the discipline and illustrates how one of these approaches might be reflected in your own research topic and question, research design and research methods.

Overarching questions to keep in mind in any research project are your 'why' questions. Why have you chosen the research topic that you will address in your paper or thesis? Why would exploring this topic further contribute to knowledge in the field of PIR? In responding to these questions, you will find that you have already made a number of methodological assumptions about how to make sense of the world around you before you have even started to work on your project. In Chapter 2, you will also be presented with tables that map key characteristics of different methodological traditions in PIR.

## Research Ethics

Part II begins with, **Chapter 3** explored research ethics. While at first you might assume that a desk-based research project poses no ethical questions, once you start to think through your research choices, you will find even the most benign research projects have ethical implications. After all, politics is about the study of the exercise of power.

Chapter 3 will highlight three dimensions of research ethics. It will start with ethics in the context of the questions we ask, then discuss ethics in the context of the research process, and then finally deal with the question of academic dishonesty.

In some cases, there is absolute clarity in terms of rules and guidelines when it comes to ethical questions that arise during the research process. However, some ethical dilemmas are more nuanced and complex. They may require you to think about a number of issues relating to your own position as a researcher, your research funders, the participants in your research, and your relations with student, professional, or academic peers. In research there is often an underlying power relationship between the researcher and the research participant. We know our project. We know what we want to get out of our fieldwork. We know how we want to disseminate our findings. Research participants, unless explicitly informed, are in the dark about all of these aspects of your research. What codes of conduct guide how we interact with those whom we will rely upon for research data? Chapter 3 will guide you through these dilemmas and stress that research ethics are an important part of every stage of the research process, such as getting institutional approval for work involving human subjects, securing ethics for approval for research projects from your home institution or research funding bodies, and adhering to standards of academic honesty when writing papers, theses, and essays.

## From Research Interests to Research Questions

After negotiating research ethics, Part II continues with a practical guide on how to launch a research project, from identifying a research topic to writing a literature review to deciding on a research design.

**Chapter 4** provides you with a guide to translating your research topic into a research question. What is the foundation for a 'good' research question? What characteristics do such research questions have in common? What makes a research question answerable in the course of a research essay, thesis, or dissertation? The relationship between your research question and your research design, the latter of which is further explained in Chapter 6, will be illuminated through examples that will place an emphasis on how research questions say something about your methodological approach. They are also closely linked to the choices you will then make in relation to research methods.

In short, the type of question you ask will impact what data you will need to gather and how you will go about analyzing your data in a way that will help you answer your question in your essay, thesis, or dissertation. Indeed, because research questions within the discipline take on many different forms, a carefully crafted research question will help you navigate subsequent research choices you will make about research design and methods.

## Doing a Literature Review

**Chapter 5** provides you with a practical guide to conducting a literature review. Your literature review is an essential, yet sometimes overlooked, component of your research project. Without a literature review, you are not able to make statements about how others have responded to your research question in the past, nor are you able to engage with existing debates on your research topic. Your literature review serves three main functions: (1) it will help you justify the importance of your question, or how your question is novel or topical; (2) it will help you to situate your own research question in the context of relevant scholarship; and (3) it will help you to introduce the major theoretical debates related to your research question.

As a researcher, it is essential to squarely place your own research in the context of existing literature on your topic. But, at the same time, the task of familiarizing yourself with the large bodies of literature that exist in relation to most issue areas in PIR may seem daunting. Chapter 5 will also guide you through this process by providing you with tips on how to quickly become familiar with major works on your topic and major scholarly journals in your field.

## What is Your Research Design?

**Chapter 6** guides you through the process of research design. Research design refers to your overall strategy for answering your research question and therefore will be closely related to the question that you have posed. Have you asked a general question about a particular practice in PIR, such as electoral system design? Is your question specific to a practice in a single country, such as Japan's electoral system? Or are you comparing two or more countries, such as electoral systems in Italy and France? Each of these research questions is geared towards a different research design that will be presented in this chapter. This chapter will thus help you to draw connections between different kinds of research questions and how these questions imply particular kinds of designs.

Particular attention in Chapter 6 is given to projects exploring a relatively small number of observations using the **case study method**. Moaz pointed out that the case study 'is arguably the most common methodology in international studies – including both international relations and comparative politics' (2002, 161). Case studies are also popular for undergraduate theses and essays. We define what constitutes a case and discuss how case selection can influence your research findings. No matter what the purpose of your case study is, whether explanatory or interpretive, the selection of cases in comparative case studies needs to be justified. This chapter will introduce some of the more common case study design strategies, such as the most similar and most different case study designs.

## Qualitative Data Collection

Part III of this textbook then moves on to outlining both qualitative and quantitative methods that can be used to collect and analyze data. Chapters introducing qualitative (Chapter 7) and quantitative (Chapter 9) methods will be followed by practical chapters on 'doing' qualitative (Chapter 8) and quantitative (Chapter 10) research in PIR. These chapters will provide guidance on how to use methods such as content and discourse analysis and statistical analysis.

**Chapter 7** opens Part III and introduces qualitative methods. The focus of qualitative research is on gathering in-depth non-numerical data on specific places, phenomena or events, and thus on a small number of cases. We begin with a discussion of what qualitative methods are and why you might want to use them. Qualitative methods are designed to deal with a small number of cases due to the constraints on a researcher's ability to gather and analyze large bodies of data. We discuss how to collect qualitative data, describing a diverse array of sources from documents to interviews and from images to physical artifacts.

## Qualitative Data Analysis

**Chapter 8** provides you with a practical guide to analyzing qualitative data. We introduce you to the process of interpreting data using qualitative methods such as historical institutionalism, process-tracing, and content, discourse, and visual analysis. We discuss the relationship between qualitative methods and causal inference. Qualitative methods have long been seen as well-suited to describing causal pathways because of their ability to describe such processes in nuanced and detailed ways. We present specific examples to help you use these tools in your own research.

## Quantitative Data Collection

**Chapter 9** provides you with an assessment of the utility and limits of quantitative research methods, while describing ways to collect quantitative data. Quantitative methods have dominated the study of PIR in North America for many years, although they are somewhat less popular in Europe. One of the reasons why many students hesitate to engage with quantitative methods is because of the perceived inaccessibility of the mathematics needed to understand them. This chapter aims to introduce you to the underlying logic of quantitative methods in an easy-to-understand manner. We explain how to translate concepts into measurable form, a process known as operationalization. We identify ways to gather quantitative data through existing datasets, surveys, and content analysis, while underscoring the importance of quantitative data quality and related concepts such as validity and reliability.

## Quantitative Data Analysis

**Chapter 10** introduces how to apply quantitative methods for data analysis in your own research. It is important to point out that the actual use of statistical tools will require additional training, some of which is available for free online. The chapter will distinguish between descriptive and inferential statistics, and explain commonly-used measures of central tendency to describe a set of data. It then goes on to explain the logic behind various statistical tests that aim to measure the relationship between two or more variables. Finally, the chapter describes the principles of formal modeling, a way to use mathematics to explain strategic interactions.

## Writing Up Your Research

The final section of this book, Part IV, will provide you with a guide to writing up and moving forward. **Chapter 11** is a guide to writing research essays, theses, and other reports. Writing often proves the most challenging part of the research process as students are confronted with the task of distilling a wide body of information collected during the research process into a cogent research paper. It is not uncommon for the writing stage of the research project to be underestimated in terms of how much time it will consume, often leading students to rush in completing an essay. This chapter addresses every stage of the writing process, from structuring your essay and thesis to strategies for making you a more effective writer. It describes the basic structure of a PIR research paper, discusses how to write an effective title, introduction, conclusion, and abstract, helps you articulate the main argument, and explains various citation conventions.

## Moving Forward

The final chapter of this book, **Chapter 12**, covers strategies to confront hurdles that students encounter in the final stages of their research project, such as writer's block. It goes on to describe how you might share your research findings with a broader audience. As researchers, we hopefully see our topics as potentially unlocking knowledge that will have value to broader society. We therefore offer advice on how to publish your research in scholarly outlets and venues for public scholarship and debate. We discuss academic publishing conventions and expectations versus those for op-eds, commentaries, and policy papers. The final section of this book contains a **Glossary** of key terms and concepts in methodology and methods in PIR.

## Chapter Summary

Research methodology and research methods are two distinct but closely related concepts. You need a strong grasp of both in order to write a coherent research essay, thesis, or dissertation. Research methodology and methods are more than specialized jargon accessible to a narrow community of scholars in PIR. Rather, are the basis for how we make claims about the world around us. They also serve as the tools we use to evaluate the policy claims we encounter on a daily basis. The pages which follow will provide you with a practical guide to both understanding these concepts and putting them to use in your own research.

As researchers, we have a responsibility to help readers make sense of our rapidly chang-ing world in a manner that a scholarly and general interest community can evaluate and debate in an open and transparent manner. By doing this, we not only help to elucidate the value of our research, but we also highlight, for a wider societal audience, why our research is of value to the broader community.

Now that you have started to reflect on questions of methodology and methods, we can now turn to Chapter 2 where these questions will be dealt with in much greater detail.

## ━━━━━━ Suggested Further Reading ━━━━━━

Harrison, Lisa, and Callan, Theresa. 2013. *Key Research Concepts in Politics and International Relations*. London: Sage.
This resource can be consulted at any stage of the research process for further information on the key terms and concepts that you will encounter in the field of PIR.

Lipson, Charles. 2005. *How to Write a BA Thesis: A Practical Guide from Your First Ideas to Your Finished Paper*. Chicago, IL: University of Chicago Press. See Chapters 1 and 2.
Lipson's practical guide to BA thesis writing provides a number of practical tips for negotiating the thesis writing process. Chapters 1 and 2 address some of the nuts and bolts issues that you should be thinking about and planning for when embarking on your research project.

Lobo-Guerrero, Luis. 2013. 'Wondering as Research Attitude.' In Mark B. Salter and Can E. Mutlu (eds.), *Research Methods in Critical Security Studies: An Introduction*. Abingdon, UK: Routledge, pp. 25-28.
This chapter provides a brief snapshot of how your interest in a topic can help you negotiate the methodological choices that you will confront during the research process.

Moses, Jonathon W., and Knutsen, Torbjorn L. 2012. *Ways of Knowing: Competing Methodologies in Social and Political Research*, 2nd edition. Basingstoke, UK: Palgrave Macmillan. For an overview of methodological perspectives see Chapter 1 (pp. 1-18).
This is an accessible text that provides in its first chapter a concise overview of the major meth-odological debates and traditions in the social sciences.

# 2

# Methodology and Methods in Politics and International Relations

━━━━━━━━━ Learning Objectives ━━━━━━━━━

- To explain the meaning of terms such as methodology, epistemology, and ontology;
- To understand how theory relates to methodology;
- To identify the main characteristics of positivist and interpretivist research paradigms;
- To elucidate the different criteria used to evaluate positivist and interpretivist research;
- To understand the value of methodological pluralism.

What distinguishes the scholarly study of PIR from punditry and opinion writing? How can we identify high-quality research that contributes to the advancement of knowledge within our disciplines? While the answer to these questions may at first glance appear to be straightforward, there are today significant debates concerning the standards by which we judge scholarly research. In this book, we will emphasize that all scholarship shares a common characteristic of following an internally consistent logic of inquiry. This means that the principle standard that we should apply to evaluating scholarly research is the *methodological standard* that an author articulates when setting out the aims and goals of his or her research project.

The focus of a broad corpus of research in PIR has as its goal to account for causality. Does one phenomenon cause another phenomenon, but if so, how? And how do we know for sure? Are PIR, as well as other social sciences, just far too complex to make determinations about causality among complex social forces? Can we ever really determine why decision-makers or elected officials opted for a particular course of action with any degree of certainty? These are some of the questions you will need to consider when making choices about research methodology and research methods. In order to begin to come up with your own answers to these questions, it is important to reflect on some of the major methodological debates in the social sciences about how we as researchers can better make sense of the world around us.

PIR encompasses fields of study with long histories of methodological contestation. These methodological debates in PIR reflect seminal points of disagreement within the broader social sciences. Precursors to contemporary debates about how we can know the world we inhabit can be traced back to antiquity, to the writings of early philosophers like Aristotle. As social scientists, our goal is to make sense of human behavior. And, as students of PIR, we aim to understand human behavior in the context of complex social institutions, such as the state, political parties, non-governmental organizations, or international bodies such as the United Nations. However, how can we as researchers generate objective knowledge about a world of which we ourselves are part? Or, to put it more simply, is objectivity even possible or desirable? Basic questions about *how we know* triggered some of the earliest methodological debates in our disciplines. This chapter aims to provide you with a snapshot of key methodological debates and how they shape research practice in our discipline today.

Because PIR are fields of inquiry that draw inspiration from a number of related disciplines, such as history, economics, law, anthropology, and sociology, they have incorporated a diverse body of methodological traditions and research methods. At times, related social science disciplines, such as economics, have left a deep imprint on PIR.

More recently, to better understand world politics, IR scholars have turned to ethnographic methods borrowed from anthropology, which rely on fieldwork and observation to analyze culture (Salter 2013, 51–58). This disciplinary diversity is increasingly considered to be one of the core features that sets research in PIR apart from other social sciences and adds value to our field of study. Indeed, the eminent IR scholar Stephen Walt has even argued that, as a community of researchers, we should see this diversity as a strength and reject attempts to impose a single methodological worldview upon the discipline (Walt 2011).

However, as we pointed out in the previous chapter, methodological plurality does not mean 'anything goes' (Feyerabend 1993, 18). Indeed, there are standards for research design. **Research design** refers to your strategy to bring together different components of your project in a coherent manner according to a logic of inquiry. Research design, in other words, is the logical process by which you will answer your research question. It will be discussed in greater detail in Chapters 4 and 6. Effective research design ensures that you will answer your research question by providing you, and your readers, with a roadmap to how, and what data, you intend to collect and how you intend to analyze that data (Vaus 2001). An effective research design must logically follow from our research question, and the quality of our findings will be evaluated in part on the basis of the research design we choose to deploy. We will explore research design in more detail in Chapter 6.

## Thinking about Methodology, Epistemology, and Ontology

There are three terms which you will encounter throughout this textbook that require further elaboration. They are **methodology**, **epistemology**, and **ontology**. In Chapter 1, we mentioned that methodology has been defined in a number of ways over the years. Here, we define methodology as *the ways through which we acquire knowledge*. Methodology is closely related to two other concepts: epistemology and ontology. **Epistemology** is *the study of knowledge*. It focuses on questions of how knowledge is produced. Every discipline makes judgments about which kinds of knowledge have value and which do not. Epistemology structures how a discipline privileges certain types of knowledge over others. **Ontology** is *the study of being*, or the nature of social entities or concepts, such as states, international institutions, or organizations. Ontology serves to frame the object of study through the construction of conceptual categories.

You should remember throughout the course of your research project that all three concepts – methodology, epistemology, and ontology – are important for establishing the why and how of our research. When thinking about each of the perspectives in Table 2.1, you will not be able to effectively provide a justification for your project.

For some research agendas, ontology is often at the center of inquiry as students and scholars attempt to reflect on the meaning of actors and concepts that we take for granted in politics. Ontological questions can also be asked about phenomena such as the nature of gender, race, and identity in domestic and world politics.

On the other hand, epistemology, or the study of knowledge and knowledge production, helps us to understand competing claims to what we value as knowledge in the field.

**Table 2.1** Perspectives on methodology, epistemology, and ontology

| Terms | Definition | What this means for research | How it shapes our research |
| --- | --- | --- | --- |
| **Methodology** | The ways through which we acquire knowledge | Relates to broader choices in the research question, research design, and how we approach research | Governs all aspects of the research process |
| **Epistemology** | The study of knowledge | Relates to questions of how knowledge is produced and what we value as scholarly knowledge | Governs how we distinguish between 'good' and 'bad' research and how we evaluate whether research contributes to knowledge in our fields |
| **Ontology** | The study of being | What are the objects that we study? | Governs those objects that we claim as building blocks for our research and for understanding |

In the following sections, you will read about positivists and interpretivists and their epistemological claims about what forms of knowledge have greater value.

Taken together, methodology, or the means of knowledge acquisition, epistemology, what knowledge we should acquire, and ontology, the study of being, constitute a core foundation upon which we will build our research agendas. Therefore, a basic awareness of methodological traditions in PIR will help unlock the appropriate research designs and methods for your research project. Decisions about what political phenomena are understudied and how to go about studying them involve ontological and epistemological assumptions.

## Methodology and Theory

Often, introductory classes on PIR leave you wondering about how abstract theories that make general propositions about social phenomena relate to real-world events that are impacting our lives. The social scientist's quest for **parsimonious theory**, or the simplest possible explanation for the broadest possible phenomenon, requires a certain degree of abstraction from social reality, which is far too complex and nuanced to lend itself to simple theories. On the other hand, if we set out to craft theory by accounting for every possible variable, what we would be left with is not theoretical analysis, but rather endless volumes attempting to describe reality.

How has this shaped theory-building in our fields of PIR? Let us take, as an example, neo-realism, a theoretical tradition in IR. IR neo-realists posit that all states are similar units, analogous to the notion of the firm in economics (Waltz 1979). They act rationally, seeking to maximize their power and defend their interests. Neo-realism does not claim to be a theory of foreign policy, nor is it meant to provide specific guidance to practitioners of international politics. Rather, it aims to make elegant and parsimonious statements about the balance of power in the world, and by extension, peace and conflict. Neo-realists, and others who engage in parsimonious theory-building projects, make simplifications about complex social organizations like states. In order to make parsimonious theoretical propositions about international politics, we need to be able to make certain assumptions about all states.

In short, one of the building blocks of research that we need in order to make sense of the complex social forces that constitute PIR is **theory**. Theory in PIR is, in its most basic form, a logical abstraction from reality that helps us understand or explain the social world. Through our research, there are generally two ways in which we can engage with theory. One is through **inductive reasoning**, where we generate theoretical propositions out of empirical observation. Alternatively, using **deductive reasoning** you start from a theoretical proposition, and test what you would expect to see if the theory were to hold true against empirical observation.

However, there is significant debate as to the purpose of theory. Is theory mainly for the purpose of explaining events? Or, is its purpose to identify and problematize certain taken-for-granted knowledge claims? Are contributions to scholarship that involve a rigorous testing of hypotheses to determine causality the only ones which have value? Or is it also valuable to question assumptions about the concepts we take for granted, such as states, actors, institutions, and ideas in international politics? While some scholars, such as Stephen Van Evera and Kenneth Waltz, have argued that theories are exclusively constructed for the purpose of explaining outcomes or events by making logical propositions related to cause and effect (Van Evera 1997, 7–8; Waltz 1979, 7), such a definition only captures one part of research practice within the field.

As you read this textbook, keep in mind that we do not aim to promote a single approach or method for our field of study. However, at the same time, PIR research methods should be held to certain standards by which all research is judged across the social sciences. Indeed, where all scholars agree is that researchers must be explicit about their choices in terms of their object of analysis, their research question, their preferred method, data collection, and data analysis (Salter 2013, 15). Therefore, one standard for all research is to explicitly justify your research choices. How you do this, and the logic that underlies it, are the subject of the rest of this chapter.

To some extent, you will be judged against the methodological standards you set for yourself. You will know what these standards are by having a solid understanding of your research question and how it in turn relates to data collection, analysis, and research design. Methods and methodology are only truly pluralistic if you have logically justified your research choices.

In PIR, we also find a wide range of cross-disciplinary methods being used by researchers. This presents a daunting task for students because, unlike fields such as anthropology, which make consistent use of core methods built around ethnography and group observation, PIR research includes a wide range of tools that have emerged from a number of disciplines ranging from economics to history and from sociology to anthropology. Sometimes these varied tools are combined in a single study.

In short, a basic grasp of social science methods spanning a number of fields is necessary. How can you make evidence-based judgments about the impact of migration or the benefits of free trade if you lack a basic understanding of how to test and evaluate theoretical propositions? A strong understanding of the core assumptions we make when carrying out our own research not only serves to help us make a contribution to scholarship, but it also reinforces the critical thinking skills that are essential for a wide range of careers such as policy roles within government ministries at the national level, local government positions, and research roles in corporations, non-governmental organizations, and international organizations.

## Methodology and Research Practice in Politics and International Relations

Most research essays or theses are drawn from the observation of some event in international or domestic politics and aim to contribute to ongoing policy debates or international crises. For example, you probably chose to study PIR because you have a long-standing interest in politics: domestic, international, or both. What you probably did not know is that PIR encompasses fields that are in part defined by both theoretical debates that try to make sense of the 'real world' and methodological debates over how we know and interpret that same world. In short, our methodological choices say something about why we theorize. And we make recourse to theory to make claims, or arguments, about how social or material forces are shaping politics.

Therefore, when you first were introduced to theories based on abstractions from reality in introductory classes to the discipline, PIR might have seemed like it was far removed from your own interests in policy-relevant issues and debates: causes of political instability, political violence and terrorism, or policy responses to climate change, to name a few examples. Now that you have been introduced to the concepts of methodology, you can begin to reflect on why theorizing is central to making sense of politics.

To make things more complicated, in IR, theoretical debates among realists, liberals, constructivists, and critical theorists often reflect underlying methodological disagreements about how we interpret and analyze data. The disagreement is often not over how to better resolve a policy problem, such as attempts to explain the cause of civil wars, but how we understand the problem itself. For example, some PIR scholars seek to understand why civil wars as a form of political violence are the subject of international attention as opposed to other forms of violence. Why don't we study communal violence on a local level? Or domestic violence?

On the one hand, there are those scholars who see their research in terms of a **positivist** tradition that draws upon the **scientific method**. They would tend to focus on the causes of civil wars. On the other hand, there are those who see their research in terms of an **interpretivist** tradition that rejects the imposition of research practices drawn from the natural sciences upon the social world, and instead draws on approaches such as ethnographic observation or discourse analysis to explore why we understand a concept like civil war as we do in the first place.

Given the highly contested nature of debates within PIR, it is not surprising that you may find starting your own research project, whether a short undergraduate research essay or a postgraduate dissertation, is a daunting task as you are faced with the challenge of translating your interest in a real-world problem or event into scholarly debates within the field.

However, before embarking on your own project, it is helpful to reflect upon how research practice has evolved over the past century. Let us turn to how concerns about war and peace have shaped the field of PIR. International Relations in particular emerged from attempts to resolve the pressing international concerns of the early 20th century. At a time when the world was grappling with the legacy of the First World War, which had ravaged Europe, scholars tried to understand how to mitigate prospects for another global conflagration. Some in the legal community proposed establishing a rule-based international order that would transform interstate violence into a criminal justice matter. From the perspective of some elites in the United States, especially then-US President Woodrow Wilson (who was trained as a political scientist), a rules-based international order was seen as offering a means by which liberal democracies could enter into collective security arrangements to secure a more peaceful world. These policies were all premised on certain understandings of the world at the time and assumptions about cause and effect. In the United Kingdom, these questions, and attempts to answer them, launched IR as a field of study when the first Chair of International Relations was established in Aberystwyth in 1919 (Burchill 2001, 4).

War and peace among states continued to be at the center of the discipline throughout the Cold War. As the risks of nuclear war escalated in the 1950s, and it became clear that the consequences of the great power war meant devastation far beyond that wrought by the two world wars of the first half of the 20th century, IR scholars sought to understand how the risk of a nuclear conflict between the United States and the Soviet Union could be prevented. Some turned to deterrence theories, grounded in rationalist assumptions regarding superpower behavior and **rational choice theory**, which was an approach to modeling behavior that emerged from the field of economics (Art and Waltz 1993). However, this state-centric worldview was also increasingly challenged by researchers in sub-fields such as peace studies who advanced approaches that questioned the orthodoxy of national interests and the pursuit of power by states.

After the Cold War, the rise of conflicts *within* states rather than *among* them expanded the focus of IR research as students and scholars sought to understand the proliferation of internal armed conflicts that seemed to defy existing theories about the causes of war and peace. Theories meant to explain conflict among states were no longer applicable. This put domestic politics squarely under the microscope of IR scholars. Furthermore, developments such as the liberalization of international trade and regional political and economic integration led to an even greater focus on domestic politics and their effect on interstate relations. In addition to this, the proliferation of international human rights treaties entered into by states led students of IR to attempt to understand what appeared to be a transformation in world politics as state interests, once argued by realists to be narrowly defined in terms of power, now seemed to encompass an expanding range of values and norms.

While the first generation of political science scholars adopted a historicist and descriptive approach to the study of politics (Lipset 1969, 1–3), subsequent generations of scholars, particularly in the United States, sought to make the study of politics more 'scientific' by applying approaches borrowed from the natural sciences. In continental Europe, however, the study of politics followed different trajectories, with its origins in faculties of law and public administration. Debates over methods and methodology are contested because introductory texts often avoid exploring how the discipline emerged and instead present the modern study of politics in a largely ahistoric context. But far from being a discipline with a shared genealogy, the study of politics differs significantly between national contexts, making it difficult to conceive of a single unified field of politics that brings together these diverse traditions from North America to Asia to Europe and beyond.

## Methodological Pluralism in Politics and International Relations

Every research article, monograph, or edited volume you will read during the course of studying or conducting research in PIR starts from the assumptions of particular methodological frameworks that can be categorized broadly between positivism and interpretivism. As we noted earlier, much of IR research during the Cold War sought to apply scientific methods to explain international conflict. Such an approach only makes sense in the context of positivist assumptions that see scientific methods as being applicable to the social sciences. Again, research practice cannot be disentangled from methodology nor can we conceive of research that contains no methodological assumptions.

We now turn to the fundamental question that will shape our research, which is also the first major choice that you will make after finding your topic of interest: *How do we understand, interpret, or explain the social world around us?* The answer to this question can be seen as defining your perspective on research practice itself. Pole and Lampard define research as 'a process we use to understand our world' (2002). With this definition of research in mind, it is not surprising that the preceding question has been at the very center of **philosophy of science** debates. The term 'philosophy of science' refers to a body of scholarship that focuses on understanding what science is and the logic of scientific thought. It has produced a wide range of responses that span from claims that the scientific method used to understand the natural sciences can be applied to the social sciences to a complete rejection of the scientific method.

The plurality of methodologies in PIR should not lead you into a circular debate about the nature of knowledge itself. On the other hand, understanding and making explicit your assumptions are essential to any research project. To be sure, even among established scholars in the field, methodological misunderstandings remain commonplace (Keohane 1988, 392).

---

## Pluralism in PIR

Pluralism in PIR methods and methodology acknowledges the interdisciplinary origins of our fields of study. Rather than meaning that anything goes in PIR research, an ethos of pluralism refers to the use of various methods and methodological traditions by different scholars.

What is important is not a dogmatic imposition of a single methodological worldview upon the discipline but rather:

1  Keeping your research choices internally consistent by understanding the underlying logic of different methodological traditions
2  Judging research by the methodological standards to which a researcher adheres

---

In the 1990s, there were growing challenges to the perceived monopoly of scientific methods in North American political science and IR. In response, a group of scholars initiated a movement known as 'perestroika', which borrowed a term that was used in the Soviet Union to describe Mikhail Gorbachev's liberalizing reforms. The perestroika movement made the case for methodological pluralism, and triggered a vigorous defense of scientific methods on the part of positivist scholars. An example of this is Robert Keohane's challenge to feminist IR scholars to articulate a research agenda that allows for conjecture and hypothesis testing, something that feminist IR scholars explicitly reject on epistemological grounds (Tickner 2005, 1–22).

Reading lists in classes are likely to contain works from both the positivist and interpretivist tradition and many of your classroom professors' own research publications will also engage with diverse methodological traditions. However, this pluralism and openness mean that PIR, unlike other fields within the social sciences, lacks a single dominant methodology or set of methods. Likewise, methods of data gathering can vary widely. Students can find themselves conducting surveys, trying to make sense of interview transcripts, or spending months in archives reading historic correspondences.

In the absence of a single unified approach to PIR research, the following chapters will take on a process-focused approach to research practice that will serve as a roadmap to the choices you will confront during the research process. However, before doing this, let us define positivism and interpretivism in greater detail.

## Epistemology and Research Practice: Positivism and Interpretivism

As we have stated repeatedly, scholarship in PIR is diverse in terms of approaches and methods. The section, for the purpose of clarity, reduces this diversity into two epistemological traditions that make distinctive claims about what we should value as knowledge. These are positivism and interpretivism. Seen as a spectrum, these two approaches set out two camps of an epistemological debate that has taken place in a number of disciplines within the social sciences and is by no means unique to the PIR. The first, positivism, argues that natural science methods should be applied to the study of the social world. The second response, interpretivism, rejects the premise that the scientific method can be applied by social scientists to better understand social phenomena.

Using the scientific method, we aim to test **hypotheses**, or conjectured relationships between two or more variables, through observation or experimentation. If our conjecture is proven false, the hypothesis is falsified. From this perspective, theoretical propositions should lend themselves to **hypothesis testing**. If through observation or experimentation, the conjecture is in line with observed reality, we can say that our hypothesis has been confirmed. Any research project which sets out hypotheses and tests these hypotheses against empirical observation is drawing upon the scientific method.

By contrast, interpretivist scholars argue that our world is not amenable to study through scientific methods such as experimentation. These scholars engage in research that interrogates the ideas, norms, beliefs, and values that underlie international politics (Hollis and Smith 1990; Linklater 1992). Lessons about the importance of interrogating such phenomena were learned long ago in ethnographic research, where researchers critically reflected upon how their own identity as an outside researcher affected both the communities they sought to study and how these communities perceived the researcher.

Most research can be situated in one of these two traditions. In fact, PIR scholars have often described 'a fundamental division within the discipline' (Burchill 2001, 2). Hollis and Smith (1990) argued that these two approaches could be classified as *explaining* on the one hand (positivism), and *understanding* on the other (interpretivism). Here we will frame the divide in terms of choices that will inform how you will undertake your own research in a manner that reflects your own assumptions and interests.

**Table 2.2** Describing the epistemological divide in PIR

| Positivism | Interpretivism |
| --- | --- |
| Causal | Constitutive |
| Naturalist | Constructivist |
| Explanatory | Constructivist |
| Explaining | Understanding |

## Positivism

As noted earlier, **positivism** is drawn from the importation of natural science research practice into the social sciences. According to Andrew Neal, positivism refers to the 'positive creation of laws, models, concepts and most importantly theories for the explanation and sometimes testing of data' (Neal 2013, 43). Therefore, as in the natural sciences, social science research should be conducted in a systemic, replicable, and evidence-based manner that leads to conclusions about causality (see Gerring 2012; King, Keohane and Verba 1994). The tools we use to study the social world are essentially the same as those we use for the study of the natural world. And the standards by which we test those theories are essentially the same. If a theoretical proposition has predictive validity–that is, if the assumptions the theory makes are not disproven by subsequent events–then the theory holds. Theoretical propositions, or hypotheses, should also be **falsifiable**. Non-falsifiable statements are those which cannot be empirically disproven.

There is a rich tradition of positivist research in politics. This is why in North America, the field is known as political *science*.[1] Many core introductory textbooks on political science research methods, such as W. Phillips Shively's *Craft of Political Research* (2013), focus predominantly on positivist methods. Positivism also has a prominent place in international relations. One of the founding fathers of North American IR, Hans Morgenthau, argued that international politics was governed by 'objective laws' (2005). In 1979, Kenneth Waltz endorsed this approach to studying international politics in his *Theory of International Politics*.

---

[1] Note that in the UK most university politics programs, at both the undergraduate and postgraduate levels, use the label Politics and not Political Science.

There are three core assumptions of positivism:

1   Politics can be studied as an objective reality: there is an observable world 'out there' which is distinct from the researcher
2   Theories are held to the standard of predictive validity
3   Hypotheses should be falsifiable

At the outset of designing your own research, it is necessary to understand what side of this divide your own interests gravitate toward. If you wish to explain the behavior of actors in politics, then the methods associated with positivism may provide tools that allow for causal claims and explanations of developments and practices in politics.

## Interpretivism

**Interpretivism** draws upon a rich tradition which rejects the application of the scientific method to the social world. Instead, interpretivists focus on how our world is constituted through processes of understanding. For interpretivists, meaning is constructed and is always context-based; the very idea that we can theorize law-like statements of certainty out of the tapestry of social reality that we are a part of is viewed with extreme skepticism. Indeed, for interpretive researchers, the value of theory should not be measured in terms of its openness to law-like propositions, but rather in its usefulness for helping us to understand particular contexts (Schwartz-Shea 2015). Unlike positivists, who aim to advance cumulative knowledge through unbiased observation, measurement, and hypothesis testing, interpretivists seek to challenge core assumptions behind the scientific theory-building project that underlie the positivist tradition. What kind of knowledge, then, do interpretive approaches aim to generate if not knowledge defined in terms of scientific knowledge? Among other things, interpretivist research agendas seek to understand identities, ideas, norms, and culture in politics.

However, if we are to move away from the positivist evaluative criteria for 'good theory,' such as its predictive power, what evaluative standards can we reference to evaluate what constitutes a 'good' essay, thesis, or dissertation in the interpretive tradition? Schwartz-Shea (2015) argues that there are four 'first-order' evaluative criteria for interpretive work. These are: (1) **trustworthiness**, (2) **thick-description**, (3) **reflexivity**, and (4) **intertextuality**.

What do these terms mean in practice? Let's start with **trustworthiness**. Schwartz-Shea points out that trustworthiness has also been used as an 'umbrella term' for all four and is ubiquitous across literature that seeks to assess evaluative criteria for interpretive work. In order to establish trustworthiness, or your reader's confidence, you need to be transparent and explicit about justifying your research choices and maintaining ethical awareness throughout the research process (Schwartz-Shea 2015).

The second of Schwartz-Shea's evaluative criteria is **thick-description**. This term, borrowed from Geertz (1973), has its roots in ethnographic fieldwork. Here, the focus is on providing sufficient narrative detail in your essay or thesis so as to be able to provide your readers with as full a context-specific reading of your topic as possible so they have a full picture of meaning in context (Schwartz-Shea 2015).

The third evaluative criterion, **reflexivity**, relates to a term that is used widely in critical IR scholarship. This term relates to a broad range of activities centered around self-reflection during the research processes and an attentiveness to your own role as a researcher involved in the production of knowledge. This can relate to your biography, as well as the biases, implicit and explicit, that you hold towards the subject of your research (Schwartz-Shea 2015). The expectation here is that 'self-reflection' during the research process will make you more aware of implicit and explicit biases in scholarship.

Examples of interpretivist literature in IR include a broad range of critical theories that focus on a reflexive problematizing of taken-for-granted assumptions about how we study world politics. For critical theorists, scientific methods, and the theories they produce, are neither neutral nor objective. Instead, they are political in the sense that they act to reproduce structures of power in world politics. It was this argument that was put forward by Richard Ashley and Robert Cox, who cautioned that the positivist epistemological position fails to question the underlying social and power structures of international politics (Ashley 1984, 225–286; Cox 1981, 126–155).

The fourth evaluative criterion that was identified by Schwartz-Shea is **intertextuality**. This final criterion, which Schwartz-Shea (2015) also designates a 'triangulation,' emphasizes that research should be multidimensional, drawing upon a number of different data sources, methods, and researchers. However, Schwartz-Shea finds the term intertextuality better suited to capture this multidimensionality as it seeks out repetition of a particular term or idea across a number of sources (Schwartz-Shea 2015).

With these four evaluative criteria in mind, we can now turn to interpretivism's contributions to PIR. A principal claim advanced by interpretivists is that the distinction between the researcher and the social world inherent in positivism should be rejected. Interpretivists argue that the researcher creates observed social realities through their own role in creating scientific knowledge and thus alters the object under study by playing a role in structuring how their object of study is understood.

Interpretivists maintain that the experimental environment of the science laboratory, in which controlled experiments can be carried out to understand causal relationships between two or more variables, cannot be replicated in the social world, where the researcher brings biases to, and influences, the phenomena under study. In the case of complex social entities such as states, experimental methods are neither feasible nor ethical. Goals at the center of positivist research agendas, such as causality, are therefore rejected in favor of an attempt to understand how identities, ideas, and other taken-for-granted concepts in PIR came to be.

A good example of one such research program would be IR feminism. Brooke Ackerly writes:

Feminist inquiry is about revealing unquestioned differences and inequalities that conceal the exercise of power, including the power to conceal those differences and inequalities, and being attentive to the power exercised when researching these. All aspects of the research process are contestable. Attentiveness to the exercise of power extends not only to a field of study but also to its manifestation through academic inquiry. (2008, 30)

Feminist scholarship's attentiveness to power has generated a rich body of empirical work on topics that explore absences and silences in international politics (Ackerly 2008, 29). One example of early feminist research that did just this was Cynthia Enloe's *Bananas, Beaches, and Bases: Making Feminist Sense of International Relations* (1989). Enloe broke new ground in research by exploring experiences that had hitherto not been the subject of attention among scholars and practitioners of international politics. With scholars focusing their attention on questions of international security and military competition, Enloe sought to demonstrate that the very practice of international politics relied upon the reproduction of gender roles in which women were relegated to a subservient position. Through case studies of military bases and military wives, Enloe elucidates how implicit gender norms acted to reproduce patriarchal practices of dominance.

Now that the distinction between positivism and interpretivism has been established, we can draw on this divide to better understand which methodology can guide your own research.

## Why Methodology Matters: Making Informed Research Choices

While students of PIR will acquire a strong understanding of core theoretical debates across a number of sub-fields in introductory texts (Baylis, Smith, and Owens 2010; Burchill et al. 2001), it is often hard for students to translate theory into their interest in real-world events (Walt 2005). However, this task is not as difficult as it seems. Often relatively straightforward questions about politics and policy reflect underlying theoretical debates in PIR. For example, consider the question of why the outside world intervened in Libya but not Syria. This question points to IR debates among realists, constructivists, and others about the underlying motivations of foreign policy decisions.

Perhaps another subject of potential interest could be the run-up to the 2003 US invasion of Iraq, where competing theoretical perspectives in IR suggested different answers to the question of whether and how Iraq's President Saddam Hussein could be deterred from his past aggressive behavior. By contrast, other theoretical debates about domestic politics offered divergent policy prescriptions toward Iraq and forecasts for the likely aftermath of the initial US led invasion.[2] Thus, if we approach theory from the perspective of a causal conjecture of what is likely to occur under certain conditions, then the bridge between policy-relevant topics of interest and theoretical debates becomes more visible.

Now that a relationship to theory has been established, the question of method arises. In order to simply start thinking about methods, recall that research methods are *techniques for collecting data* (Bryman 2008, 31). These can include quantitative methods to interpret large datasets or qualitative methods which allow a researcher to delve more deeply into specific events, places, organizations, or personalities. However, before embarking upon

---

[2] Stephen Walt makes a parallel argument in relation to both the former Yugoslavia and Iraq (2005, 28).

data collection it is imperative that the researcher has a clear idea of what data to collect, a key step in the research design process.

## Illustrative Research Projects

One challenge that you might encounter when studying research methodology and research methods is that often you are presented with examples of research design, case selection, data collection, and data analysis techniques in the abstract. One feature that we have included in this textbook is that of two expository research projects that aim to help you see how the concepts discussed are concretely applied. We will return to these projects in each of the forthcoming chapters to illustrate how your research choices will shape how your own project will take shape.

The first of these projects focuses on *populist political parties*. Populism has been in the news a great deal over the past five years, and from North America to Western and Eastern Europe, populist politicians and political parties have enjoyed growing support. The study of electoral and political party systems has long been central to the field of comparative politics. Events such as the Brexit referendum in 2016 and Donald J. Trump's election to the White House the same year suggest that electoral politics in western democratic states have experienced dramatic changes during the 2010s. What accounts for the electoral success of populist political parties in certain western democracies? Why is there significant variation across states when it comes to the electoral appeal of populist political parties? How and why did issues such as migration, which is seen as driving populist support, become politically salient during the 2010s? Think about which methodological tradition (positivism or interpretivism) can best provide a framework for answering the question and why.

The second project, which we will reference throughout the book, focuses on how *human rights* matter in the policies of western states. Traditionally, IR explored questions of war and peace among states, and thus had a marked state security focus. For IR realists, the focus has been on explaining state behavior through the pursuit of power and relative power distributions among states. As such, the study of human rights was peripheral to early theoretical debate; however, this changed in the 1990s as the end of the Cold War brought about a new-wave impetus to understand how and why human rights came to be perceived as increasingly important. How and when did the idea of human rights come to matter in international politics? Was it because of a post-Cold War wave of democratization and the end of the superpower standoff opened up new space for the development of human rights institutions? Or was it because of transnational networks of NGOs gaining growing influence among transnational publics? When do western states such as European countries and the United States emphasize human rights in their foreign policies? Is it only when there is an absence of countervailing interests, or is a deeper commitment to values at play? Do media and public opinion drive western leaders to turn to human rights? Just as you have done with questions drawn from the populist political parties project, reflect upon which methodological tradition (positivism or interpretivism) can best provide a framework for responding to these questions.

## Chapter Summary

Research design is about choices. After having decided upon your research topic, you should begin to ask why your topic is of interest to a wider community of interested readers. What is it that you hope to learn, and for others to learn, from engaging with your research?

From the very outset of the research process, you are confronted by choices that will inform what kind of research essay or thesis you will write. Although students of PIR have no trouble identifying policy-relevant topics of interest such as international terrorism, human trafficking, migration, and civil conflict, the gap between student interest in a particular topic and the process of distilling that interest into a methodologically cogent and theoretically informed research paper often results in essays which fall into the trap of either overgeneralization ('I have studied a particular case and claim, without the proper research design, and make the argument that my findings can explain all cases') or making unsubstantiated claims ('I argue that there exists a relationship between two variables, but have not designed my study in a way that actually substantiates this claim').

PIR is a field of study defined by theoretical and methodological plurality. As such, a diversity of theoretical approaches to explaining or understanding politics exist alongside a diverse range of research methods. When embarking upon undergraduate or postgraduate essay- or thesis-writing, there are a number of questions that should be settled long before thinking about a research question.

These questions are:

- What is your topic of interest and how is it relevant to both the real world and PIR?
- What is the purpose of your study?

  o   Is it to explain a certain event, trend, or phenomenon in politics?
  o   Is it to interrogate the meaning of a particular concept, identity, or practice in politics?

- Where does your research question fall on the positivist/interpretivist divide?

Your response to the first question should be fairly straightforward, but will require some review of the literature to make sure that your topic is novel and to begin thinking about how to situate it within the existing body of research. The second requires you to think about what it is you want to do. What kind of knowledge do you want to contribute? Once you have settled on a response to this question, you are then able to situate your own research among the two broad traditions in PIR research presented in this chapter.

In order to disentangle a divide between contested approaches that often fail to directly engage with one another, the positivist–interpretivist epistemological debate in PIR was presented to help you to evaluate the relative utility of the method's tools, which will be presented later in this book. Your research topic and interests should be the guide toward methodology and epistemology. Start from your topic and purpose and ask yourself: do you want to explain events in the world 'out there'? Or do you want to question the social meaning of a particular practice, entity, or concept in politics?

Once you have established your research topic and purpose, you can then go on to formulate your research question with an awareness of how the question you pose will determine which methods are most appropriate for your research. However, before going any further, we first turn to research ethics, the subject of the next chapter.

## Suggested Further Reading

Burchill, Scott, Linklater, Andrew, Devetak, Richard, Donnelly, Jack, Nardin, Terry, Paterson, Matthew, Reus-Smit, Christian, and True, Jacqui. 2013. *Theories of International Relations*, 5th edition. New York: Palgrave Macmillan. See the Introduction, pp. 1-31.
Burchill introduces you to broad debates on research practice in the field of International Relations. Burchill uses the terms 'explanatory' versus 'constitutive' theory in order to highlight the positivist/interpretivist divide that is described in this chapter.

Gerring, John. 2012. *Social Science Methodology: A Unified Framework*, 2nd edition. Cambridge, UK: Cambridge University Press. For an overview of an empirical perspective on science, see 'Chapter 1: A Unified Framework', pp. 1-23.
Gerring provides an impassioned argument as to why methodological pluralism is not desirable in social science research and instead makes the case for a positivist approach to research in PIR.

Hollis, Martin, and Smith, Steve. 1990. *Explaining and Understanding International Relations*. Oxford: Clarendon Press.
Hollis and Smith use the dichotomy of 'explaining' versus 'understanding' to highlight the positivist/interpretivist divide in International Relations research. This is a useful and accessible text that will help you to understand some of the earlier debates on methodology in International Relations.

Jackson, Patrick Thaddeus. 2010. *The Conduct of Inquiry in International Relations*. New York: Routledge.
Jackson's text makes the case for pluralism when it comes to methodology in International Relations.

King, Gary, Keohane, Robert O., and Verba, Sidney. 1994. *Designing Social Inquiry: Scientific Inference in Qualitative Research*. Princeton, NJ: Princeton University Press. See Chapter 1 (pp. 3-33) for an introduction to causal inference and the scientific method in the social sciences.
For many years, King, Keohane, and Verba's text has been part of the canon of methods literature in political science programs across the United States. Similar to Gerring, King et al. make the case for a unified logic of inquiry built around causal inference.

Moses, Jonathon W., and Knutsen, Torbjorn L. 2012. *Ways of Knowing: Competing Methodologies in Social and Political Research*, 2nd edition. Basingstoke, UK: Palgrave Macmillan.
For an introduction to the empirical, or as Moses and Knutsen refer to it, naturalist, approach, see Chapter 2 (pp. 19-51). And, for an overview of an interpretivist, or as Moses and Knutsen refer to it, constructivist, approach, see Chapter 8 (pp. 169-203).
Moses and Knutsen provide a deep historical overview of both naturalist (positivist) and constructivist (interpretivist) traditions in PIR research that traces these debates back to antiquity.

Salter, Mark B., and Mutlu, Can E. (eds.). 2013. *Research Methods in Critical Security Studies: An Introduction*. London: Routledge. For an introduction to interpretive research, see in particular the Introduction (pp. 15–24).
Salter and Mutlu's edited volume contains numerous valuable essays on critical methods in security studies that include a wide range of reflections on topics ranging from research design to specific approaches to conducting research.

Shively, W. Phillips. 2013. *The Craft of Political Research*, 9th edition. Boston, MA: Pearson. See Chapter 1, pp. 1–13.
This introductory text includes a basic introduction to positivist research in political science. In Chapter 1, Shively presents two types of theories in politics research: positive theory, which closely aligns with how we have defined positivist research in this chapter, and normative theory, which reflects some interpretivist characteristics.

# 3

# Research Ethics

━━━━━━━━ Learning Objectives ━━━━━━━━

- To critically reflect on how research ethics and research integrity matter throughout the research process;
- To gain an awareness of conflict of interest and other dilemmas involved in securing research funding;
- To understand ethical standards in the data collection, analysis, and writing up stages of research;
- To recognize the importance of academic honesty.

PIR research, like other social sciences, is at its core about understanding human behavior, and as a PIR researcher you are likely to engage with other people, including research subjects. Therefore, it is likely that you will think about the ethical issues that may arise long before you even begin to collect or analyze data. In some cases, existing research ethics codes, policies, and written guidance provide clear guidance on ethical issues. Rules are most explicit when it comes to questions of outright fraud, such as data manipulation or **plagiarism**. However, many questions students face about ethics-related dilemmas in their research are often much more nuanced. Because of this, research ethics should not be thought of solely in the form of transgressions, but rather as a set of guidelines that will help you produce better quality, more credible research and maintain your reputation as a professional.

In what contexts might you find yourself faced with dilemmas related to research ethics? To take a plausible example, you might encounter issues related to securing **informed consent** for interviews. Informed consent is the requirement that all research participants are made aware of the nature of the project in which they are participating. Many research ethics bodies stipulate that you must secure the written consent of all interview participants. What would you do if some of your interview participants were hesitant to provide written consent and instead prefer to only provide verbal agreement? How will you present the data they provide in your essay or thesis? In the course of carrying out your research, you might find yourself asking ethics-related questions that your thesis supervisor or course professor might not be able to easily answer.

This chapter will address three dimensions of ethics you may confront in your research project (see Table 3.1). The first is reflexivity. It relates to why we ask our research questions, how we expect our research to be used by practitioners, and the impact our research is expected to have upon society. This includes, for example, ethical dilemmas about our sources of research funding. For example, a foundation in a repressive state might have an interest in funding research that somehow justifies the policies of the ruling regime. Thus, while it may not always be immediately obvious, there is a prospect for a conflict of interest in PIR research. Funding from philanthropic foundations, private corporations, and governments have all become sources of support for research in PIR. As such, both students and scholars must pay greater attention to how the agendas of donors may shape both research outputs and the external perceptions of our work.

The second dimension explores the ethics of the *research process* in relation to data collection and analysis. The principle of 'do no harm' should inform every part of the research process. This principle is of particular importance in relation to our interaction with research subjects, whether through interviews, focus groups, or surveys. As advances in technology have allowed authoritarian states, such as the People's Republic of China (PRC), to more effectively monitor their own citizens, researchers using **human subjects** must be aware of the potentially harmful impact of the very act of speaking to citizens of such countries, whether in person or electronically. For example, one recent study of anti-authoritarian demonstrations in Hong Kong, which relied on experimental methods to elicit protester motivations (Cantoni, Yang, Yuchtman, and Zhang 2019, 1021), generated significant debate among scholars on social media as to the potential harm such field experiments could do to participants who may have been under the surveillance of the authoritarian Chinese state.

Even assuming that an interview can take place securely, there is still the need to protect the identity of your interviewee when reporting the outcomes of your research. Often, part of 'doing no harm' includes **anonymizing** how we identify our research participants and handling the data we collect in a responsible manner that will not lead to accidental breaches of anonymity.

The third dimension addresses *academic dishonesty* and **plagiarism** and covers a wide range of acts that include tampering with or manipulating your research data, or using other people's ideas and words without proper attribution. In the United States, a PhD student fabricated data from an experiment whose results purportedly demonstrated that contact with gay canvassers (volunteers who go door to door encouraging people to vote) could change potential voters' opinions on the issue of gay marriage. The findings, published in the journal *Science*, were retracted once it was demonstrated that the data on which this experiment was based were entirely fabricated (Gelman 2015). Proper attribution is also critical to maintaining our integrity as researchers, and even renowned scholars have lapsed at times, hurting their reputations. An example is Doris Kearns Goodwin, a celebrated biographer of US presidents, who resigned from the Pulitzer Prize Board in 2002 due to allegations of failure to properly attribute sources (Wall Street Journal 2002). All of these practices constitute significant breaches of academic trust. The norms of honesty and transparency also extend to how we report our findings: we should be humble about our conclusions and their predictability and generalizability.

**Table 3.1**  Three dimensions of research ethics in PIR

| | |
|---|---|
| **Reflexivity** | Why do we ask the research questions we ask? |
| | Why do funders prioritize certain research agendas and not others? |
| | What are the ethics of research funding? |
| | What is the impact of our research on society? |
| **Research Process (Data Collection/Analysis)** | How does participation in our research impact the lives of research participants? |
| | What measures should we take to protect research participants from harm? |
| **Academic Dishonesty and Plagiarism** | What are our responsibilities to maintain the integrity of academic research? |
| | How do we ensure that we effectively guard against plagiarism? |

## Reflexivity, Research Ethics, and Societal Impact

As students of PIR, we have an interest in carrying out research that informs the world around us, and maybe even helps to create change. The quest for *objectivity* in our scientific research should not signal disengagement from what is relevant and important in the political world. There are many examples of PIR research that engages with the most pressing issues of the day. For example, in 2018 the political scientists Steven Levitsky and Daniel Ziblatt published a best-selling book which drew on PIR research about the erosion of democracy (2018). Rarely do books based on PIR theories make it this big: even former US president Barack Obama read and recommended it. Provocatively titled *How Democracies Die*, its publication coincided with a growing fear that democratically-elected leaders such as US president Donald Trump were threatening independent institutions and, by extension, democracy itself.

There are in fact many ways that researchers engage with the real world. PIR scholars have long contributed to the public policy debate by writing op-eds (opinion and editorial articles) and being called upon as experts in the print and broadcast media. These days, PIR researchers are also sharing their research findings in venues such as *The Monkey Cage* and *The Conversation*, two prominent blogs where academics write for a broader audience (a topic we discuss in Chapter 12). These outlets have been designed to make rigorous academic research accessible to a broader public. Other scholars bring their expertise to the public debate on Twitter and other social media. Researchers have also contributed to the public good by serving as expert witnesses in trials. Yet others have taken on public service roles, serving as advisers to elected officials. Unlike economists, who often rely on abstract models with unrealistic assumptions, students and scholars of PIR deal with politics and thus are often better equipped to offer policy advice that is not only theoretically possible but also politically viable.

It is great to be relevant. But if PIR is about the exercise of power, then relevance can sometimes mean engaging with power structures in some way, or perhaps even being part of those structures. In other words, it is hard to completely divorce PIR from power itself. Herein lie some of the ethical dilemmas of research. Power is exercised by elites, and so PIR researchers gravitate toward them. In some cases, they might have been part of that elite themselves. How will this influence their methodology and results? This is why some PIR scholars take a self-conscious step away from their own personal biases and beliefs as individuals, a step advocated by positivists like Keohane, King, and Verba (1994). On the other hand, interpretivists see such an attempt to erase one's own positionality as being fraught with ethical risk. **Positionality** is the social and political context that creates your identity according to factors such as race, class, gender, sexuality, and ability status. Positionality also describes how your identity influences, and potentially biases, your understanding of and outlook on the world, which in turn influences how you approach your research.

## Reflexivity, Critical Theory, and Feminist Research Ethics

Certain kinds of research will organically reveal the author's agenda, ideologies, and affiliations. Interpretivist research has long asked probing questions about the relationship between the researcher and their research, and why certain research agendas and research questions have been privileged over time at the expense of others (Ackerly and True 2008, 693–707).

The need to reflect on your own positionality as a researcher is often acknowledged as being a core component of interpretivist research design. Critical theory research traditions have a long-established tradition of putting ethics at the center of academic inquiry by paying special attention to marginalized voices and groups in society, politics, and the economy. There is also much attention paid to ethics in feminist research methodologies. Harding and Norberg write:

> These theorists and researchers have argued that conventional standards for 'good research' discriminate against or empower specific social groups no less than do the policies of legal, economic, military, educational, welfare, and health-care institutions; in fact, these standards actually enable the practices of these institutions. (2005, 2009)

Building on earlier feminist methodological reflections, Ackerly and True elaborate upon what they refer to as the *feminist research ethic* as containing four core commitments that require attentiveness to:

1   The power of knowledge and epistemology
2   Boundaries, marginalization and silences
3   Relationships and their power differentials
4   Our situatedness as researchers (2008, 695)

Not only is positionality important to consider when reflecting on your research question and research design, but also in the context of your interaction with research participants.

## Research Ethics, Research Funding, and Conflicts of Interest

Before you can publish your research in academic journals, you will likely be asked if you have any potential conflict of interest to declare to your publisher and eventually to your readers. Conflicts of interest may arise from research funding sources. Engaging with power in PIR means accepting research funding from structures of power, which runs up against core research values such as impartiality and independence. In some cases, researchers cultivate fruitful and mutually beneficial relationships with their research funding bodies. At other times, the relationship between researchers and research funders is fraught with controversy. Take, for example, the debate in the United States among anthropologists over conducting research in support of US military counter-insurgency operations in Afghanistan and Iraq. After the September 11, 2001 attacks on the United States, the US government invested heavily in developing deeper cultural and linguistic knowledge about regions of the world where the US military was deployed. It was neither new nor unique to the United States that a state should direct research funding to issues and countries of strategic concern. During the Cold War, significant funding was provided to institutions of higher education in the United States to train students in area studies and languages that were deemed critical to national security. The Russian language and 'Soviet studies' were prominent among them (Bonnell and Breslauer 2004, 218–219). Indeed, Cold War-era US government research funding for a number of disciplines arguably enabled the rise and phenomenal growth of famous American universities, such as Columbia, MIT and

Stanford, not to mention the industries around them (think Silicon Valley). Scholars such as Steve Smith have similarly argued that US national security priorities during the Cold War left a deep imprint on the discipline of PIR (Smith 2002, 67–85).

However, there are drawbacks to research funding that is driven by the foreign policy agenda of a given state. Returning to the post-9/11 example, the US Army *Human Terrain System Project*'s funding of social science research in places like Iraq and Afghanistan (Sims 2015) provoked significant debate among anthropologists (American Anthropological Association 2007). Indeed, from the perspective of the American Anthropological Association, the Army's project was seen as putting both researchers and those who researchers came into contact with in combat zones at intolerable levels of risk. On the one hand, there was a convergence of interest between anthropologists and the US government, both of whom sought to better their own, and society's, knowledge of understudied cultures. On the other hand, the research was funded to support a military-led counter-insurgency campaign. Where are the ethical boundaries for individual researchers to be found?

To provide another example, tens of millions of dollars in funding from Gulf Arab states have poured into Washington, DC-based think-tanks, putting the independence of their research and advocacy at risk. Table 3.2 summarizes foreign donations to a number of American think-tanks. While this does not mean that scholars at well-known research institutions such as the Center for Strategic and International Studies write propaganda pieces praising the Saudi or Emirati monarchies (indeed, the benefactors themselves understand that this would lead the think-tanks to lose any semblance of credibility), it is not hard to find a tendency toward dampened or avoided criticism at certain institutions and among certain experts.

**Table 3.2** Examples of US think-tanks and foreign funding

| Name | Notes on Foreign Funding |
| --- | --- |
| Atlantic Council | Over two dozen foreign donors make up between 5 and 20 percent of the budget |
| Brookings Institution | 12 percent of the budget is from foreign countries Qatar is one of the biggest donors |
| Middle East Institute | Major donors include the Arab Gulf countries |
| Center for Strategic and International Studies | Foreign donors include China and Arab Gulf countries |

*Source*: Lipton, Williams, and Confessore (2014)

Research questions in PIR are likely to be of interest to non-scholarly audiences who wish to make use of results to address the challenges they are facing. In some countries, this is seen as being largely positive and even incentivized through programs meant to evaluate the 'impact' of scholarly research on policy, or through 'valorization' practices meant to translate scholarly research into real-world applications. The United Kingdom and the Netherlands are two examples of countries where national research bodies use the metrics of social impact or valorization to assess the potential value of research.

Moreover, in the absence of broad interest in certain topics, countries, or regions, government funding may be the only source of support for research. But not all sources of government funding, even from the same government, are equal in terms of the independence they afford the researcher. Some, like the very popular and prestigious US government-sponsored Fulbright grants, give the researcher complete autonomy after they are granted. Furthermore, as noted earlier, non-government sources of funding (such as corporate or industry grants) might possibly come with more strings attached than government ones.

Nevertheless, there are real concerns over the extent to which the academic community should permit government funding priorities – whether that funding comes from domestic or foreign governments – to shape research agendas (Collini 2011). Unfortunately, the codes of conduct for research ethics discussed in this chapter do not provide absolute clarity when it comes to the dilemma of government funding. It is up to the individual researcher to weigh the ethics of accepting certain funding sources for any given project. Moreover, whatever external funding you accept, you must be transparent about it, listing in your thesis or essay all funding bodies that have contributed to your research. Today, as noted earlier, many academic journals require researchers to disclose any funding they received to support their research and any potential conflict of interest that may exist. What constitutes a conflict of interest? If we turn to one major academic publisher, Taylor and Francis, we see the term defined as follows:

> A conflict of interest can occur when you (or your employer or sponsor) have a financial, commercial, legal, or professional relationship with other organizations, or with the people working with them, that could influence your research. (2019)

Note that a conflict of interest may not arise solely from the source of your research funding. In fact, as a conflict of interest can arise from financial, commercial, legal, or professional relationships that could influence your research, a conflict can also arise from a wide range of activities. These include consultancies, employment, advocacy groups, research grants, fees and honoraria, patents, royalties, or even stock or share ownership.

## Research Ethics in Data Collection and Analysis

The second dimension of ethics is that which relates to the research process. At some point, you will have to go out and collect your data and analyze it. Some research projects will require you to interact directly with human subjects, or research participants. In others, your interactions will be more indirect, but, at the very least, you may interact with fellow researchers. These interactions have ethical implications.

### Values and Research Integrity

Research integrity is at the center of ethics. It refers to the harmony between your actions as a researcher and the values of the community to which you belong, in this case the PIR scientific research community. Key values in this community include collegiality and impartiality, and of course a commitment to rigorous research. Collegiality describes the quality of your relations with fellow students and scholars. If you continue in PIR research or practice in some capacity, you will find that the community is smaller than you think. The use of social media has shrunk it further. This makes it all the more important to uphold norms of politeness in electronic and in-person interactions. You never know when you will encounter someone again, and you may need assistance one day with reference letters or reviews. Responding to emails in a timely manner is one simple way to uphold collegiality, but in general striving to be a professional, kind, and accessible colleague is the way to go.

Impartiality does not mean that you can't have a strongly-held opinion about an issue related to your topic, or that this opinion can't motivate your research agenda. Indeed, as we have noted in other parts of this book, your **normative beliefs** will inevitably shape your research agenda. You may think populist parties pose an existential threat to democracy, or fervently believe that western states should use their power and resources to promote human rights. On that basis, you might decide to pursue a research project on why populists are successful or one explaining when western states decide to intervene on behalf of human rights. Each project would reflect your beliefs and interests. However, impartiality means that you will compartmentalize your prejudices and ideologies when designing your research and let the data guide your conclusions. Your research will not be taken seriously if it is seen as overly polemic and lacks serious engagement with the existing literature, or if you misrepresent the data you have gathered to support a position you fervently hold.

## The Tension between Transparency and Protection of Human Subjects

**Transparency** – the principle that every PIR researcher should make the essential components of his or her work visible to fellow scholars – is among the most important of values associated with research integrity. The American Political Science Association has recognized three dimensions of transparency (data transparency, analytic transparency, and production transparency), all of which are described by Andrew Moravcsik (2014):

- **Data transparency** ensures that the reader of your research has access to the evidence used to support empirical research claims, thereby permitting 'readers to appreciate the richness and nuance of what sources actually say, assess precisely how they relate to broader claims, and evaluate whether they have been interpreted or analyzed correctly' (2014, 48).
- **Analytic transparency** gives your readers access to information about how you analyzed your data: 'the precise interpretive process by which an author infers that evidence supports a specific descriptive, interpretive, or causal claim' (2014, 48). In other words, your research should show that you have weighed alternative processes and interpretations.
- **Production transparency** provides readers of your research with access 'to information about the methods by which particular bodies of cited evidence, arguments, and methods were selected from among the full body of possible choices' (2014, 49). It helps reassure your readers that you did not handpick sources, for example. Production transparency mandates that you explain how choices of evidence, theory, and method were made, giving 'readers a better awareness of the potential biases that a particular piece of research may contain' (2014, 49).

Moreover, some PIR journals now require that data be made available once an article is published. A number of electronic repositories host and distribute PIR datasets, such as the Interuniversity Consortium for Political and Social Research (ICPSR). Other journals have proposed the pre-registration of research proposals (including details about variables and statistical tests) that can later be compared with an actually executed analysis to ensure that the researcher did not tweak data or methods to achieve a particular result. But it is difficult to imagine how this would work for observational, interpretive, and various kinds of qualitative research.

To maintain research transparency in projects employing qualitative research methods, Andrew Moravcsik (2014, 51) mentions tools such as data archiving, qualitative databasing, hyperlinks, traditional citation, and active citation. Data archiving is the practice of preserving field data, including interviews, ethnographic notes, and informal documents (though, as described below, it is challenging because of human subject-related ethics issues). Databases (using applications such as Access, Filemaker, or Atlas) can help you manage qualitative data for small-N research designs. Hyperlinks may work when an article is published and read electronically, but websites change over time (a link may disappear entirely) and may be blocked by paywalls. Of course, conventional footnotes and endnotes are the most basic way to ensure transparency, but Moravcsik argues that they often fail to provide adequate data, analytic, or production transparency.

To remedy the limitations of these transparency tools, Moravcsik advocates **active citation**. Active citation, he writes, 'envisages that any empirical citation be hyperlinked to an annotated excerpt from the original source, which appears in a "transparency appendix" at the end of the paper, article, or book chapter.' Active citation requires 'that the citation be complete and precise' and its 'distinctive quality' is a 'transparency appendix' attached to the research product (Moravcsik 2014, 51). Each citation in the main text is hyperlinked to an entry in the transparency appendix, while each of these entries contains:

1    A copy of the full citation
2    An excerpt from the source, presumptively at least 50-100 words
3    An annotation explaining how the source supports the claim being made
4    Optionally, an outside link to and/or a scan of the full source

However, the goal of transparency runs into serious conflicts when it comes to human subject involvement in various kinds of qualitative research methods, such as ethnographic work in certain settings. As we suggested earlier, when research involves human subjects in authoritarian or conflict settings, their lives may be endangered if their identities are made public. Even large-N data collection methods, such as surveys, require the researcher to guarantee the anonymity of his or her respondents lest they receive less-than-honest responses. The tension between the ethical responsibility to be transparent and the parallel ethical responsibility to protect one's research subjects was cast into sharp relief by the intense controversy which surrounded the sociologist Alice Goffman's widely read study (Goffman 2015) of young African-American men caught up in the US criminal justice system. Some critics who questioned Goffman's methodology and research ethics requested that she hand over her field notes and other original data for public scrutiny, but Goffman argued that this could endanger her research participants, some of whom were wanted by law enforcement authorities. PIR and other social science disciplines are still grappling with how to deal with such dilemmas. Below, we discuss your ethical responsibilities *vis-à-vis* human subjects in greater depth.

## Data Collection Ethics: Human Subjects and Experimental Interventions

Even before the research process begins, students and scholars in North America, Australia, Japan, the United Kingdom, and other countries have to secure research ethics-related clearance from their institutions to carry out research directly involving human subjects. The scope and breadth of ethics clearance committees has grown significantly in recent years. At some institutions, this process requires you to submit a human subjects research application to a specialized ethics committee that will evaluate your project on a number of criteria, among them the need to 'do no harm' in the research process. The UK's *Economic and Social Research Council* provides a list of six core research ethics principles:

1   Research should aim to maximize the benefits for individuals and society and to minimize risk and harm.
2   The rights and dignity of individuals and groups should be respected.
3   Wherever possible, participation should be voluntary and appropriately informed.
4   Research should be conducted with integrity and transparency.
5   Lines of responsibility and accountability should be clearly defined.
6   Independence of research should be maintained and, where conflicts of interest cannot be avoided, they should be made explicit. (Economic and Social Research Council 2019)

As you can see from this list, research ethics touches on the entire research process from start to finish. Here, we focus on those elements that relate to potentially doing harm to research participants.

## Research Ethics Principles – A Dutch Perspective

While the principle 'do no harm' generally informs most aspects of research ethics, some national research funding bodies have attempted to further specify and define the core principles of research ethics. In the Netherlands, *The Netherlands Organization for Scientific Research* (NWO) sets out five research ethics principles that should guide all scholarly research:

1   **Honesty:** This is defined in respect [of] reporting research findings and taking into account other perspectives in scholarship in your own research. It also refers to not trying to make claims that are unfounded by inflating your findings or fabricating data. Results should be presented honestly and not misrepresented to support a particular perspective.
2   **Scrupulousness:** This refers to the use of rigorous and appropriate methods, careful research design and dissemination of research findings.
3   **Transparency:** This commits researchers to being explicit about stakeholders and methods, how they obtained and analyzed their data, and researchers should aim to make their research publicly available, if possible.

4   **Independence:** Non-scholarly pressures, political or business, should not impact your research choices or findings.
5   **Responsibility:** This is a broad principle that requires the researcher to take into account their research subjects, funding bodies, and the environment. It places an emphasis on research being scientifically and/or societally relevant and on maintaining the 'virtues' of a good researcher.

*Source*: The Netherlands Organization for Scientific Research. 2018. *Netherlands Code of Conduct for Research Integrity*, pp. 13-14. Available at: www.nwo.nl/en/documents/nwo/policy/netherlands-code-of-conduct-for-research-integrity

Since many students and scholars ask research questions that require them to gather data from research subjects at home or abroad in regions scarred by conflict, there is a corresponding need for greater attention to be paid to research ethics as they relate to potential harm to the researcher and research participants. Thus, much of the debate over research ethics during the data collection process has centered around the principle of 'do no harm.'

## Codes of Conduct and Ethical Guidance

### American Political Science Association (APSA)

The APSA has published an extensive guide to professional ethics that encompasses both ethical questions related to research and professional conduct as a scholar in general. The APSA's *Guide to Professional Ethics in Political Science* (2012) can be found at: www.apsanet.org/portals/54/Files/Publications/APSAEthicsGuide2012.pdf

### Economic and Social Research Council (ESRC)

The ESCR provides a detailed research ethics framework that is accessible on its website at: https://esrc.ukri.org/funding/guidance-for-applicants/research-ethics/

### Japan Society for the Promotion of Science (JSPS)

The JSPS provides a comprehensive guide for researchers and students in Japan in its booklet, *For the Sound Development of Science*, which is available online at: www.jsps.go.jp/j-kousei/data/rinri_e.pdf

### Netherlands Organization for Scientific Research (NWO)

The NWO has also published a publicly available guide for ethics. *The Netherlands Code of Conduct for Research Integrity* (2018) can be found at: www.nwo.nl/en/documents/nwo/policy/netherlands-code-of-conduct-for-research-integrity

Concern about research involving human subjects was brought into focus by the grotesque scientific experiments carried out on human subjects in Nazi Germany and Nazi-occupied Europe. These experiments, to which imprisoned and coerced human subjects were subjected, were widely publicized during the Nuremberg trials (Shuster 1997, 1436–1440). Criminal trials of Nazi medical doctors who had perpetrated such crimes resulted in the drafting of ethics rules known as the Nuremberg Code for medical research ethics. This document was later described as 'the most important document in the history of the ethics of medical research' (Shuster 1997, 1436). Furthermore, within the medical sciences, the ethics of using data from Nazi experiments in contemporary research continues to cause controversy decades after the Nuremberg trials (Bogod 2004, 1155–1156; Moe 1984, 5–7).

Although the Nuremberg Code's focus was on medical ethics, this did not prevent many of its core principles from making their way into the social science ethics codes that emerged later in the 20th century. Today, many of the core principles of the Nuremberg Code, such as informed consent and do no harm, are included in most codes of research ethics in the social sciences. But how could research in PIR potentially harm research participants? After all, our field is very far removed from the medical sciences and medical experimentation.

Let's return to Cantoni, Yang, Yuchtman and Zhang's study of what drives individuals' decisions to participate in political protests (2019). The authors drew their sample of experimental subjects from the student population at a Hong Kong university. Students were recruited through an email distributed to the entire student body and paid approximately US$25 for completion of their surveys (Cantoni, Yang, Yuchtman and Zhang 2019, 1035–1036). However, given mainland Chinese allegations that anti-authoritarian protestors are puppets of western states, serious risks might arise if student activists are identified. Emails can be easily hacked by the security services of authoritarian states. Moreover, paying research participants creates additional ethical and methodological issues. Are the respondents being truthful? How do we know it is not a biased sample? These are the kinds of questions that an ethics review committee would ponder when reviewing proposals to carry out research involving human subjects.

Moses and Knutsen have observed that **experimentation** (or experimental methods) in the social sciences has become increasingly mainstream (2012, 54). Druckman, Green, Kuklinski, and Lupia observed that 'the number and influence of experimental studies is growing rapidly, as political scientists discover ways of using experimental techniques to illuminate political phenomena' (2006, 627). However, one factor that separates experimentation in the social sciences and the natural sciences is the difference in our ability to control variables within a laboratory setting and within a social science setting. This, in turn, has serious implications for ethics.

The nature of experimentation in the social sciences brings with it many questions about how your research participants' involvement in your project will impact their well-being or even social standing. But it is not just experimental methods where we need to be attentive to the risk posed to research participants. An additional consideration is that any time we conduct interviews or collect data from anyone, from subject-matter experts to the general public, there is a risk that we may be exposing research participants to harm that even the participant might not be aware of. While we may consider our research project to be benign, we need to always account for how our interactions with research participants may impact those who volunteer their time to participate in our research.

In Chapter 2, we noted that a social scientist is confronted with trying to make sense of the social world, which is made up of, and experienced by, people – a community of which the researcher is a member. This is different from the natural world – from which the researcher is detached. When natural scientists observe the interaction between two chemical elements, they observe and record their findings as a detached, impartial observer. When countries go to war with each other, images of armed conflict are broadcast on television or are viewed on websites, evoking a number of emotions which preclude us from merely bearing witness as a detached observer.

Some social scientists reference our inability to detach ourselves from our object of study to argue that experimental methods, such as those conducted in the natural sciences or even medicine, have no place within the discipline. Moreover, no matter how carefully we design social experiments, it is impossible to recreate a laboratory setting that would allow us to isolate variables with precision. Indeed, as Moses and Knutsen observed in relation to the study of war, 'While we can assume that many generals long for a better understanding of the nature of war, ... it would neither be cheap nor appropriate to explore these topics through research projects that apply the experimental method' (2012, 53). Given the fact that experiments involving human subjects are increasingly mainstream within PIR, the Nuremberg Code's guidance on human subjects is of growing relevance to researchers in our field.

Thus, while it goes without saying that laboratory experiments for social phenomena such as armed conflict are beyond the scope of any feasible research design, either in an ethical or a material sense, in the study of politics we often conduct small-scale experiments with targeted groups of people in order to improve our understanding of specific populations. Whether we want to better understand attitudes toward political parties, issues, race, or religion, experimental methods have proven useful. For example, Roman David's study of the social impact of efforts to deal with the legacy of the communist past in Central and Eastern Europe made use of experimental methods to understand the causes behind divergent attitudes toward the authoritarian past (David 2011).

No matter how benign we may perceive our experiments to be, as researchers, we have a responsibility to fully disclose to participants in our research the purpose and nature of our study and not to harm those with whom we interact. One notorious application of the experimental method was the Milgram experiment, where, arguably, the researcher did not consider the psychological effects of having one group of research participants believe they had inflicted harm on another group. In an attempt to study obedience, Milgram designed an experiment that required the researcher to deceive research participants (1963, 371–378). As a result, the Milgrim experiments are often taken as a textbook example of the risks of not adequately considering ethics in experimental research design (Tavris 2014).

In addition to experiments, data collection methods and fieldwork techniques have evolved rapidly and challenged some core ethical principles, such as informed consent, that guide social science research. Increasingly, digital experimental methods are transforming how we encounter our research participants. For example, using email lists as a means to target potential research participants would not have been possible decades ago.

Sometimes researchers aim to insert themselves into real processes, such as how politicians interact with their constituents. For example, researchers might harness social media for the purpose of experimentation. They could post certain questions or messages on the Facebook page of a politician to test when and how they respond. While the intention is good, and the underlying research question is a valuable one, the kind of manipulation involved in carrying out such an experiment interferes with and perhaps influences the very social and political realm you are trying to study. While good PIR research should engage with the real world, the idea that it could *interfere* with processes in the world is quite controversial at best. In 2014, a group of PIR researchers sent messages to more than 100,000 voters in the US state of Montana, in which they informed respondents of the ideological leanings of candidates for the state Supreme Court to test for what they call 'emotional contagion'. The messages contained the official seal of the state. The experiment became a scandal once it became public. By assigning ideologies to formally apolitical judges, the research may have affected the election outcome and thus interfered with the democratic process (Willis 2014). To give yet another example, researchers manipulated Facebook newsfeeds to test whether the emotional state of the social networking site's users could be influenced by the content of what users were viewing (Kramer, Guillory, and Hancock 2014, 8788–8790). This research design provoked widespread criticism as it entailed the manipulation of user content for the purpose of an experiment without the knowledge or consent of participants (BBC News 2014). Why not simply gather observational data from publicly available data that people generate through social networking sites? Can we use statements extracted from these sites for our research without the consent of those who maintain personal or professional profiles on these networks?

When doing research on political activism, Facebook profiles may provide a potentially rich resource for those seeking to understand specific activist communities. However, just because a person on Facebook has posted something you might wish to use in your research does not mean this person has consented to having this post, intended for a community of friends, reproduced in your publicly available research. Could using it in such a way bring harm upon the friend? These are questions you should ask yourself. You should always request the permission of those whose words you are using, especially if you have obtained them from a private or restricted medium.

In short, the digitalization of research has expanded the realm of interaction with human subjects, but also created new ethical dilemmas, some of which are not easily solvable. As such, experimental interventions in the digital realm should be carefully considered and implemented.

## Institutional Review Boards and Your Research Participants

Most universities, or publicly funded research institutes, will require you to go through a process of ethics review prior to securing permission to carry out research on human subjects. While institutional review processes vary considerably across institutions, there are commonalities. First, you will be asked to describe why and how your research will involve human subjects. What kind of data collection method will you use: interviews, focus groups, or surveys? Will your data be observational, or will you be asking participants to take part in an experiment?

Second, you will be asked to describe and provide evidence of how you will secure informed consent from your research participants. Informed consent requires you to inform all participants in your research not only of their participation in your research, but also the purpose of your research project. This can be provided in an informed consent form, which is a short document providing evidence that your research subjects have voluntarily consented to participate in your project. Your interview consent form should include a paragraph describing your research in accessible terms (also see the discussion on interviewing in Chapter 7). You should also identify how your research is being funded, and describe the levels of anonymity you will be providing to participants. In the case of interviews, you can offer your participants varying degrees of anonymity that could include:

- Full anonymity, where no identifiable information will be provided in published research results (on background)
- Some general information about the participant's profession or authority to speak on the matter being provided in published research results (off the record)
- No anonymity, where the individual will be referenced by name and affiliation (on the record)

As we noted earlier in the section on the inherent tension between transparency and protecting human subjects, there is a benefit and cost to each kind of consent in terms of the level of transparency. For example, if you were able to interview a knowledgeable high-level government official about a key foreign policy decision in which they were involved, but did not receive permission to reference this person by name, the strength and validity of your findings may appear weaker. In order to provide maximum transparency in the research process, and balance against our obligation to do no harm to research participants, in published research interview consent forms can provide participants with a sliding scale of anonymity in order to give them a greater degree of choice:

- I consent to the use of my name, position and affiliation in published research.
- I consent to the use of only my position and affiliation in published research.
- I consent to the use of only my affiliation in published research.
- I do not consent to either the use of my name or affiliation in published research.

However, protecting the anonymity of participants is only one dimension on which your project will be evaluated by the research ethics boards. You will also need to assess whether or not there is the potential to harm your participants. Harm could be physical, psychological, or even professional. Could your research participants suffer career consequences after speaking to you? Will you harm participants by asking them to talk about a traumatic life experience, such as conflict? Institutional ethics boards exercise particular caution if your research engages with vulnerable adults, such as those who do not have the capacity to make informed decisions about participating in research, and children.

## Ethics Checklist

1   Are there any underlying ethical questions posed by your research question?
2   (In the event you are conducting funded research) Is there a potential conflict of interest between my research funders and my research?
3   Is there a potential conflict of interest between you, the researcher, and your research question?
4   Does your research design require you to interact with human subjects?

The Ethics Checklist provides a checklist of overriding ethics-related questions that you should ask yourself throughout the research process. There are probably very few research questions that would allow you to answer no to Question #1. Question #2 is one you should ask yourself in the event of your research being funded by a third party, while Question #3 is something that may come up if you find yourself emotionally too close to a particular topic to write about or research it dispassionately. Finally, if you answer yes to Question #4, you should next think about what kind of people you will be interacting with: members of a particular profession, employees of an organization, or activists in a certain political party. If you are likely to work with children or vulnerable adults, you should consult closely with your institutional ethics committee to ensure that you have the appropriate permissions and training to carry out your research.

## Honesty in Reporting Research Outputs

As a PIR researcher, like researchers in other academic disciplines, you have an obligation to be ethical in the way you report research findings and cite the work of others. This includes proper attribution of ideas and data taken from other researchers and sources, truthful analysis and reporting of the data you have gathered, and disclosure of funding sources and vested interests.

Elsewhere in this chapter, we mention the case of the voting researcher who fabricated data and published them in a prominent journal (the fraud was uncovered relatively quickly by others attempting to replicate the findings). Making up or editing data to fit a favored hypothesis or simply to 'make a splash' is among the worst ethical violations one can imagine in any research community. Besides destroying your reputation, it can harm the credibility of the field as a whole. A similarly grave ethical violation would be the selective reporting of data, quantitative or qualitative, as a way to support a favored argument. It is important to report all of your data and the story it tells, even if this story challenges what you expected to find.

Plagiarism, the partial or wholesale use of someone's else's work (here we mean not just ideas or results but also sentences and phrases) without giving proper credit, has been a growing problem among students as internet technology has enabled easy access to a growing body of knowledge. The term 'plagiarism' is derived from a Latin root ('plagiarius') meaning 'kidnapper.' In defining plagiarism, it is useful to examine the multiple forms that plagiarism can take. Forms of plagiarism include blatant plagiarism, technical plagiarism, patchwork plagiarism, and self-plagiarism. Blatant plagiarism is a deliberate act intended to deceive others; in this case, a person copies work and knowingly omits citing or giving credit to the original source. Acknowledging and citing the work of other scholars is an important part of the scientific process, and it is vital to establish good habits around this norm from the earliest stage of one's career. It is not only ideas and data that must be cited, but also sentences and phrases that are close to that which appears in another person's work. The common practice of paraphrasing, or reducing the sense of a passage in another text to one or more sentences, is acceptable so long as you cite the author and passage being paraphrased. Just as technology is an enabler of plagiarism, it can also help you acknowledge others' work more efficiently. Open-source tools such as Google Scholar, as well as the electronic catalogues of most university libraries, allow you not only to quickly locate articles, book reviews, and even entire e-books, but also to export citations quickly and easily to your own work.

## Chapter Summary

As the American Anthropological Association notes in its *Principles of Professional Responsibility*, 'As a social enterprise, research and practice always involve others – colleagues, students, research participants, employers, clients, funding agencies (whether institutional, community-based or individual)' (AAA Ethics Forum 2012). Given the complexity of research ethics, a number of professional and funding bodies have drafted codes of research conduct to provide researchers with guidance on some of the dilemmas and challenges they might face during the course of their research.

It is natural that PIR research should engage with the real world, including human subjects, and contribute to better policy-making. However, engaging with real structures of power and people suggests important ethical considerations we have surveyed in this chapter. Certain kinds of research, especially those employing interpretivist and critical theory approaches, argue that researchers should not only recognize their place in existing power structures, but also work to reform those structures. But all kinds of PIR research – positivist and interpretivist, qualitative and quantitative, observational and experimental – have certain shared ethical standards to which you should strive to adhere. These include many values associated with research integrity: impartiality, independence, and academic honesty.

Research ethics thus inform every step of the research process, from thinking about how to formulate a research question to the implications of research funding for academic independence. Thinking about ethics is also essential if we plan to interact with human subjects. Anytime we ask people to participate in our research, we should take into consideration whether or not we have secured their informed consent. We should also consider whether or not there is a prospect for harm to the researcher or research participants. We also need to remember that serious breaches of academic trust, such as plagiarism and data falsification, have far reaching consequences for the researcher and for trust in the academic community as a whole. Now that we have reflected upon the ethics of the research process, we can begin the process of formulating a research question, the topic of the next chapter.

### Suggested Further Reading

Ackerly, Brooke, and True, Jacqui. 2008. Reflexivity in Practice: Power and Ethics in Feminist Research on International Relations. *International Studies Review*, 10(4), 693-707.
This article provides an introduction to reflexivity. It does this through an interrogation of questions of power and ethics in research.

Bryman, Alan. 2008. *Social Research Methods*. Oxford: Oxford University Press. See Chapter 5, Ethics and Politics in Social Research, pp. 112-136.
Bryman provides an overview of research ethics and standards that are relevant to a broad range of social sciences.

Jacobsen, Karen, and Landau, Lauren B. 2003. The Dual Imperative of Refugee Research: Some Methodological and Ethical Considerations in Social Science Research and Forced Migration. *Disasters*, 23(3), 195-196.
This article is a helpful introduction to many of the practical and ethical dilemmas faced by researchers conducting fieldwork with vulnerable population groups.

Lipson, Charles. 2005. *How to Write a BA Thesis: A Practical Guide from Your First Ideas to Your Finished Paper*. Chicago, IL: University of Chicago Press. See Chapter 3: Taking Effective Notes and Avoiding Plagiarism, pp. 37-65.
Lipson provides some good practical tips and strategies for research that will help you to minimize the risk of misattribution of sources or failure to attribute sources.

# 4

# Your Research Question

━━━━━━━━━━━━━━ Learning Objectives ━━━━━━━━━━━━━━

- To understand how to translate a research topic into a research question;
- To familiarize yourself with the characteristics of good research questions;
- To consider the relationship between theory and your research question;
- To differentiate between exploratory, explanatory, evaluative, and reflective research questions.

Now that you have chosen your research topic, settled on a general research approach, and accounted for issues of research ethics, it is time to translate your topic into a research question. Most research in PIR today is **question-based**, which means that it begins with the posing of an explicit question at the outset, and responds to that question through a carefully-conceived research design in a paper or thesis (Lamont 2015, 30). This requires the translation of an idea into a single sentence that simultaneously captures your research interests, articulates the task you want to accomplish, and suggests your line of inquiry and how it contributes to PIR as a field. The research question thus also suggests the general methodology that will be used to answer it: positivist or interpretivist. To remind you of these terms, positivism encompasses research questions that attempt to find a causal relationship between two or more variables, while interpretive questions help us improve our understanding of how meanings assigned to PIR phenomena shape actions, institutions, and actors. In sum, to complete your next task, it is necessary to translate your topic into a question, and think about how your question will inform a body of theory and be relevant and interesting to your readers.

Assessment of your work will reflect how successfully you have responded to the question posed. But what constitutes a good research question? As noted in Chapter 2, PIR is defined in part by the plurality of methodological commitments and methods used by researchers. This plurality, in turn, is reflected in the types of questions we ask in our research. There is no single formula for designing an effective research question in PIR. At the same time, this does not mean that anything goes as both positivist and interpretivist research traditions provide a set of standards for evaluating good research questions.

In this chapter, we discuss the importance of formulating a good research question, focusing on a number of issues related to the task. We will guide you through how to go from a general research interest in a topic to a clearly formulated research question. It is here we will discuss how to distinguish between *exploratory*, *explanatory*, *evaluative*, and *reflective* research questions. Then we will conclude with a discussion of how theory relates to our research question and provide an exercise that will help you to formulate your own research question.

## The Rationale for a Good Research Question

Formulating a good research question will be among the most important steps you take in the research process. A well-conceived question lays the foundation for everything else you will do. It may help determine whether someone will actually want to read your research by capturing their attention. 'But wait!' you may say, 'my only reader is my professor, and she has no choice but to read and assess my paper. So why would I want to capture *her* attention?' You are right that at this stage your readership consists of exactly one person. But if you plan to do any kind of writing in the future – and chances are that you will – the need to frame your memo, article, analysis, or other product around a compelling question is a vital skill to develop. Getting someone's attention is becoming increasingly competitive. This is why the internet is full of outrageous 'clickbait,' and even well-regarded media outlets must use certain kinds of headlines to get people's attention. Good questions function as a kind of clickbait for your audience, whether those are readers of an academic journal, your colleagues and managers at a company, or consumers of a policy paper in the United Nations.

Given your personal interest and investment in a particular topic, it may seem inherently fascinating from your perspective. But a broader public also needs to find it fascinating. The research question will help suggest why. Perhaps you have just returned from a stint studying abroad in Morocco, where you have learned about women's activism in rural areas. This inspires you to write an undergraduate thesis on the topic. It is easy to assume that everyone else will automatically be equally passionate about Moroccan women activists, but most people are busy with their own interests (not to mention the massive amounts of news and information thrown at them by their smartphones on a daily basis) and don't necessarily share your enthusiasm. But your reader, or at the very least your professor, will share with you a broader interest in important areas of PIR inquiry, such as social movements or gender and politics. Thus, it is important to come up with a question that not only zeroes in on your topic, but also points to broader concerns in the discipline. In other words, you need to relate your topic to theoretical PIR debates. The way your question is formulated should immediately allow an educated reader to understand why and how it relates to some bigger issues. Let's say you translate your interest in Moroccan women's activism into the following question:

*What impact has the rise of women's organizations had on local politics in Morocco?*

You will see later on that this is an explanatory question, focusing on how one phenomenon impacts another. Beyond those interested in Moroccan politics, the question should also capture those interested in gender, civil society, and local politics, thereby suggesting a number of literatures (Chapter 5) and theoretical traditions in PIR.

Another reason that a clear, interesting, and theoretically relevant research question is important is that it will serve as a guide for you throughout the research process. In the middle of that process, when you are drowning in data and other research materials and perhaps losing sight of what you are doing and why it all matters, having a research question to return to and restore focus will be extremely helpful. This question will also aid in your discussions with your professor, advisor, or thesis supervisor. At any stage of the research process, you should ensure that all of your efforts ultimately come back to the task of responding to this question in a manner that upholds the highest ethical and research standards. In short, without a cogent research question, it is difficult to write a convincing essay or thesis.

## From Research Topic to Research Question

The process of formulating a research question is related to the choice of a logic of inquiry. As you begin to translate topic to question, think about the following issues: Does your topic encompass an unexpected outcome which does not conform to theoretical expectations or conventional wisdom? For example, perhaps an influential theory suggests that high levels of economic inequality increase support for populism, but you have found a case in which populist parties are weak despite the existence of inequality. Alternatively, there may be something about your topic that constitutes an overlooked gap in the existing literature. Perhaps the existing scholarship on the foreign policies of the European Union (EU) neglects to describe and explain when and why the EU pursues a human rights-centered approach. In other words, your topic should have an underlying logic of inquiry to guide your research project. Research, after all, should always consist of more than anecdotes or simple description. And your research question, in turn, should point to how you will augment knowledge or contribute to solving a problem in PIR.

Although framing your research question might at first glance appear to be a rather straightforward task, in fact it requires careful reflection because it will become an important factor in establishing what kind of research design you use and which methods are most appropriately suited to your project. In other words, there must be logical consistency between your research question, your research design, and your methods. What we mean by this should become clearer in the forthcoming sections, as well as the ensuing chapters.

Before we can get to formulating your research question, we need to take a step back in the research process and ask ourselves how we arrived at our topic in the first place. Usually, the choice of topic stems from a personal interest in something in the social world. While the role of curiosity is often downplayed in methods textbooks, it is natural that our own curiosity and passion about a given topic serve both as a catalyst and propellant of a research project over time. In fact, often the best papers and theses are written by researchers who have a personal commitment to a topic. In academic books, such personal motivations are frequently described in a preface section. The political scientist Barbara Geddes even suggests that rather than starting from gaps in the literature, a research topic should start from your own 'unfocused curiosity' (2010, 29). The process of refining your topic into a question helps bring this curiosity into focus and contextualizes it within the arena of scholarly debates in PIR.

## Geddes on Finding a Research Topic

Contrary to the advice about looking for holes in the literature, good research in the comparative field often begins either with an intense but unfocused curiosity about why some event or process has happened or with a sense of sputtering indignation at the patent idiocy of some particular argument advanced in the literature. Sometimes political commitments or an aroused sense of injustice drive this curiosity or indignation. Potential researchers who feel little curiosity, intuition, or indignation in response to the social world and the arguments published about it should consider the possibility that they have chosen the wrong job.

Barbara Geddes. 2010. *Paradigms and Sand Castles: Theory Building and Research Design in Comparative Politics.* Ann Arbor, MI: University of Michigan Press, p. 29.

If you, as Geddes suggests, have come to your topic out of an 'intense but unfocused' curiosity, then you might want to begin to ask yourself probing questions about what it is exactly that has produced this curiosity about your topic. Is it that you are unsatisfied with conventional wisdom about what has given rise to a particular political phenomenon, such as populism? Or, perhaps your interest isn't about cause and effect at all. You might be asking yourself: how has a certain way of doing things come about? Why do human rights discourses dominate in the United Nations even as the body is unwilling or unable to actually enforce human rights norms? This process is described by Lobo-Guerrero as 'wondering' (2013, 25–28).

## Lobo-Guerrero on Wondering

Wondering is an attitude to approach research material on the grounds of its very existence. Its starting point is to encourage the researcher to pose questions on why something has been presented or analyzed in a particular way; what needs to be in place for a particular idea, which appears obvious or simple, to be possible, and indeed, thinkable; and what role do those ideas and thought play on the way the world is portrayed?

Luis Lobo-Guerrero. 2013. Wondering as Research Attitude. In Mark B. Salter and Can E. Mutlu (eds.), *Research Methods in Critical Security Studies: An Introduction*. New York: Routledge, p. 25.

Through this process of self-reflection and 'wondering' about your topic, you are now beginning to think about your topic in the form of question-based research. As noted in the introduction to this chapter, how you frame your question will be critical to determining how your research is evaluated by others. Take a moment to reflect on why you have selected your research topic and what you wish to learn from the research process. Having completed this step, you will now also be able to think about whether your research will be *exploratory*, *explanatory*, *evaluative*, or *reflective*. While this typology does not necessarily capture all the types of question we ask in PIR, it can assist in getting you to think about your research question in a more structured manner.

Your research topic is something that you likely already had in mind before picking up this textbook. You may have derived the topic on the basis of your own interests, or perhaps you were assigned a list of topics in class, and you selected the one most closely related to your interests. Topics are commonly articulated as broad subjects. While human rights and foreign policy is a research topic, it is not a research question. There are numerous ways one can approach this topic, from highlighting how state interest impedes a values-based foreign policy to explaining how human rights develop as a norm in international organizations. In short, there are many different aspects of any research topic that can generate a number of valuable questions. There is no shortcut formula to arriving at your research question. However, once you have decided which aspect of your topic is of greatest interest, you should be in a good position to begin formulating a question.

For example, imagine your narrowed topic of interest is the growth of populist political parties in post-communist Central and Eastern European countries. Observing the growing influence of these parties in recent years, you might ask if their increasing popularity can be explained by a particular phenomenon or event. As noted above, how you frame your question and the words you choose will also say something about your perspective on methodology, research design, and the methods you will use to gather and analyze data. This is because your research question will set out the topic and goals of your research project and will also hint at your methodology.

## A Good Research Question...

- Is short and grammatically simple
- Is precise
- Is open-ended
- Is researchable
- Is rooted in scholarly debates
- Is theoretically interesting
- Refers to general concepts rather than specific variables
- States the research goal
- Implies the research approach
- Is not normative or speculative

Exploratory research aims to stake out new ground or bring to the table new knowledge on a given subject. Its general purpose can be to open avenues for future research that can later confirm or refute theory (Gerring 2004). One way this can be achieved is an exploratory study that classifies or creates new categories. For example, a project could be to map populist parties in a particular country. In practical terms, this could mean responding to questions like: who are they, who leads them, what are their platforms, who votes for them, and what distinguishes one from another? Alternatively, an exploratory essay might outline a future research agenda on populist political parties. For example, the existing scholarship on populism might rely heavily on surveys, but you might want to advocate a research agenda that employs focus groups and experiments as a way to better understand the roots of populist support. There are many ways that a research question might suggest an exploratory research agenda. Here, the goal is not generalization or causal inference (though it may be indirectly related to both of these). For the example above on new directions in studying populism, a possible question could ask: 'how can we uncover why populism is on the rise?' Alternatively, an exploratory question might simply call for description as part of the task of characterizing a particular phenomenon. For instance, we may ask: 'what is the nature of nationalism in contemporary Europe?' Finally, exploratory research questions may be initiated with the words 'what role,' such as: 'what role did social media play in mobilizing protests during the 2011 Tunisian revolution?' Exploratory research questions can lead to the development of new categories or concepts that will then be used by scholars to pursue various avenues of research.

Explanatory research aims to explain why a particular event or outcome occurred, and is thus inherently positivist in its orientation. A positivist question, in turn, tends to generate 'why' or 'what explains'-type questions. You might pose one of the following explanatory questions, for example: 'Why did Donald Trump win the 2016 US presidential election?' Or, 'why did France, the UK, and the US decide to intervene in Libya in 2011?' Here the focus is on identifying causal mechanisms, thereby suggesting a research design that will allow for causal inference. Your choices in this regard will be described in Chapter 6.

A third category of research is evaluative. Evaluative research focuses on measuring the effectiveness of a particular policy, institution, or action and is associated with 'how effective'-type research questions. For example, you might ask: 'how effective are international courts in prosecuting war crimes?' or 'how effective are environmental agreements in reducing harmful emissions?' Notice that evaluative questions are well suited to policy analysis. If you peruse the research output of think-tanks, or look at the reports of governments and international organizations, you are likely to find many examples of evaluative research.

The fourth and final category worth mentioning is reflective research. Reflective research problematizes norms and practices that are otherwise taken for granted in order to draw attention to how disciplinary knowledge privileges certain kinds of research questions over others. 'How'-type questions are often well-suited to reflective research projects. For example, we might ask: 'how has PIR research on nationalism in Southeast Asia shaped popular understanding of the causes of conflict in the region?' The idea is that we need to problematize how PIR researchers define and deal with a complex phenomenon like nationalism. Has it been based on western or postcolonial biases? How has their framing of nationalism affected how western policy-makers have dealt with countries in Southeast Asia?

One last note is in order. The interrogative pronoun (what, why, how, etc.) you choose to begin your question does not necessarily indicate the type of question it is. An explanatory question can begin with 'what' (i.e., 'what explains?' or 'what has been the impact of?') just as it can open with a reflective question (i.e., 'what is the meaning of?').

## Logic of Inquiry and Research Questions

Note that each of the above types of research and associated research question terms has its own distinct logic. For example, explanatory questions ('why' and 'what explains') focus on causality and explanation. These questions can be broken down into **independent variables** (the explanatory factors) and dependent variables (what you are attempting to explain). For example, in one of the 'why' questions mentioned above, US, UK, and French intervention is the dependent variable, and the question suggests that the research project will identify the independent variable or variables which explain when Western states choose to intervene militarily. Another question in the explanatory category, that about the 2016 election similarly does not specify any independent variables. That is OK. However, explanatory research questions can also be written in such a way that you hint at the independent variable. Research questions that suggest testing a hypothesis often explicitly name the independent variable whose influence you want to test for. An example: 'How did social media influence the 2011 Arab uprisings?' In this case, social media is the independent variable whose relationship to popular uprisings (the dependent variable) you want to examine.

Questions such as these, which focus on causality, constitute the core of positivist research design. Some political scientists, such as King, Keohane and Verba (1994), argue that all social science research questions should be causal. However, as we noted in Chapter 1, such an injunction is too narrow to encompass a field as diverse as PIR.

There are also simply what Howard (2017, 36–37) describes as 'what happened'-type research questions. While there is often a push for explanation in PIR, sometimes we need to step back and describe complex political processes and phenomena. It is often difficult to understand what happened; hence the countless volumes on certain key historical events, such as the Second World War. 'What happened' research questions also allow us to delineate concepts, though in a less critical and deconstructive way than reflective approaches. Given their focus on understanding and measuring concepts, 'what happened' questions are closely tied to issues of operationalization and measurement, described in Chapter 9.

Reflective and other kinds of interpretivist research questions, as noted above, explore the social and political construction of objects of study that are otherwise taken for granted. For example, they may grapple with the question of how a concept such as 'states' came into being. Or ask if the way we conceive phenomena such as 'nationalism' makes sense. Scholars associated with critical theory approaches emphasize that explanation should not be the sole intellectual goal of our research. Critical theory emerged from the Marxist tradition and it was developed by a group of sociologists in Germany who referred to themselves as The Frankfurt School. Critical theory has a normative goal: it aims at critiquing and changing society as a whole rather than merely understanding or explaining it. Critical theory's aim is to uncover the assumptions that prevent us from grasping how the world really works.

## Interpretivism and Causality

It would be incorrect to assume that interpretive research has no interest in causal inference due to its focus on meaning. **Emergent causality** offers an alternative to positivist explanatory approaches by focusing instead on how a particular identity, movement, or practice emerged in the first place. Emergent causality assumes that the effects of emergent social practices cannot be knowable at the outset. This is because what is 'being produced could not be conceptualized before its production' (Connolly 2004, 343). We will revisit this concept in Chapters 6 and 8.

To sum up, your research question helps define the type of research you need to answer it. It indicates whether your research will be exploratory, explanatory, evaluative, or reflective, and whether it will build theory or test existing theories, as a subsequent section elaborates.

## General Characteristics of a Good Research Question

Epistemology and ontology notwithstanding, there are some common features of any good research question. Note, for instance, that all of the example questions we have mentioned thus far avoid normative starting words like 'should' or 'ought.' Normative issues, or issues to which you have a values-based commitment, can serve as an excellent motivator when you are searching for a topic. A paper or thesis can have normative implications, but normative concerns should not serve as the basis for a research question. Rather, normative questions require moral, ethical, ideological, philosophical, or political arguments. Moreover, a good research question in PIR should not speculate what will happen in the future. If you are asking an explanatory question, you can certainly make predictions based on your causal findings in the conclusion to your paper or thesis. And others can test to see whether your theory holds against future cases in order to see whether or not your theory has predictive validity. But a 'crystal ball' question should not serve as the foundation of your research design.

## Normative and 'Crystal Ball' Questions

Should the United States keep its military in northern Syria?

Will the United States and China go to war over the South China Sea?

Your research question, furthermore, should be brief, structurally simple, precise, and open-ended. Avoid long questions: 'less is more' should be the guiding principle. Keep editing your question until no further word can be deleted. Do not bring unnecessary clarifications or conditions into the question. Distill it to its very essence. Avoid composite questions, such as 'what is the state of democracy in Zimbabwe and why?' These are two separate projects, and the first is descriptive (an exploratory question) while the second is explanatory.

Speaking of exploratory questions that suggest description, here is another one: 'what was the international community's response to the humanitarian crisis in Yemen?' The problem with such a question is that it invites a response that would simply chronologically state what had happened with no additional analysis. While exploratory questions do sometimes appear in PIR journals, most research paper assignments will ask you to go beyond mere description. Thus, rephrasing the question above along these lines could make it theoretically relevant and more desirable. An example of such a question is: 'why didn't the doctrine of Responsibility to Protect (R2P) lead external states to intervene in Yemen and alleviate widespread civilian deaths and humanitarian suffering?' This question would in turn allow you to explore what role, if any, the emergent doctrine of R2P played in international debates.

Moreover, research questions should not contain implicit answers: 'how' questions can stray into this territory. For example, if you ask 'how does Confucianism explain party politics in South Korea?,' your question already presupposes that culture has an important causal role. But you don't know that for sure yet, or at least have not proven it. It would be better to rephrase this question so that it is more like the one above about the impact of social media on the 2011 Tunisian revolution: 'What role does Confucianism play in shaping party politics in South Korea?' This reformulation of the question implies that Confucianism may or may not be the main causal factor, or may be one cause among many. A question implying that you will examine a specific case (such as South Korea) is acceptable (Chapter 6), but it may be less easily justifiable in terms of its generalizability, and thus value to social science. Thus, the question about social media and Tunisia might be expanded to include the entire Arab Spring of 2010–2011, and the question about South Korea might be reformulated to encompass other societies where Confucianism is deeply rooted.

Research questions should also be related to existing scholarly debates. When thinking about your question, survey what authors are writing about promising directions for future research. Have a look at how scholars writing about your topic answer the question 'who cares?' In choosing your topic, you have probably engaged in some kind of early literature review to get a sense of what scholars are discussing in academic journals, books, and online fora. You may find, for example, a lively debate among scholars and pundits about why Jair Bolsonaro won the 2018 Brazilian presidential election. That there is such a debate is intuitive, but as you start to work on your literature review (Chapter 5), you will want to dig up the scholarly work that engages the question. Google may at first glance be a tempting way to find this literature, but getting hundreds of thousands of hits on a topic like Bolsonaro's victory is fast, but not so useful. Instead, consider consulting the *Annual Review of Political Science*, which captures the latest scholarship. Don't have time to read entire articles? Have a look at review articles and essays published in most journals. Look for conventional wisdom, and think about whether it can be challenged. Let's say many analysts assume that Bolsonaro prevailed because of his promises to root out corruption. Perhaps you will see that inadequate attention has been given to the collapse of the Left in Brazilian politics, and choose to focus on that as an explanatory factor. But here we stray into Chapter 5 territory. The box presented earlier in this chapter ('A good research question…') summarizes the preceding discussion.

## Research Questions and Theory

Theory is what distinguishes scholarly work in PIR from opinion pieces, think-tank reports, and other forms of non-fiction writing. If numbers in PIR are intimidating for many students (Chapter 9), so is theory, in part because it tends toward abstraction. Stephen Van Evera argues that theories 'are general statements that describe and explain the causes or effects of classes of phenomena' (1997, 7–8). Here, we find two critical assumptions. The first is that theories should be 'general statements.' In other words, they should not be overly specific or descriptive. Furthermore, the emphasis is on parsimony, or being thrifty with your words. A theory that is too specific will have less explanatory power across a broad range of cases. The second assumption is that all theories describe or explain cause and effect. But this is a positivist assumption: the body of theory associated with interpretive research will have a different set of assumptions and focus on the question 'how do we know what we know about PIR?'

Whether in the positivist or interpretivist tradition, theories deliberately simplify reality. Their purpose is not to explain or describe every facet of a phenomenon in PIR. No theory attempts to explain it all. Rather, theories pinpoint specific elements of a process. They not only predict certain outcomes, but also help us to understand what is important.

So you should not approach theory with inflated expectations, but you should understand that theories set the research agenda, help us identify puzzles and debates, and thus powerfully inform how we formulate our research questions. The first step toward understanding the role of theory in formulating your research question is to place the question on the positivist–interpretive spectrum.

## Positivist Theory

From the positivist perspective, theories can be translated into arrow diagrams that clearly show the relationship between variables. For example, democratic peace theory (Kinsella 2005) posits that a democratic system of governance is the independent variable that accounts for an absence of war among democratic states (the dependent variable).

(Independent Variable)           ⟶         (Dependent Variable)

Democracy                        ⟶         Peace

Let's return to the example of populist political parties in Europe. Existing theories might suggest that growing levels of immigration generate higher levels of support for populist political parties. The idea behind this theory is that voters feel unsettled by the changing demographics associated with mass migration, and will seek comfort in parties who appeal to nativist sentiments while promising to curb immigration. In your research, you would like to engage with this theory, and you come up with the following question:

> *Does an increase in migration result in increased levels of support for populist political parties?*

Here your question is clearly positivist in that you are seeking to explain a particular phenomenon – the electoral success of populist parties. The independent variable whose effect you have chosen to test is migration. Perhaps you would like to test a theory and find out whether the assumptions hold or were disproven when subjected to empirical tests. These are positivist *theory-testing questions*. This type of research question is perhaps the most straightforward to connect with a body of scholarship as every issue area in PIR – be it electoral politics, political party system development, or international security – contains numerous opposing theoretical debates. As noted earlier, theory usually comprises general cause-and-effect statements. As a result, specific hypotheses of what we should expect to see, if the theory holds, are easily deducted from these general statements. Using the research question above, we might come with the following hypothesis:

> *An influx of migrants into Austria in 2015 strengthened the electoral prospects of the Freedom Party.*

One part of our data analysis would be aimed at testing this hypothesis for the Austrian case. This, in short, is a cause-and-effect statement that can be tested.

## Interpretivist Theory

Many questions asked by scholars of PIR do not conform to the mold of positivism. Scholars working in the interpretive tradition ask research questions which focus on identifying the core relations that are under study. When describing what constitutes a research question, Mark Salter posits that '[a] clean research question identifies the core relations that are under study, but does not seek efficiency or coherence, or even parsimony of explanation of those relations' (2013, 16). Here, Salter focuses on whether or not the research question adequately links the case or case studies chosen by the researcher with concepts or theoretical debates. Salter takes issue with a perceived positivist bias towards parsimony – the simpler the theory, the greater the theory's potential explanatory power. Moreover, Salter seeks to expand the scope of theorizing to include research agendas that do not seek causal inference.

Patrick Jackson observes that there exist two strands of reflexive research, and that the first more closely aligns with traditional, or positivist, approaches in that the researcher attempts, to the best of their ability, to take on an impartial and disinterested approach to their subject of study (Jackson 2016, 187). Here, when contemplating your research question, you will acknowledge the core ontological-epistemological assumptions of interpretive research that were discussed in Chapter 2. This might mean that you will acknowledge that there are multiple perspectives on your topic, and your own positionality as a researcher, but you will seek to minimize your own biases as you approach your research.

Interpretive research is based on the assumption that social reality is not singular or objective, but rather constructed by human experiences and social contexts, and is therefore best studied within its socio-historic context by reconciling the subjective interpretations of its various participants. As interpretive researchers understand PIR phenomena as inseparable from their cultural, historical, and social context, they interpret the reality through a 'sense-making' process rather than a hypothesis-testing process.

In Jackson's study of post-Second World War German reconstruction, we find examples of 'why' research questions that fit within the interpretive tradition (Jackson 2006):

- Why was a German state rebuilt so soon after the end of the Second World War - a war that had, after all, been fought against a German state?
- Why did the United States take the leading role in rebuilding the western zones of occupation?
- Why was this reconstruction carried out primarily through the Marshall Plan and NATO, placing the BRD [Federal Republic of Germany] on somewhat of an equal footing with the other members of what quite recently had been an anti-German coalition?

Jackson argues that the answer to his question lies in the Federal Republic of Germany's use of civilizational discourse, which firmly embedded the new post-Second World War state in the West. The questions above are formulated such that they can be seen as closely related to the 'why' or 'what explains' question presented earlier. Indeed, some research questions can be approached from a positivist or an interpretivist perspective. However, Jackson points out that in addition to his empirical puzzle, good research should also account for human agency. What Jackson means by this is that what we study is not stable and fixed, like a rock, but rather is social and dynamic and constructed by human beings, scholars included.

## Exercise

By translating your research topic into a research question, you have a clear idea as to what methodological assumptions you are making (positivist or interpretive) and the overall aim or goal of your project. In the exercise below, write your research question and specify what kind of question you have asked. This will help you later in making choices about research design and research methods.

Having completed the exercise, you might want to take into consideration research questions that should be 'important' to the real world. Whether or not something is important to the real world is highly subjective, but at this point you should at the very least be able to answer the 'so what?' question in relation to your own research question. Try to assume that you have completed your research project, or you have responded to your research question, and ask yourself: what is the significance of what you have found or what you have not found? Why does it matter to your reader?

---

## Exercise: Formulating a Research Question

Research Question:_____

_____

What is the importance of your research question (so what)?

Is your research question positivist or interpretivist? And why?

What is the significance of your question word (why, how, what, etc.) for your question?

What kind of research question (exploratory, explanatory, evaluative, or reflective) have you asked? And why?

---

## Chapter Summary

One of the first steps to take in the research process is to translate your topic into a research question. This chapter has discussed why research questions are vital and explained how to craft a good question. It has also demonstrated that research questions can come in many different forms. How you arrive at your research question will be determined by what facets of your research topic you find interesting or puzzling. All good research questions will have an underlying logic of inquiry, whether they be positivist or interpretive. Your research question should provide a solid foundation for the rest of your project.

Having formulated a question, you can begin to think about your research design, which is the topic of Chapter 6. For now, you might want to begin to understand the link between your research question and your research design. One of the choices you will face in terms of research design is whether to pursue the study of a single case or a small number of cases, or whether you will employ statistical analysis of a large number of cases (large-$N$ design). Interpretive research questions that focus on understanding processes, concepts, or ideas, often lend themselves to small-*N* case study research. But, as Chapter 6 will highlight, the small-*N* comparative case design is also well equipped to deal with causality. Often, however, PIR researchers aiming to test certain theories or specific hypotheses turn to large-*N* research and various statistical tools (see Chapters 9 and 10). However, the immediate next step you will take is to research and write a literature review, the subject of the next chapter. As we suggested above, your research question will help to direct you to the literature that is most relevant.

## Suggested Further Reading

Baglione, Lisa A. 2020. *Writing a Research Paper in Political Science: A Practical Guide to Inquiry, Structure, and Methods*. Los Angeles: Sage.
Contains valuable advice on how to write different kinds of research questions.

Geddes, Barbara. 2010. *Paradigms and Sand Castles: Theory Building and Research Design in Comparative Politics*. Ann Arbor, MI: University of Michigan Press.
Geddes takes issue with standard positivistic designs for arriving at a research question, and instead argues that research questions should be driven by your curiosity.

Howard, Christopher. 2017. *Thinking Like a Political Scientist: A Practical Guide to Research Methods*.
An excellent book on methods that includes a discussion of various kinds of research questions and their underlying logic of inquiry.

Lobo-Guerrero, Luis. 2013. Wondering as Research Attitude. In Mark B. Salter and Can E. Mutlu (eds.), *Research Methods in Critical Security Studies: An Introduction*. New York: Routledge.
Like Geddes, Lobo-Guerrero challenges positivist prescriptions for research questions and argues that the research questions should reflect your sense of curiosity about a research topic.

Shively, W. Phillips. 2013. *The Craft of Political Research*, 9th edition. New York: Pearson. See Chapter 2: Political Theories and Research Topics, pp. 14-32.
Shively presents a guide to developing research questions to test causal (positivist) theories in PIR.

# 5

# Compiling and Writing a Literature Review

━━━━━━━━━━ Learning Objectives ━━━━━━━━━━

- To understand the purpose and value of a literature review;
- To identify strategies for locating and gathering scholarly sources for a literature review;
- To learn how to structure, organize, and write a literature review.

As discussed in Chapter 4, your topic and research question, in addition to being interesting and relevant to the wider world, should also engage with some larger issues of interest to other scholars and students of PIR. The next step in the research process is to think about how to situate your project in the existing body of PIR scholarship. The purpose of a **literature review** (also sometimes called the 'lit review') is just that. A literature review is an analytical survey of published research on a topic related to your research question. It analyzes, organizes, and contextualizes the existing scholarship so as to identify gaps that your essay, dissertation, or thesis will address while situating your approach and argument in that scholarship.

While it may be tempting to start by writing the introduction to your research paper, you will have a much more effective thesis or paper if you begin by compiling and writing a proper literature review. (In fact, as we suggest in Chapter 11, the introduction should probably be written last.) Students often assume that a literature review involves searching for articles and books which cover exactly the same ground as their proposed question. For example, if you are interested in the causes of the populist surge in Europe, you might be inclined to gather research articles which describe and explain the rise of populism in one or more European countries. Indeed, this material may be helpful, empirically and theoretically. But a literature review should also engage with the scholarship covering concepts and theoretical frameworks which transcend your empirical focus alone. In the example of a project on populist parties, theoretically and conceptually relevant literature might include that on voting behavior, the politics of grievance, and social movements – whether or not it focuses on Europe.

In this chapter, we introduce you to the process of compiling and writing a literature review. We first explain why a literature review is important and then go through the process of compiling and writing one, step by step. We provide examples of how the various components of a literature review might look based on a fictional research project on US intervention in Libya. We cover topics such as searching for scholarly materials in electronic library databases, using review essays, note-taking, and structuring a literature review. The 'Suggested Further Reading' section at the end of the chapter includes recent examples of review essays, which serve both as a model of an expanded literature review and a source of materials to include in your own review.

## Why a Literature Review?

You probably have already encountered literature reviews. They are part of almost every **peer-reviewed** journal article or scholarly book that you have read for a class. If your instructor has assigned **review essays**, which provide an overview of the state of the PIR literature in a given area, you may have read what amounts to a lengthy literature review (Wesley 2008, 369–385).

Literature reviews constitute a sometimes underappreciated, yet essential component of every research paper, thesis, or scholarly publication. Indeed, a thorough literature review is the foundation upon which your research design, either positivist or interpretive, as well as your conclusions, will be built. Because interpretivist approaches are often concerned with tracing the meaning PIR phenomena acquire over time, some interpretive research papers might even have the feel of an elongated literature review that engages extensively with how a particular concept has been analyzed by other authors. For example, you might be writing a paper on the ways in which western PIR scholarship has dealt with 'political Islam' and how in turn this has shaped our understanding of phenomenon.

The bibliographic work you will carry out early in the project serves as a foundation for the literature review. Some professors may ask you to prepare an **annotated bibliography** as part of the first stages of a research process. An annotated bibliography is a list of citations followed by a brief paragraph (the annotation) which notes the importance of the source for your project. As we will emphasize in Chapter 11, whether or not you prepare an annotated bibliography, it is important to be meticulous in keeping notes during this stage, not only for the sake of the literature review itself, but also for **referencing** purposes. As we will also discuss in Chapter 11, the literature review is typically the section that appears right after the introduction, but it should also be able to stand alone as a coherently written essay.

The term 'literature' of course also denotes fiction or novels, but here it is used to refer to a scholarly body of work. The purpose of a literature review, however, is not simply to list relevant articles and books but rather to contextualize your research question by describing how other scholars have answered it while evaluating the strengths and weaknesses of each of their approaches. The literature review thus requires you to read and describe the existing literature in a systematic manner so that it can later be organized according to various approaches to your research question. Consequently, the literature review also helps demonstrate the relevance, importance, or novelty of your research question. It highlights to scholars in your field why and how your research contributes to, or advances, existing debates in the field. It will not only signal to the reader why and how your own research agenda relates to existing debates, but it will also instill confidence in the reader that you are well versed in the literature of your field. Many literature reviews culminate by highlighting one or more approaches as the most compelling, thereby helping to locate and articulate your **main argument.**

By contrast, an incomplete literature review will leave readers of your work with an impression that you are unfamiliar with the existing PIR scholarship and debates relating to your topic, making even the most convincingly argued and methodologically sound papers fall short. Readers might point out that your research question has already been addressed by another author, perhaps one who even made use of the exact same cases. Or you might find that you have misunderstood a particular theoretical approach, or have focused on testing an obscure theoretical model that has already been debunked by others. The literature review, in other words, also can provide vital information that leads you to revise your project in important ways. A literature review might also compel you to further reflect upon, or even modify, your research question. Or perhaps a literature review will reveal that your question points you toward an intellectual dead end. If this is the case, you can draw inspiration from the debates that you have encountered in your literature review to recraft your question.

Depending on its focus, the works you cite in your literature review may also become a source of empirical data for other parts of your thesis or essay. For example, if your topic is human rights and foreign policy, when reviewing the constructivist IR literature on the spread of human rights norms, you might happen upon empirical data about cases that you could then cite in your data analysis (see Chapters 7–10).

## Where Do I Start?

In reading review essays and literature reviews in peer-reviewed journal articles, you might have noticed that literature reviews assume diverse forms and can be organized in a number of different ways. PIR scholarship has grown exponentially in recent decades as the number of journals has expanded. Commensurate with this growth has been an increase in ready electronic access to most journals and many books. Long gone are the days when students thumbed through library card catalogues to locate the needed materials. Indeed, given the breadth and extent of literature on any topic of interest in PIR, the heightened access to this scholarship afforded by electronic databases, and the diverse forms that literature reviews assume, the task of condensing potentially large bodies of literature into a concise literature review may at first appear to be daunting. Thus, when confronted with the task of putting together a literature review on your research question, the first issue that comes to mind might very well be where to start.

One of the skills you will need to conduct an effective literature review is the ability to distinguish scholarly, peer-reviewed work from non-scholarly, non-peer-reviewed work. While this may appear to be stating the obvious, you should keep in mind that, even among scholars, the growing number of academic journals has meant that it is difficult to discern genuine peer-reviewed journals from a growing number of predatory journals that have the outward appearance of scholarly publications, but do not maintain their standards. In order to be sure that what you are using meets the highest standards of peer review, you could also start by looking for journals that have appeared on course syllabi designed by recognized professors at reputable institutions. Syllabi are readily available online through a simple Google search, but you might consider using syllabi databases such as that maintained by the American Political Science Association. Consider also using journals like the *Annual Review of Political Science,* which compiles the latest scholarship. Alternatively, while subjective, you might be able to find lists of the most highly respected journals in your field through the websites of professional organizations such as the International Studies Association (ISA). Table 5.1 contains a list of major journals in the PIR field. Note that this list is not meant to be comprehensive, but rather to highlight a few highly-regarded journals in some of the disciplines' sub-fields.

This does not mean, however, that you cannot sometimes include other, non-peer-reviewed kinds of work, such as the reports of think-tanks or international organizations,

**Table 5.1** Major journals in PIR and their associated sub-fields

| Journal | Sub-field |
| --- | --- |
| International Organization | IR |
| International Studies Quarterly | IR |
| International Security | IR |
| World Politics | IR |
| European Journal of International Relations | IR |
| Journal of Conflict Resolution | IR |
| Review of International Studies | IR |
| American Journal of Political Science | mixed |
| Quarterly Journal of Political Science | mixed |
| American Political Science Review | mixed |
| Comparative Politics | comparative |
| Comparative Political Studies | comparative |

trade books, or even some media products, in your literature review. This work still undergoes review of some sort, though it is usually internal to the institution or publication. However, it is less likely to be theoretically informed in the way that a peer-reviewed journal article or book is, and thus less amenable to be included in a literature review organized around alternative approaches. Nevertheless, non-peer-reviewed reports and articles may take a position on an issue in a way that will fit within your literature review's categorization of the scholarship. For example, the report of a UN agency on human development deficits in a given country might be included in a literature review which addresses how development affects political stability.

One of the best ways to ensure that you are accessing high-quality, peer-reviewed PIR scholarship is to use your university's library site to find articles and books rather than using an open internet search engine. To do this, you will need an ability to navigate your institution's electronic library search platform. Each one is different, as are the subscriptions your university holds to different journal databases. Your library staff are likely to offer online or in-person training on how to most effectively harness the available resources. Once you are comfortable with navigating the library site and its resources, you might want to try a **keyword search** which will give you access to major e-journal databases such as *JStor* or *EBSCOhost Academic Search Premier*. These databases have numerous helpful features, including the ability to save, export, and organize citations. A list of popular e-journal databases containing PIR and other social science journals appears in Table 5.2. Google Scholar can also be of assistance in searches for academic articles and books, but keep in mind that it does not provide you with the same degree of quality control as a library site or e-journal database, and it is sometimes more difficult to sort through. One helpful feature of Google Scholar is that it allows you to evaluate the extent to which a peer-reviewed article has been cited, and even who has cited it. If you notice an article on your topic that has a very high citation count, then you can be certain that this article has had a significant impact on debates related to your topic. Thus, it may be helpful to use Google Scholar as a tool alongside the e-journal databases.

**Table 5.2**   Popular e-journal databases

| |
| --- |
| JSTOR |
| Project MUSE |
| Sage Research Methods |
| ScienceDirect |
| Web of Science |
| ProQuest Central |
| Academic OneFile |
| Academic Search Complete |

Keyword searches will take some practice as different databases and library search engines have their idiosyncrasies. One major challenge in performing searches of databases is narrowing your results: as we mentioned, there is a lot out there in the PIR publishing world. In the event that your subject keyword returns too many results, you might try to narrow your search by modifying your search terms. For example, a search for 'authoritarianism' on *EBSCOhost's Academic Search Premier* returns tens of thousands of responses. However, by narrowing the search to 'presidential authoritarianism,' your search returns a much more manageable 700 or so responses. In addition to this, you may find it relevant to limit your search to a specific timeframe. Some electronic journal databases have archives going back to the 19th century. Such a broad time horizon for articles may not be relevant to your topic and research question. Thus, in the sidebar you can restrict the scope in time that you would like to search. By narrowing the timeframe to between 1990 and 2019, you will find that the number of total responses in a search for 'authoritarianism' is reduced to 23,622. Other filters will allow you to further narrow the scope of responses. For example, you can choose to display only results that were published in scholarly peer-reviewed journals. Once you have familiarized yourself with the relevant scholarship on your topic by compiling lists of articles and books, you will have to decide what merits inclusion in your literature review.

## Note-Taking for the Literature Review

As you gather articles and books for the literature review, it is vital to take notes. Good note-taking will not only help you to be a better writer, but it will also help you avoid any questions being raised about academic honesty, which we covered in Chapter 3. Plagiarism is often not intentional, but the result of sloppy note-taking on the part of the researcher. Good note-taking is a skill that is relevant not only to the literature review, but is also necessary throughout the entirety of the research process.

In the past, researchers used cards to take notes. Today, students and scholars have moved on from paper and pen to digital note-taking. There are a number of software packages that can help you to organize your notes and link them to bibliographic entries that you can later easily deploy in your paper or thesis. Note-taking can also be done directly on digital copies of journal articles and books by using the highlighting or comments features in a PDF reader. With digital note-taking, it is still important to ensure that you have transcribed full bibliographic entries and page numbers (more on this in Chapter 11). As we take notes, we might find that we have forgotten to provide a reference for some key observations that will be included in the literature review – or worse yet, forgotten what reference it came from. More often than not, attempting to track down a lost source a second time is an unnecessary and time-consuming exercise. Being meticulous from the outset will pay great dividends later on.

As you read and take notes, you should also be mapping out the schools of thought or approaches you will later analyze. You can do this by grouping together authors who make similar arguments and identifying points of disagreement with opposing perspectives. One helpful technique for doing this is to map out different perspectives using a table, matrix, or spectrum in which you place authors and works according to the orientation or position they have taken in a theoretical debate. To use an example from the study of ethnicity, nationalism, and politics, some of the main fault lines in the scholarship around this topic have to do with the degree to which ethnic identity is an innate or 'primordial' characteristic versus the extent to which ethnic identities are mobilized by 'identity entrepreneurs' to achieve political ends. Some scholarship lands between these two camps. In this case, you might create three lists reflecting this spectrum of theoretical approaches (i.e., primordialism, political mobilization, and a combination of the two). On each list, you would not only record bibliographic entries for articles and books fitting that paradigm, but also annotate them with brief descriptions of the argument and contributions of the work. You might also include in this annotation page numbers for key quotations and passages you might later cite. Here, too, technology helps PIR researchers to more efficiently perform tasks that once took much longer. For example, electronic book readers such as Kindle have useful highlight and note-taking features that allow you to quickly locate and reference passages.

## What to Include and What Not to Include in a Literature Review

How do you know which authors, articles, and books are the most relevant and important? As noted above, reading review essays and perusing syllabi will help you identify them. One obvious way to start finding relevant literature is to identify peer-reviewed articles which pose research questions similar to yours. As your research progresses, you will undoubtedly see certain names and titles pop up repeatedly. Eventually you will realize the gains of what is known as 'snowballing:' reputed scholarship will introduce you to yet more books and articles which you may choose to include in the literature review.

Depending on the nature of your research project, your literature review may be a narrow survey of selected literature on a topic or a more expansive analysis of scholarship on a larger question in PIR. A 10-page essay on the 2016 US election and Donald Trump's victory could draw on the extensive analysis of that electoral contest and divisions among scholars and analysts over whether Trump won due to cultural or economic dissatisfaction. But in a longer research paper or thesis, you could also widen the literature to studies of previous US elections. But there is no reason to limit your literature review to just studies of US elections: indeed, you might also consider how other Trump-like, populist candidates have won in diverse countries across the world. Notice that as you expand the scope of your literature review, you are also speaking to broader audiences. In the first version, you may have been speaking mostly to experts on American politics. In the expanded version, you are also engaging comparativists and experts on political parties and voting behavior.

If you are writing a thesis about how and when regional international organizations, such as NATO, the United Nations, the African Union, and the Arab League, deal with human rights issues and carrying out a quantitative analysis of dozens of cases (**a large-N design**), your literature review might be a more comprehensive analytical survey of theoretical literature on your topic. For example, it is likely to group the scholarly literature in international relations (IR) into realist, liberal, and constructivist explanations for the behavior of international organizations. In addition to organizing the literature by schools of thought, you will also discuss the merits and drawbacks of each IR school.

Once you have located the relevant articles and books, read the abstract and/or introduction, and then find the literature review section. More often than not, literature reviews will not be labeled as such, but you should easily be able to recognize the portion of the article (or book) that discusses the existing literature and theoretical debates. Other scholars will lay out the debates for you in their own literature reviews, simultaneously giving you a sense of the schools of thought that exist and the major works associated with each school.

As you read other literature reviews, look at the footnotes, works cited, or bibliography to find titles, authors, and journal names. This is not an invitation to simply use another scholar's literature review as your own, but to harness existing literature reviews as sources for both relevant work and as a way to identify PIR scholarly debates. For example, if your research question is about the determinants of populist party success, even a cursory glance at a literature review in an existing study of populism might identify a number of common answers, such as: (1) elite mobilization around identity politics; (2) economic inequality; (3) migration; and (4) media and social polarization. Gidron and Bonikowski (2013) review some of the political science literature on populism. Alternatively, if you are writing about the causes of the Arab Spring, you will most certainly turn to the very large literature on violent and nonviolent revolutions.

If you are still finding it difficult to identify major debates related to your topic, one point of reference might be introductory textbooks in your field or review articles or articles that present the state of the art of research on your topic. Introductory textbooks will often present major theoretical debates that might help you organize your own theoretical framework. For example, in the IR sub-field of international political economy, some introductory texts introduce students to different theoretical traditions that range from liberalism to Marxism. Review essays, which are mentioned above and examples of which are listed in the 'Suggested Further Reading' section at the end of the chapter, are another useful source since they place current research publications in the context of recent debates in your field. Word of mouth can also be an excellent way to identify relevant literature and debates. Ask around. What do your colleagues and professors recommend as the most important works and authors in a field? Finally, don't hesitate to consult reference librarians: in the age of electronic databases, they often have more time than you might assume and would be delighted to help you locate more material for your literature review. Finally, the process of identifying articles and books for your literature review also entails making a conscious decision to stop searching. There is a lot out there in PIR, and you can't read or reference it all. Too much material in a literature review can be overwhelming, for you and your reader.

## The Anatomy of a Literature Review: Analyzing, Organizing, and Situating

The purpose of a literature review is not simply to provide a summary of everything written on your topic. Instead, the goal is to *analyze* scholarly contributions related to your research question, *organize* major debates found in these contributions, and *situate* your project among them. In doing all of this, you will point out any gaps in the existing literature as a way of both situating and justifying your research.

At some point, you will also need to come up with a title for the literature review and write an introductory paragraph. Don't title your literature review section the 'Literature Review.' It would be supremely awkward. When choosing a title, think about how you can communicate the purpose and content of the section as it applies to your project. A good approach here is to have your literature review title suggest the various approaches to your question. Returning to the determinants of populist support example, you might call your literature review 'The Roots of Populism: Four Views.' Such a title signals to your reader that she or he should expect to find in your literature review four distinct approaches to analyzing the phenomenon of populism.

Before or after deciding on the title (though titles are often best left for last), draft an introductory paragraph or section which provides an overview to the literature review. In this paragraph, you might mention that (1) there is a scholarly debate on your research question; (2) each school offers a specific answer; and (3) each approach has its associated strengths and weaknesses. In the introduction, you will preview which approach best answers your question. For example, let's say you are interested in the general topic of when the United States incorporates human rights promotion into its foreign policy. More specifically, you wish to examine the determinants of US support for human rights-related resolutions in the United Nations Security Council (UNSC) since the end of the Cold War. The research question in this case is:

*What explains US votes for human rights-related resolutions in the UNSC?*

Consider the larger theoretical issues raised by this question: for example, how states behave in the international system, and why they behave in this way. This theoretical issue, in turn, suggests a number of related questions. Do states act according to an *a priori* objectively identifiable set of interests having to do with maximizing their power and protecting their access to economic resources? Or are these interests more dynamic and dependent on institutions, norms, culture, values, and other factors? These questions point to debates among the traditional schools of thought in international relations, especially realism, liberalism, and constructivism. Each of these schools explains state behavior in a different way.

However, you might also look at this research question as raising theoretical issues concerning the foreign policy decision-making process. How do elites decide on certain policies, as individuals and in groups? How do psychological factors and group dynamics shape foreign policy decision-making? Relating to these questions, you will find a substantial body of scholarship on the dynamics of decision-making and how it affects foreign policy choices, sometimes referred to as foreign policy analysis (Houghton 2013). This literature includes theories with roots in social psychology that examine how dynamics such as analogical reasoning and 'groupthink' shape foreign policy outcomes (Houghton 2013). Other theories in the foreign policy analysis tradition include the bureaucratic politics paradigm, which focuses on the institutions that formulate and implement foreign policies. The premise of these theories is that bureaucracies have their own particularistic interests and deploy bargaining power to shape policies. Thus, your literature review could draw on one or both of these bodies of scholarship. For example, you could have two major sections in your literature review: one would be titled 'IR Theories' and the second 'Foreign Policy Analysis Theories,' noting that each set of theories seeks to explain different facets of state behavior. Combining them, you might be able to account for US voting behavior on the Security Council. Consider the following example of an introductory paragraph drawing on the previous example of a research project on US support for human rights-related resolutions:

> Scholars of US foreign policy have long sought to understand its determinants. Here I discuss the scholarship associated with three dominant approaches to explaining US foreign policy decisions: the role of the individual, bureaucratic politics, and group dynamics. I will evaluate the strengths and weaknesses of each in terms of their ability to explain the 2011 decision on the part of the Obama administration to advocate an R2P-based intervention in Libya in the UN Security Council.

When organizing major approaches, you will categorize authors into theoretical traditions, approaches, or schools of thought. You shouldn't organize the literature review around authors themselves. It would be difficult to follow, not to mention cumbersome for your reader. Then, you should label each of these schools. The next step is to briefly outline and evaluate each approach, noting when it appeared or became popular, and specifying its major adherents and mentioning some of their contributions. You may also briefly mention the strengths and weaknesses of each approach in a general sense, thereby foreshadowing their utility in answering your questions specifically but not going into specifics just yet. Using the example above, for realism, you would likely discuss how it became popular at the height of the Cold War, and note key proponents of realism, such as Hans Morgenthau, Kenneth Waltz, and Stephen Walt. The following paragraph is an example of how you might summarize the bureaucratic politics approach:

Derived from organizational theory, the bureaucratic politics approach to US foreign policy decision-making was developed in the 1960s and 1970s by scholars such as Graham Allison (1971), and despite massive change that has ensued in the world since then, its insights remain strikingly relevant for understanding US foreign policy decision-making today. This literature's key assumptions are that: (1) the instinct of any organization is self-preservation; (2) US foreign policy does not result from the intentions of any one individual; (3) US foreign policy is not based on a rational calculation based on interests, costs, and benefits; and (4) foreign policy bureaucracies may resist the preferences of presidents and other political leaders. Thus, a decision that appears like a strategic US move on the world stage may in fact represent a shaky compromise between rival elements within the US government. While the bureaucratic politics approach can successfully describe outcomes on more routine foreign policy issues, it is less adept at explaining the high-profile decisions in which the president is personally involved. Moreover, it is sometimes hard to distinguish bureaucratic from individual interest – in other words, is the Secretary of State channeling her own view, or that of the bureaucracy she leads? (based on Boduszyński 2019)

Third, and this is the very important part, you will systematically discuss the utility and limits of each approach in answering your question. These in turn may correspond to specific hypotheses (educated guesses purporting to explain some feature of the political world) about foreign policy decisions in which you are interested. To do this, you have to get inside the mind of proponents of various approaches and consider, in a non-judgmental way, how each would address your question. For positivist research questions, you will think about how well each approach would explain your dependent variable. Returning to the human rights and US foreign policy example, you might note that realism is adept at predicting cases of US support for human rights resolutions in the Security Council where there are *no realpolitik* concerns, but cannot account for those cases where the US votes to promote human rights *despite* the existence of countervailing security or economic interests. You might then note that constructivism, with its focus on identities and norms around human rights, compensates for some of realism's limitations as an explanatory factor. Let's look at a more specific excerpt from a literature review drawing on a research project which attempts to explain the US decision to intervene in Libya in 2011:

The bureaucratic approach alone has limits in accounting for Obama's decision to intervene. It is unlikely that individuals like Samantha Power and Susan Rice would have changed their beliefs on Libya if they had worked for different bureaucratic actors. As US Ambassador to the UN, Susan Rice was a part of a larger State Department bureaucracy whose Near Eastern Affairs Bureau did not rally behind intervention. The rebuilding of contacts with Libya had been a long, painful process, and at least some State Department diplomats did not want to destroy all that had been accomplished since the rapprochement of the early 2000s. Instead of acting based on institutional interest or culture, Rice viewed Libya 'as an opportunity to enact a new form of humanitarian intervention, one contemplated for nearly a decade' (Blomdahl 2016, 151-152). As for Power, had she been driven only by the bureaucratic interests of the institution she represented, she might not have opposed her own boss at the helm of the NSC, Tom Donilon. Moreover, she might have cared more for the substantial political risk to Obama of the Libya intervention. (based on Boduszyński 2019)

Note how the author points to the limits of the bureaucratic politics approach in order to build up to the main argument, which advocates for the individual actor approach.

Fourth, you will situate your approach among these schools. In a best-case scenario, this will flow naturally from the first two stages (analyzing and organizing) as you would have already noted the strengths and weaknesses of various schools of thought, thus setting up your 'punchline.' This is where you will say, though not in these words exactly: 'Aha! This is why my approach makes the most sense.' This is also where you will outline your main argument, which you would have already summarized in the introduction to your thesis or paper. In this final part, you will also summarize the literature review and provide a solid transition to the next phase of your work. You want to finish strongly, leaving no doubt about the direction in which you are heading in terms of your argument and how it fits into the debates you have just outlined. Here is an excerpt from a literature review which is a continuation of the previous one (framing the US decision to intervene in Libya in 2011) and shows how to transition from the analysis to outlining the main argument, which in this case highlights the central role of individual foreign policy-makers (in this case, Samantha Power and Susan Rice, two top Obama advisors) in explaining the outcome:

> The limits of the bureaucratic policy approach underscore the importance of considering individuals. The policy preferences of both Power and Rice reflected their individual beliefs, which featured a career-long advocacy of humanitarian intervention, driven by the analogies derived from the Balkans and Rwanda. As political appointees who were not constrained by the career- and organizational culture-based caution of the State and Defense Departments and viewing the events in the Middle East as a sign of a new era, Power and Rice were in a position to frame US interests in Libya in a fresh way. Power and Rice were in a position to sway Obama not only because of the power of their ideas but also because of their direct line to the president. In the end, the decision to intervene in Libya was not a compromise based on bureaucratic bargaining as the bureaucratic politics model might predict, but rather the victory of one group of individuals – those with a pre-existing ideological commitment to intervention – and their beliefs over another one. If we were to construct a counterfactual scenario in which these individuals did not exist – that is, if key advisors with privileged access to the president who held strong humanitarian intervention beliefs were not at the policy-making table as the Libya uprising began – then it is hard to imagine that President Obama, with his obvious reluctance to entangle the US in an Arab country, would have acted. (based on Blomdahl 2016 and Boduszyński 2019)

But it's also OK to decide that your contribution to a scholarly debate is to pick a middle ground, to combine existing approaches, or even to say that they are all right. In this case, you would summarize why *both* bureaucratic politics and individual influence might explain the Libya intervention, and in the data analysis section you would offer evidence of why this is the case. Real political phenomena are complex, after all, and picking one side in a debate often does not make sense empirically. You can also qualify your argument, both in the literature review and in the conclusion, by noting the plausibility of alternative hypotheses rooted in other literatures. Here is another excerpt from the Libya intervention example:

> However, some opponents of intervention may have been working not only from personal belief but also based on bureaucratic interests. The Pentagon often worried about military overextension and getting involved in a conflict without clear long-term objectives, which may account for the stance of Secretary of Defense Robert Gates. The military at the time was facing spending cuts in response to the recession, thereby constraining military operations. Gates was also adept at bureaucratic obstructionism, at times instructing his subordinates to withhold information from the White House to discourage a military option in Libya.

Table 5.3 provides you with a template for compiling the information for your own literature review. To complete it, find two peer-reviewed articles on your topic. Locate the literature review section and respond to the following questions in the adjacent blank spaces.

**Table 5.3**  Analyzing, organizing, and situating

*For the following worksheet, find two peer-reviewed articles on your topic. Locate the literature review session and respond to the following questions in the adjacent blank spaces.*

| Article 1 | Article 2 |
|---|---|
| Article reference information: *author, title, journal, volume, issue, year of publication, page numbers* | Article reference information: *author, title, journal, volume, issue, year of publication, page numbers* |
| How many pages or paragraphs long is the literature review? | How many pages or paragraphs long is the literature review? |
| Which authors and works are identified in the literature review? Why have these particular authors/ works been identified for the purpose of this article? | Which authors and works are identified in the literature review? Why have these particular authors/ works been identified for the purpose of this article? |
| Which theoretical debates have been identified in the literature review? How do these debates relate to the work's theoretical framework? | Which theoretical debates have been identified in the literature review? How do these debates relate to the work's theoretical framework? |

As you wrap up your literature review, ask yourself these four questions to ensure that your literature review is complete:

- Does your literature review contextualize and situate your research question in existing scholarship and debates?
- Does your literature review analyze, organize, and structure these debates?
- Does your literature review identify specific gaps in scholarly knowledge on your topic?
- Does your literature review lead up to your own argument and position?

When reading literature reviews in scholarly articles, you might have found authors build up an opposing point of view only to tear it down later. An example of this in international relations is John Mearsheimer's well-cited article, entitled 'Back to the Future' (1990). In this article, Mearsheimer sets out the core liberal and constructivist assumptions on the future of peace in Europe in order to later make the case that realism provides a more compelling case for instability in Europe after the Cold War. When presenting competing approaches, it is imperative to present as thorough and as nuanced a perspective as possible in order to avoid misrepresenting the arguments of others in your literature review.

While it might be tempting to oversimplify opposing perspectives with which you disagree, misrepresenting an opposing argument for the purpose of making it an easier target will harm the credibility of your own research. This is called **straw man argumentation**. Straw man arguments refer to the oversimplification or misrepresentation of an opposing argument so as to make it easier to disprove. A well-written literature review will give equal weight to all approaches. By doing this, you will ensure that the data analysis, which you will carry out later in the project, is adequately contextualized in existing debates and that any conclusions you reach will be more convincing to the reader.

Once you have a first draft of your literature review, you may find it necessary to revisit your research question. Do not be alarmed if this is the case. Research and writing in PIR is not a linear step-by-step process. You are not assembling a piece of furniture purchased from IKEA. You are engaged in an intellectual exercise. This means that it is common practice to go back and rethink certain steps or research choices that you made earlier in the process. This shows reflexivity as a researcher and openness to competing perspectives on your topic, and in the end, will help you write a stronger essay, paper, or thesis.

## Chapter Summary

All scholarly writing is about participation in an ongoing conversation. Research papers are never stand-alone products. They attempt to extend, refine, or challenge what we know about PIR-related phenomena. Moreover, they are written with the aim of inviting critique and response. In order to accomplish this goal, readers should be able to recognize not only your own arguments, but also how your arguments relate to what has been written in the past about your topic. For these reasons, the literature review is a foundational component to every essay, thesis, or dissertation in PIR. It is also an essential part of writing proposals for research grants.

In a literature review, you analyze scholarship related to your question and the main concepts with which you will grapple. You identify the most important authors and summarize their contributions, noting how they have influenced other scholars. You consider which of their arguments are compelling, and why. In short, you are explaining to your reader how others have addressed your research question, both in terms of your more specific topic and the larger theoretical issues it raises. Every good research question can be either supported or negated. While for positivists the test of a good research question is falsifiability, interpretive scholarship too insists upon clearly stating how your topic relates to ideas and debates in the field and formulating a question that is contestable. The literature review, thus, also plays an important role in justifying the scholarly relevance of your research question.

Once you have completed your literature review, and you are confident that your research question contributes to scholarly debates and knowledge in PIR, you are ready to reflect on your research design, and what strategies for data collection and data analysis are best suited to responding to your question. These are among the topics of the next chapter.

## Suggested Further Reading

Bates, Robert H. 1997. Comparative Politics and Rational Choice: A Review Essay. *American Political Science Review*, 91(3), 699-704.
A great example of a review essay which can serve as a model for a literature review.

Bean, F.D. 2016. Changing Ethnic and Racial Diversity in the United States: A Review Essay. *Population and Development Review*, 42(1), 135-142.
Another review essay to consider.

Cotton, J. 2018. A Century of Wilsonianism: A Review Essay. *Australian Journal of Political Science*, 53(3), 398-407.
Yet another review essay, this one in the field of IR and foreign policy studies.

Gidron, Noam, and Ziblatt, Daniel. 2019. Center Right Political Parties in Advanced Democracies. *Annual Review of Political Science*, 22(1), May, 17-35.
A review essay on the literature on center-right parties.

Guo, S. 2018. Political Science and Chinese Political Studies: Where is Chinese Political Science Headed? *Journal of Chinese Political Science*, 23(2), 287-295.
This review essay covers the PIR literature in China.

Lipson, Charles. 2018. *How to Write a BA Thesis: A Practical Guide from Your First Ideas to Your Finished Paper*, 2nd edition. Chicago, IL: University of Chicago Press. See Chapter 5: How to Build a Reading List, pp. 70-75.
A useful chapter on literature reviews in a helpful textbook.

Miragliotta, N.L. 2017. Elections and Electoral Politics: A Review Essay. *Australian Journal of Political Science*, 52(4), 615-625.
A review essay on scholarship about elections and electoral politics.

Roselle, Laura, and Spray, Sharon. 2012. *Research and Writing in International Relations*. New York: Pearson. See Chapter 2: Getting Started on Your Literature Review, pp. 15-31.
Some additional guidance for a literature review.

Weldon, S.L. 2019. Power, Exclusion and Empowerment: Feminist Innovation in Political Science. *Women's Studies International Forum*, 72, 127-136.
A review essay on feminist scholarship in PIR.

Wood, M. 2014. Bridging the Relevance Gap in Political Science. *Politics*, 34(3), 275-286.
Some thoughts on the importance of relevance real-world in PIR.

# 6

# Research Design

========= Learning Objectives =========

- To understand how the purpose of your research relates to your choice of research design;
- To consider how your choice of cases might impact your findings;
- To think about how to justify and explain your own research design;
- To become familiar with comparative and case-oriented research design strategies.

You now have a topic and research question. You have considered ethical questions. You have drafted a literature review, identifying the body of research and theory which your paper will engage. Finally, you have considered your logic of inquiry and the various methodologies available to address your question. Now it is time for you to think about your research design. Research design refers to the 'roadmap,' or overarching strategy that you will use to answer your research question. Every research project, whether it is positivist or interpretivist, needs a logically consistent research design. Research designs are numerous, but some of the main types include experimental design, case-oriented design, or large-N, variable-oriented design. In this chapter, we will (1) discuss the relationship between your research purpose and the research design you choose; (2) define a case and highlight how case selection impacts research findings; (3) introduce you to several kinds of research designs; and (4) explain how the comparative case study research design works.

**Cases** provide the empirical material with which to make your argument and, if your purpose is to uncover causality (the positivist approach), to test hypotheses about relationships among variables. One of the big decisions you have to make vis-à-vis research design is whether to analyze a single case, a small number of cases, or a large quantitative dataset of cases to answer your question. You also have to decide *which* cases you will examine, a process known as **case selection**. This chapter highlights one of the most widely used research designs in Politics (especially comparative politics) and International Relations – the comparative **case research design**.

In fact, research that engages with only one or a relatively small number of cases can be used for both hypothesis testing and **thick interpretive description**. The latter method is widely used in ethnographic research and is based on intensive observation (Geertz 1973, 3–20). In either instance, you must select the cases you will use, a subject which this chapter also covers. Which cases will you focus on? How many cases will you include? How might your choice of cases influence your findings? Here, we cover small-N designs, while research designs that deal with large numbers of cases ('large-N') are covered in Chapters 9 and 10.

## From Question to Design to Method: What is Your Purpose?

In Chapter 4, we discussed various kinds of research questions. Let's briefly return to this topic by highlighting three varieties of research questions with unique purposes – two implying a positivist approach and the third an interpretivist one:

1    A study of a single historical event.

a    Sample Research Question: What factors explain the outbreak of the French Revolution? (Skocpol 1979)

2    A study of multiple outcomes in a particular issue area, over time.

b    Sample Research Question: Why do states comply with human rights commitments? (Lamont 2010)

3    A study that will deepen our understanding of a particular concept or idea.

c    Sample Research Question: How do war memorials in Europe shape a society's collective memory of the past? (Pavlaković 2014)

Hopefully, it is immediately clear to you that the first two questions are positivist because the purpose of the research is to uncover a causal relationship. Both specify a dependent variable (the outbreak of the French Revolution in the first; human rights compliance in the second). The third question, by contrast, seeks not so much explanation but rather interpretation (though here too there is some implied causality – how war memorials affect memory). Because the first two questions are positivist, your research design will seek to maximize causal inference (the process of drawing a conclusion about a causal connection). As will be explained further in this and subsequent chapters, maximizing causal inference will depend either on having an adequate number of cases (for a large-$N$ statistical study) OR an appropriate case selection strategy (for a small-$N$ case study design).

For positivist questions such as 1 and 2 above, you can test hypotheses through either **experimental** or **observational research designs**. An experimental design affords you significant control over variables in your study. You would assign subjects randomly to control and treatment groups. What does this mean, practically, for PIR research questions, as in the examples above? In reality, there is no way to run an experiment that would test why the French Revolution, or for that matter, any revolution, takes place. As we will note below, you cannot control the environment of entire societies. But you could conceive an experiment that tests the psychological roots of why people join movements that aim to overturn the existing order. You could expose one group of people to a certain kind of information (the treatment group), and survey their reactions compared to a control group, for example. Of course, as Chapter 3 noted, there would be ethical considerations involved. But PIR researchers are increasingly turning to experimental methods, for instance using social media to test how people react to certain kinds of information. Some recent experimental PIR research is listed among the works in the 'Suggested Further Reading' list at the end of this chapter. One major advantage of experimental methods in PIR, in spite of their ethical and practical complications, is the fact that they have high **internal validity,** meaning that the results are accurate and true for the cases we are studying.

Observational research designs, by contrast, do not afford us this same level of control. Here, we have to work with the cases, variation, and control available to us in a sample that we have selected. However, this is the reality with which most PIR researchers must contend. Unlike our sisters and brothers in chemistry or biology, as social science researchers we cannot manipulate certain phenomena to test for cause and effect. We cannot, for instance, change the ethnic diversity of a country, or assign natural resources to one society while taking them away from another. Nor can we assign people to genders, ethnicities, sexual orientations, and so on. The best we can do is observe what is actually out there. This means that observational designs have high **external validity**. External validity denotes our ability to generalize the findings to a larger set of cases. But given the real limits of controlling for various **confounding factors** (third variables that distort a causal relationship) in observational designs, their internal validity is generally lower than that for their experimental counterparts.

In the first question, your aim is to identify the factors that explain a single event. This question lends itself to a **single case study design**. Single case study designs can yield rich causal stories. However, they are unlikely to generate findings that allow you to make **generalizable** claims; in this case, regarding the causes of revolution in general. The causes of the French Revolution, in other words, may be particular to just that case, i.e. to France. The causes of revolution in China may be entirely different.

However, design is not analogous to method, and you will still need to select among various methods (see Chapters 7–10) to prove the causality. Since the first question is a study of a single case, qualitative methods are the most likely choice. You could use **process-tracing**, which involves developing a causal story that links a causal variable to an observed outcome (the dependent variable), to show how certain explanatory factors led to the outbreak of revolution in France. Process-tracing is described in Chapter 8. Or, you could use **formal models**, a quantitative method described in Chapter 10, to depict the strategic interactions among various actors (the Church, Jacobins, aristocracy, etc.) that led to the French Revolution. As for the second question, it clearly implies not only a positivist quest for causal inference, but also a **multiple case study design**. This could mean a focused qualitative comparison of several instances of compliance and non-compliance with human rights norms over time (Lamont 2010), or a large-N quantitative study of patterns of compliance over many years.

The third question (to which we return toward the end of this chapter) suggests a study that could either employ a single case study design (e.g. focusing on a particular Holocaust memorial in Germany) or a multiple case study design covering memorials in one or several countries. However, because it is interpretive rather than positivist (i.e., seeking causal relationships among variables is not the primary goal), the research design and methods have to be appropriate to the purpose of uncovering and questioning the underlying meanings and how they are constructed. For example, you might employ qualitative data collection methods (Chapter 7) such as **open-ended interviews** or **focus groups** with a sample of people who have visited a museum, a detailed description of the design and features of a memorial, or an examination of political discourse around the chosen site(s) of memory. But you might also gather such data through **content analysis** or **surveys** (Chapter 9), which would then likely necessitate **quantitative methods** to analyze the results (Chapter 10). Nevertheless, case-oriented designs are often the most logical choice for interpretive research questions. Daniela Lai and Roberto Roccu have argued for the **extended case methodology**, which 'has a flexible approach to theory building, ... is concerned with contextually rich, complex accounts of the social world' and is 'consistent with the ontological and epistemological commitments of several critical IR approaches' (2019, 67–69).

## Cases, Case Selection, and Case-Oriented Research Designs

Case selection is an important step in the research design process. A case – an individual observation of an empirical phenomenon – should not be confused with the term *case study*. Nearly all empirical research projects are case studies. Usually, they also contain cases which are randomly chosen (the large-$N$ design), assigned (experimental design), or deliberately paired to isolate potential causes (the comparative design – a major subject of this chapter). A public opinion survey of 2000 randomly selected British citizens about their attitudes toward Brexit is a case study of British public opinion containing 2000 individual cases of Brits, each with a particular opinion. It is also a large-$N$ quantitative design based on a survey as a form of data collection. For more on analysis in large-$N$ designs associated with quantitative methods, turn to Chapters 9 and 10.

In order to address any research question, positivist or interpretive, you will have to choose an empirical case or case(s) to examine in depth. If you choose to investigate a large number of empirical cases, you will likely be relying on an existing quantitative dataset, and the cases have been chosen for you by someone else. As Chapters 9–10 elaborate, for a large-$N$ research design, you may have less control over case selection, but you can ensure that the organization or person that collected the data for you did so according to scientific standards. Or, if you are the data collector, you can uphold these standards. If someone else did the data collection, you should be sure that the data was gathered in an unbiased way, and that it is **valid** and **reliable** (see Chapter 9 for a discussion of validity and reliability). If the data collection occurred via a survey, then you want to be sure that it was **randomized** (that is, the individual cases were selected without any deliberate or unintended bias).

For research designs that focus on one or a small number of cases, the logic around case selection is different. You are no longer randomly drawing observations from a pot, but rather deliberately selecting cases based on their attributes. Let's consider the example of a research project about Turkey's foreign policy. Perhaps you have decided on the following research question: 'What has shaped Turkey's foreign policy?' This question meets the standards we discussed in Chapter 4. It is specific, relevant, and implies a logic of inquiry (positivist). You have a clearly-defined dependent variable: outcomes in Turkey's foreign policy. Hopefully you have thought about how to identify and operationalize key concepts, a subject that is discussed in Chapter 9. For example, you may have decided to operationalize Turkey's foreign policy by looking at statements issued by President Erdogan and other top Turkish officials. But you have yet to select your case or cases of Turkish foreign policy.

Returning to our example of populism, a research paper on populist parties in Poland, Hungary, and Romania would form a small-$N$, comparative case design focusing on party politics in East-Central Europe and containing three country cases (and likely further, within-country cases of populist and non-populist parties). Cases may also refer to multiple observations *over time*. For example, if you are looking at local governance in Japan over different periods, what at first glance appears as a single case study (Japan) may in fact include several within-country cases, given that both modes of local governance and the factors influencing them have evolved over time.

**Case-oriented research design** thus relies on one or a small number of observations. Drawing on one or a handful of cases has its inherent limitations. But, for many undergraduate research paper topics in PIR, it is often the most attractive choice. This is because the quantitative analysis and statistical tools associated with large-$N$ designs and survey or experimental methods require advanced experience and training. Case-oriented research design is also well suited to undergraduates who wish to explore an empirical observation in greater detail. For instance, many undergraduates are inspired by their experience of studying overseas and want to write in depth about the country they got to know, perhaps drawing on sources in a new language they have acquired.

The case-oriented approach is primarily a qualitative one, but this does not mean it eschews numerical data entirely. Indeed, it can deploy **descriptive statistics** (numbers which summarize the characteristics of a dataset) as well. For instance, if you are comparing two populist parties in Europe (one successful and one not), you will likely present numerical election results to describe your dependent variable. But this still leaves the issue of which cases to include in a case-oriented design. Returning to our previous example, Turkey's foreign policy is a case study of one state's foreign policy. But which instance of Turkey's foreign policy will you analyze? After all, there are lots of choices out there – and over many hundreds of years, if we include the predecessor to the modern Turkish state, the Ottoman Empire, which colonized large swathes of south-eastern Europe, the Middle East, and North Africa. More recently, Turkey has joined NATO, negotiated with the European Union, and sent troops to Iraq. Each of these is a case of Turkish foreign policy. How many of them will you consider and why?

Case selection needs to be carefully considered if you want to answer the question of what has shaped Turkey's foreign policy in a rigorous, generalizable way. As discussed elsewhere in this book, most questions studied by PIR scholars are not easily subjected to experimental and quasi-experimental design. Psychologists might divide research subjects into control and treatment groups to examine the effect of a certain stimulus. But there is no feasible, much less ethical, way to test what determines Turkey's foreign policy through experimentation. A large-$N$ design is also not so practical. You could, in theory, design a statistical study, randomly choosing dozens or hundreds or even thousands of individual acts of Turkish foreign policy. But this might not be realistic for a number of reasons. For example, the task of generating such a dataset may be too complex.

In fact, studies of foreign policy behavior in the larger field of PIR often rely on a smaller number of observations, or cases. The choice of these cases is extremely important, as it will determine whether you can make *generalizable claims* from your findings. But if your research design includes a poorly chosen set of cases, you may be telling an interesting story, but you will not necessarily be capturing larger truths about what shapes Turkish foreign policy, or the foreign policy of states more generally, which is, after all, one of the goals of a PIR research paper.

Let's say you choose to focus on the Turkish response to the Syrian uprising in the year 2011. Based on the fact that Turkey seemed to support the revolution, you may conclude that Erdogan's foreign policy thinking was driven by identity-based factors highlighted by the constructivist tradition in international relations. Namely, some have argued that Erdogan was driven by his personal desire to support fellow Sunnis in Syria, and Turkey's desire to be seen as a leader in the Sunni Islamic world (Ayman 2014). However, using a single instance of Turkish foreign policy at a particular time and toward a particular state may not be representative. The Syrian uprising was a specific and unexpected event.

Before the uprising, Erdogan enjoyed positive relations with Syrian dictator Bashar al-Assad. And by 2018, Turkish policy toward Syria seemed to flip again toward engagement with the Assad regime.

Therefore, if you add other cases of Turkish foreign policy to your research design, such as Ankara's relations with Tehran, the idea that Sunni identity is the singular or even primary motivator of Turkish foreign policy under Erdogan is quickly dispelled, as Erdogan has also maintained purposeful relations with his Shia neighbors in Iran. Here, the addition of an additional case helped to eliminate a potential causal factor (identity) and perhaps disqualify a theoretical approach in IR, constructivism, which highlights state identity.

The addition of more cases may change the picture further. Perhaps it would be helpful to see how Turkey responded to the Bahraini uprising of 2011, which was driven largely by Shia protestors rather than Sunni citizens, to test whether the 'Sunni identity' thesis can be sustained in other cases. This line of reasoning – thinking about how the addition of cases helps to isolate or eliminate potential causal factors – is the essence of the comparative case design, further discussed below. In fact, as you will see, the case study method is simultaneously a research design and a research method by which we can achieve the positivist goal of causal inference through the careful selection of cases.

Single cases can be helpful too, in terms of developing, revising, and challenging theories. But this will depend on the purpose of your project. For example, if you wish to challenge a large body of literature which claims that Turkish foreign policy is based on realist motivations and a strategy of 'hedging' relations with neighboring states so as to prevent potential conflicts and realize trade benefits, then the single case study of Erdogan's support for the Syrian uprising can be a powerful theory-challenging one. Why would Turkey deliberately harm relations with an important neighbor? If your research purpose is to contribute to theories about state behavior more generally, you could also conceive your research on Turkish foreign policy as a single case study of a state's foreign policy. If Turkey behaves in the international arena in a way that is very different from other states, you may be able to use the case of Turkey to undermine or delimit the scope of existing theories. Or you may argue that it behaves in a way that is very much in line with other states.

## The Logic of Small-N Comparative Research Design

Both small-N and large-N designs rely on the power of comparison to achieve the goal of causal inference. In large-N studies, that comparison is 'hidden' in a statistical model. In small-N studies, the comparison is more explicit in the case selection, and is meant to help control for confounding explanatory variables while 'isolating' the independent variable of interest.

How many cases qualify for a comparative research design, and at what point does one reach the threshold for a quantitative, large-N research design? There is no definite answer to this question. You could run a statistical regression with a handful of cases, though there is little utility in doing so, as Chapters 9 and 10 explain. Alternatively, you could set up a complex comparative design and study several dozen cases in depth, though this would be analytically difficult for you and challenging for your reader. As a result, most small-N comparative research designs examine two to a dozen cases.

Small-$N$ studies are, at times, the only choice available to a researcher when there is not a sufficiently large number of observations available to generate a **statistically significant** sample, or when the possible explanatory variables are too numerous, nuanced, or complex to code. Let's say you want to understand how ethnic diversity versus homogeneity influences the prospects for democracy in a particular region of the world, such as Africa. Your **unit of analysis** in this case is an individual African state (Zambia or Algeria, for instance), because your dependent variable, our outcome of interest, is levels of democracy at the national level. You potentially have enough cases in Africa (54) to run a statistical regression, and you could come up with an **operational definition** (see Chapter 9) of ethnic diversity (let's say: the proportion of ethnic minorities relative to the total population). The statistical model would allow you to control for factors such as economic development or colonial legacy – in other words, to ensure that it is indeed ethnic diversity, and not these factors, which are driving outcomes in democratization.

But what if it is not the *fact* of ethnic diversity, but the *content* of ethnic relations, which may differ significantly among African countries, that matters? Ethnic relations are based on complex patterns of interaction and long histories that may be hard to capture quantitatively, even with the best operational definitions. The fact of ethnic plurality in one country may mean something different in another. In other words, your operational definition of ethnicity may not be valid. In this example, a large-$N$ design may be a useful way to frame a study, but more meaningful research results might be obtained through a thoughtfully-designed small-$N$ comparison of two or more African countries.

As mentioned above, the comparative case design relies on the logic of comparison. Comparison is part of our daily lives (Toshkov 2016, 259). In fact, it is hard to imagine human reasoning and decision-making without the aid of comparison. You think about your favorite restaurants in terms of how they compare to others. City officials think about how their counterparts in other municipalities have solved a similar problem, such as homelessness. Foreign policy-makers turn to analogies from the past to consider their options and their implications (Houghton 2013).

While we draw upon comparisons in everyday life, choosing cases for a small-$N$ comparative research design in PIR requires more careful reflection. To some extent, the rationale behind choosing cases for a comparative case design is not so different from that which underlies experimental studies. For small-$N$ comparative designs, we also want to control for the influence of certain factors. If your hunch is that permissive immigration policies are the key factor driving support for populism, then we need to somehow create a situation in which only the hypothesized factor (i.e., the role of immigration policies) differs and everything else remains the same. You cannot create a laboratory to test this proposition experimentally, nor do you have enough cases of a large-$N$ design and statistical analysis. Three basic approaches are available if you are using a small-$N$ comparative research design.

The first begins with a theoretically-driven question, such as 'What is the impact of immigration on levels of support for populist parties?' This question leads the researcher to select a small set of carefully selected cases (sometimes as few as two) designed to control for causal variables other than immigration, conduct an empirical analysis, and then confirm or disconfirm the hypothesis that served as the catalyst for the research question.

The second approach begins with a set of cases (such as immigration policies in five major European states) and examines their political consequences. This approach can produce some interesting empirical narratives, and provide the basis for new hypotheses, but it is not so strong on causal inference. Either of these first two approaches can be easily adapted to an interpretivist research question.

The third approach relies on a single case and **within-case analysis**. Within-case analysis provides limited insights on causality by evaluating competing hypotheses against the evidence in a thorough examination of that single case. If your goal is to explain one specific and yet pivotal historical event (like the French Revolution above; or the sudden victory or defeat of populists in a particular country), a single case study buttressed by an extensive empirical account might actually provide a stronger causal account than a research design that relies on a larger number of cases but can only weakly explain causality. Yet, then we again confront the problem of generalizability. Perhaps the case you are examining is simply exceptional – an **outlier.**

The remainder of this chapter describes how to create a research design for the first approach, the small-N comparative case study design, which often appears in two general forms: most similar systems (MSS) and most different systems (MSD).

## Most Similar Systems (MSS) Research Design

Keep everything the same while letting your main explanatory variable of interest vary across the cases: this is the core principle of the **most similar systems (MSS) research design**. More specifically, in MSS you know the values of the hypothesized independent variables and have determined that they vary across the cases, while other possible explanatory variables remain constant. Table 6.1 contains a simple illustration of an MSS design using an empirical example from democratization studies.

**Table 6.1** Most similar systems design: democratization in the Balkans

| Possible determinant | Albania | Macedonia |
| --- | --- | --- |
| Level of economic development | Low | Low |
| Pre-war experience with democracy | No | No |
| Ottoman colonial history | Yes | Yes |
| Ethnic plurality | No | Yes |
| Level of democracy (Dependent variable) | ? | ? |

Source: Based on Boduszyński (2010)

In this study, the researcher is testing for the influence of ethnic plurality versus homogeneity (the independent variable) on the dependent variable of interest, democratization in two Balkan states. Importantly, the values for the independent variable differ between the two cases: Albania is ethnically homogeneous, while Macedonia's population is ethnically plural. The question marks for the dependent variable indicate that in theory we neither know the outcome nor care about it during the design stage (in practice, of course, we often do know the outcome, and that is fine).

The important thing is that we have chosen cases so that we can hold constant all other possible independent variables which might explain the levels of democratization: Ottoman colonial history, pre-war experience with democracy, and level of economic development. It does not matter what the values of these variables are, as long as they are the same for both cases, and if they are the variables we wish to hold constant. Albania and Macedonia happen to have a shared history of Ottoman rule, but if they didn't – let's say they were both under Habsburg rule – that would be OK too in terms of the MSS design.

Yet, it is critical that when selecting control variables, you are considering those that, theoretically speaking, might have some influence on the outcome. For instance, you might find that both Albania and Macedonia are mountainous countries: but there is no obvious connection, nor any theories suggesting a connection between mountainous geography and democracy (or any existing research that examines the relationship between the two).

The next step is to look at the outcome of interest, or dependent variable: in this case, the levels of democratization in Macedonia and Albania over a given time period. There are many useful indices of democratization available to student researchers, among them Freedom House scores and the Varieties of Democracy (V-Dem) database, based at the University of Gothenburg in Sweden (freedomhouse.org; v-dem.net). If the average of V-Dem scores for the two countries over the same period of time turns out not to vary, then you can conclude that the hypothesized variable (ethnic plurality) cannot be a sufficient condition explaining democratization. On the other hand, if the levels of democratization are significantly different, then perhaps you are on to something – maybe ethnic makeup does have something to do with democratization.

The above MSS design is a good first step toward hypothesis testing and causal inference in a small number of cases. But it has inherent weaknesses. There might be other key variables you are missing. You may be measuring variables inaccurately. Even assuming substantial variation on the dependent variable (level of democracy), how do you know which way the causality runs? In other words, how do you know that ethnic divisions affects democracy and not the other way around? In some countries, elections have exacerbated ethnic tensions (Chua 2004). Alternatively, the explanatory variable (ethnic plurality) may be interacting with another variable to produce the result in a way that this MSS design does not capture.

Of course, you could dig deeper into the cases themselves to deal with such issues. This is what small-$N$ case-oriented research designs often do, using methods such as process-tracing to show that the variable of interest really did affect the outcome. For instance, your thesis or paper could include a detailed history showing how ethnic tensions in Macedonia helped preclude the kind of cooperation necessary to build an inclusive political order, and instead led to the rise of an authoritarian populist regime.

But a careful selection of additional cases can also help address the issues noted above. For example, let's say you were interested in the reason European Union candidate states in the Balkans adopt legislation mandated by Brussels as a condition for membership. By looking at a number of similar cases (let's say Albania, Macedonia, Moldova, and Kosovo), you are controlling for a number of potential causal factors, such as administrative capacity, executive–legislative relations, and types of political systems. Adding additional cases may reveal more nuanced causes, such as party politics. Grzegorz Ekeirt (2015) reviews the extensive literature on the determinants of post-communist outcomes.

## Most Different Systems (MDS) Research Design

The logic of the **most different systems (MDS) research design** is based upon choosing cases that are as different as possible on conceivable independent variables but nevertheless have a common outcome on the dependent variable. Like MSS, MDS design tends to be highly inductive and thus better at theory generation than hypothesis testing. It is also subject to the aforementioned limitations of other small-$N$ designs. Thus, as with MSS, adding additional cases can help, but so can the use of methods such as process-tracing, within-case analysis, and moving beyond binary measures of variables.

Table 6.2 presents an MDS research design drawn from an actual study by the scholar Marc Morjé Howard (2003). Howard found an interesting puzzle based on an observation: despite a decade having passed since the collapse of communism, citizens of post-communist countries were still far less likely to join voluntary organizations than people from other countries and regions of the world. He asked the following research question: 'What explains this distinctive pattern of weak civil society in post-communist countries?' Based on the pioneering work of Jowitt (1992) on the Leninist legacy, he hypothesized that communism was by its nature uniquely detrimental to the development of the kind of societal trust needed for civic engagement. Howard developed a compelling causal argument about the powerful impact of the communist experience on its countries and citizens. He argues that the communist practice of forced participation in state-controlled organizations, the development and persistence of vibrant private networks, and the disappointment with post-communist democracy have imbued post-communist citizens with an antipathy to voluntary organizations.

Howard's research design is equally innovative. It has a large-$N$ component, in which he uses statistical analysis on data from over 30 democratic and democratizing countries in the World Values Survey (worldvaluessurvey.org). By including post-communist and other post-authoritarian countries in his statistical model and controlling for other factors (a benefit of statistical analysis we will highlight in Chapters 9 and 10), Howard is able to show the unique influence of the communist legacy as compared to the legacies of other authoritarian states. He finds that other post-authoritarian societies (for instance, those in Latin America) do not exhibit nearly the same aversion to civic participation as post-communist ones.

But the important part of Howard's research design for our present discussion is the case-oriented one. Namely, to bolster his argument about the unique impact of communism, Howard presents extensive and original evidence from his own research in the former East Germany and Russia, including in-depth interviews with ordinary citizens and an original survey. He chooses to pair two cases that are very different on many key structural explanatory variables, such as levels of economic development, exposure to western intellectual and cultural norms, and pre-war experience with democracy. But he also chose two cases with a shared experience of decades of communist rule, a factor which he hypothesized could be the key variable affecting levels of civic engagement (which Howard operationalized by looking at membership in voluntary organizations, as measured in the World Values Survey). He found that per capita membership in voluntary organizations in both countries was low compared to other countries undergoing transitions from authoritarianism, such as those in Latin America, thereby underscoring the unique causal effect of communism. Thus, Howard's research design is a **multimethod** one, including both small-$N$ and large-$N$ components.

**Table 6.2** Most different systems design: civic engagement in Russia and the former GDR

| Possible determinant | Former GDR | Russia |
|---|---|---|
| Level of economic development | High | Low |
| Pre-war experience with democracy | Yes | No |
| Western cultural heritage | Yes | No |
| Communist legacy | Yes | Yes |
| Civic engagement (Dependent variable) | ? | ? |

*Source*: Based on Howard (2003)

## Research Design for Interpretive Questions

While the above examples of research design sought to maximize causal inference, there are also case study research designs that ask ontological questions about concepts, entities, and practices in PIR that are often taken for granted. As you will recall from Chapter 2, ontology refers to what something 'is' – or an object of interest, or research on context-specific meanings (Schwartz-Shea and Yanow 2013, 23). Let's consider the interpretive question posed earlier: 'How do war memorials in Europe shape a society's collective memory of the past?' Here, we see how interpretive questions are focused on understanding a certain object – sites of memory in this case – and the social meaning of the object in the context of collective memory. Interpretive questions seek to understand how certain objects acquire social meaning over time. Here, as with positivist questions, you will face dilemmas related to case selection. For example, you could explore a specific site of memory, or you could compare collective practices of Holocaust remembrance across various countries in Europe. While the primary research purpose in this example is not necessarily causal inference, interpretive research can come close to offering suggested explanations for outcomes through the concept of emergent causality. Rather than focusing on grand theoretical claims through making claims to direct causality between variables, emergent causality is a notion developed by William E. Connelly (2004) which sees causality as an emergent condition that opens up possibilities for action.

For example, Connolly (2005) poses the following question: 'What is the connection today between evangelical Christianity, cowboy capitalism, the electronic news media, and the Republican Party?' He argues that linear models of cause and effect can't disentangle each of the elements in his question, which tend to blend into one another. Rather, the connections among these disparate phenomena are constructed through particular acts, such as George W. Bush's driving of an SUV at a NASCAR racetrack during the 2004 US presidential campaign. Connolly writes:

> The crowd responded to the SUV as a symbol of disdain for womanly ecologists, safety advocates, supporters of fuel economy, weak-willed pluralists, and internationalists.

Bush played upon the symbol and drew energy from the crowd's acclamation of it. Resentment against those who express an ethos of care for the world was never named: a message expressed without being articulated. (Connolly 2005, 879)

In international relations, research on the concept of **ontological security** serves as another example of an interpretive research agenda that does not adhere to positivist conceptions of measuring cause and effect (Gustafsson 2014, 71–86). As we just recalled above, ontology refers to the study of being, or what 'is,' in politics. Ontological security is the study of state security identities: how they emerge, are constructed, or reproduced, and how they shape possibilities for action in foreign policy. Ontological security assumes that states seek to protect their own sense of identity, which might be defined in terms of values in addition to protecting the physical integrity of the state. Interpretivist research designs can require us to understand the role of narrative and collective memory in constructing this sense of state identity (Subotic 2013).

When designing your interpretivist research project, you may start out with a number of purposes in mind such as accounting for the emergence of a particular concept. For example, you may wish to focus on the concept of national sovereignty, and how changes in perceptions of this concept have altered foreign policy practices over time. You are thinking not in terms of precise causal claims, but in terms of emergent causality, or structuring possible foreign policy responses. Alternatively, you may also be interested in narratives and identities in politics. In this case, you will look to 'the stories states tell' to better understand the processes of state identity construction and how they either restrict or open up space for foreign or domestic policy formulation and implementation.

In short, the logic of interpretivist research design departs from the logic of positivist research designs. Unlike positivist designs, interpretivist ones do not attempt to reproduce the logic of the scientific method and its inherent search for causal inference. Moreover, with interpretivist questions, you will likely already have your case in mind. This is because interpretivist research often requires previous in-depth knowledge of a particular case and its position within a given historic and cultural context. If you are to add cases to your study, the focus will be on understanding processes rather than outcome. As such, the scientific methods for case selection we discussed above for positivist questions often do not apply for interpretivist ones.

## Chapter Summary

Research design refers to the roadmap which will guide your thesis or paper. PIR researchers can choose from a number of different research designs. Each kind is associated with certain advantages and disadvantages. Early on in the process, you will make a choice about whether to engage a small or large number of cases, and which cases to choose. Both decisions are related to a number of factors: your research purpose, the availability of data, and the kind of question you pose. If causal inference is your goal, and you wish to examine a small number of cases, case-oriented comparative designs such as MSS and MDS provide a way to address causality while also examining an observation in some depth. Case-oriented designs, even those analyzing a single case, can also help generate new ideas and theoretical insights, as well as paths forward for further research. Experimental designs, by contrast, offer high levels of control over confounding explanatory factors and thus high levels of internal validity. Experimental designs themselves come in several kinds, such as **laboratory experiments** or **field experiments**.

Large-$N$ designs are well suited to quantitative analysis. We have discussed such designs less here, but you will delve into quantitative data collection and analysis in Chapters 9 and 10, respectively. However, these days, many scholars combine multiple designs, using what is known as multimethod research. The PIR literature is replete with multimethod designs, such as the example of Howard's book described above (Howard 2003). To give another example, Dara Kay Cohen (2013) conducted a study of rape during wartime using a large-$N$ statistical analysis of 86 wars over three decades, but combined that with an in-depth single case study of the war in Sierra Leone.

This chapter has heavily focused on case-oriented designs, especially the small-$N$ comparative case design. As we have demonstrated, careful case selection allows for research designs that might illustrate how what are at first seemingly trivial differences among societies, states, or time periods shape very different outcomes. Case-oriented research, whether positivist or interpretive, might also suggest that there are greater commonalities among diverse cases than is evident at first glance. Finding these common patterns, in fact, is among the most exciting things about research.

Once you have selected a research design, it is time to think about data collection, and then analysis of that data using qualitative or quantitative techniques. The next four chapters cover these topics. Chapter 7 deals with data collection for qualitative research, while Chapter 8 presents tools for qualitative analysis. Chapter 9 is about quantitative data collection, while Chapter 10 introduces tools for quantitative analysis.

## ▬▬▬▬ Suggested Further Reading ▬▬▬▬

Bennett, Andrew, and Checkel, Jeffrey T. (eds.). 2015. *Process Tracing*. Cambridge, UK: Cambridge University Press.
An introduction to process-tracing as a way to account for complex causal processes.

Berg-Schlosser, Dirk. 2012. *Mixed Methods in Comparative Politics: Principles and Applications*. London: Palgrave Macmillan.
Mixed method designs have become increasingly popular. This volume describes how to use them.

Bevir, M. 2000. *Interpretive Political Science*. Thousand Oaks, CA: Sage.
An introduction to the principles of interpretive research by a noted political theorist.

Blatter, Joachim, and Haverland, Markus. 2012. *Designing Case Studies: Explanatory Approaches in Small-N Research*. London: Palgrave Macmillan.
A primer on the small-N design.

Brady, Henry E., and Collier, David (eds.). 2010. *Rethinking Social Inquiry: Diverse Tools, Shared Standards*. Lanham, MD: Rowman & Littlefield.
A seminal volume on the shared scientific standards of quantitative and qualitative methods.

Caramani, Daniele. 2008. *Introduction to the Comparative Method with Boolean Algebra.* Thousand Oaks, CA: Sage.
An advanced text on the comparative case study method.

Doyle, Michael W., and Sambanis, Nicholas. 2000. International Peacebuilding: A Theoretical and Quantitative Analysis. *American Political Science Review*, 94(4), 779–801.
A good illustration of innovative research design.

Dunning, Thad. 2012. *Natural Experiments in the Social Sciences: A Design-Based Approach.* Cambridge, UK: Cambridge University Press.
An influential political scientist tackles experimental designs.

Geddes, Barbara. 1990. How the Cases you Choose Affect the Answers you Get: Selection Bias in Comparative Politics. *Political Analysis*, 2, 131–150.
An important article on case selection.

Horiuchi, Yusaku, Imai, Kosuke, and Taniguchi, Naoko. 2007. Designing and Analyzing Randomized Experiments: Application to a Japanese Election Survey Experiment. *American Journal of Political Science*, 51(3), 669–687.
An example of how to use experimental design.

Imai, Kosuke, et al. 2011. Unpacking the Black Box of Causality: Learning about Causal Mechanisms from Experimental and Observational Studies. *American Political Science Review*, 105(4), 765–789.
Discusses causality in two kinds of research designs.

Krook, Mona Lena. 2010. Women's Representation in Parliament: A Qualitative Comparative Analysis. *Political Studies*, 58(5), 886–908.
An illustration of the comparative case study method.

Mahoney, James, and Goertz, Gary. 2006. A Tale of Two Cultures: Contrasting Quantitative and Qualitative Research. *Political Analysis*, 14(3), 227–249.
The trade-offs between two research approaches.

Pepinsky, Thomas B. 2019. The Return of the Single Country Case Study. *Annual Review of Political Science*, 22(1), May, 187–203.
A defense of the value of single case study designs.

Ragin, Charles C., and Becker, Howard Saul. (eds.). 1992. *What is a Case? Exploring the Foundations of Social Inquiry.* Cambridge, UK: Cambridge University Press.
Leading experts on methods describe the case study method.

Schwartz-Shea, Peregrine and Yanow, Dvora. 2013. *Interpretive Research: Concepts and Processes.* London: Routledge.
An overview of the interpretive approach to research.

Shapiro, Ian and Smith, Rogers M. 2004. *Problems and Methods in the Study of Politics.* Cambridge, UK: Cambridge University Press.
A classic guide to PIR methods.

Small, Mario Luis. 2011. How to Conduct a Mixed Methods Study: Recent Trends in a Rapidly Growing Literature. *Annual Review of Sociology,* 37, 57-86.
Another article on mixed method design.

Yin, Robert K. 2017. *Case Study Research and Applications: Design and Methods.* Thousand Oaks, CA: Sage.
More on the case study design.

# 7

# Collecting Data for Qualitative Methods

━━━━━━━━━ Learning Objectives ━━━━━━━━━

- To define various kinds of qualitative methods;
- To distinguish between different reasons for using qualitative methods;
- To justify your use of qualitative methods;
- To become familiar with qualitative data collection strategies.

If you have decided to explore a single case, or a small number of cases, you will need to find a suitable strategy for *data collection* and *data analysis*. **Qualitative methods**, which provide a number of different tools in this regard, may be well-suited to your project. Qualitative methods are widely used in PIR and encompass a number of different means of data collection and analysis that will be surveyed in this and the next chapter. In fact, you have also been exposed to some aspects of qualitative methods in the previous chapter, which introduced you to comparative case study designs such as the most similar systems (MSS) and most different systems (MSD). These approaches are not only research designs, but also methods of analyzing qualitative data, the subject of the next chapter.

Qualitative methods refer to a way of doing social science research which focuses on the collection, interpretation, and analysis of non-numerical data. There is a misconception that qualitative methods are not rigorous (Levy 2002, 131). In fact, qualitative methods strive for the same rigor as their quantitative counterparts. Qualitative methods, moreover, are not exclusive to any particular epistemological tradition in PIR. They are neither inherently interpretive nor positivist. Qualitative work has been discussed by positivists, such as King, Keohane, and Verba (1994), who argue that the logic of causal inference, or what has been referred to throughout this text as the positivist tradition, unites what they consider to be good qualitative and quantitative research design. What they mean by this is that qualitative methods and quantitative methods use a different set of tools, but rely on common standards and aim to accomplish the same goal: explaining causal relationships between variables.

Numerous methods textbooks explicitly address the diverse set of qualitative practices available to researchers in PIR. Some will be of more interest to those undertaking interpretivist research (Klotz and Prakash 2008; Salter and Mutlu 2013; Yanow Shea-Schwartz 2015). However, other texts focus exclusively on qualitative methods from a positivist perspective. These texts assume the goal of your study is to make some kind of causal inference (George and Bennett 2005; Gerring 2007; King, Keohane, and Verba 1994). This chapter includes examples drawn from both positivist and interpretivist research.

We begin by defining qualitative methods, and then go on to discuss justifications for their usage. This is followed by a presentation of ways to collect qualitative data, including document-based research and content analysis, interviews, focus groups, the internet and social media, and visual research. You might even be able to engage in **field research** – travel to a particular site relevant to your project – to collect qualitative data.

## What are Qualitative Methods?

Given the breadth of research that fits under the qualitative label, what are some common characteristics of qualitative methods? We define qualitative methods to be research tools, techniques, and strategies that help us to collect, interpret, and analyze non-numeric data. Scott and Garner (2013) argue that the key difference between qualitative methods and quantitative methods is that qualitative researchers study a small number of cases, but a large number of variables – or data points – associated with their cases. By contrast, quantitative researchers study a large number of cases, but only a few variables associated with each case (Scott and Garner 2013, 9).

Qualitative methods, it should be noted, are also not exclusive to the study of PIR. Indeed, the qualitative data analysis tools used in PIR often draw on a number of related disciplines. As such, the concepts and tools that you will be presented with later in this chapter, and also in Chapter 8, are those that are also widely used by historians, sociologists, and ethnographers, in addition to political scientists and students of IR.

In the previous chapter, you read about the comparative case design strategy, which adheres to King, Keohane, and Verba's definition of shared standards for causal inference. But other qualitative designs and methods do so too. For example, Morgan's recent work on populism and gender in France aims to make a causal argument using qualitative methods. Morgan asks 'Why have gender-based forms of oppression, as opposed to other criticisms of immigrant communities, become part of integration policies and debates?' (2018, 889). In order to answer this question, Morgan presents the reader with an inter-temporal comparison of France in the 1990s and France in the 2000s, and employs process-tracing 'to reveal the confluence of actors and events shaping integration policy' (Morgan 2018, 891).

However, qualitative methods are also widely used by interpretive researchers who reject the logic of causal inference and instead seek to understand the meaning of political phenomena. For example, an interpretive research project might engage the assumptions we often make about what states want. It may ask what taken-for-granted terms in International Relations, such as 'national interest,' mean in the first place. How is the 'national interest' constituted? These are the questions that were posed by Weldes in a qualitative study of national interest (Weldes 1996, 275–318). Another example is an article by de Carvalho, Schia, and Guillaume (2019), who undertake an ethnographic study of participants in a US government-funded initiative that enables participants from Liberia to receive an education in the United States and then return home to work in government ministries (de Carvalho et al. 2019, 179–202). Rather than seek to make a causal argument in the positivist sense, the aim of the authors was to 'make the case for understanding peacebuilding settings through the politics of sovereignty by bringing the discourse on sovereignty to bear on the policy of local ownership' (de Carvalho et al. 2019, 180). In other words, these authors seek to understand how discourse and policies shape how we understand phenomena such as peacebuilding and development.

Qualitative methods generally rely on inductive reasoning. This is because qualitative researchers tend to generate theoretical propositions out of empirical observation (Bryman 2008, 366; Yanow and Schwartz-Shea 2015). For example, an in-depth case study on a populist political party in Germany might generate new theoretical propositions about the German party system. Or it might act to falsify a more general theoretical proposition that already exists in the literature. Take, for example, Charles Lees' recent article on right-wing populism in Germany (2018, 295–310). Lees starts off with a theoretical puzzle: the rise of the Alternative for Germany party, a populist and nationalist group, seems to contradict established assumptions in the literature, drawn from Historical Institutionalism (HI), about Germany's historical experience, and how post-Second World War political institutions acted to marginalize anti-European populist political parties within institutional and normative structures that favored deepening European integration. We will describe HI in the next chapter. Through a case study of the electoral performance of the Alternative for Germany, Lees reaches the conclusion that the 2017 German federal elections constituted a **critical juncture** in German party politics (Lees 2018, 297–299). Critical junctures will be explained in Chapter 8.

## Qualitative Methods

Qualitative methods are data collection techniques and data analysis strategies that rely upon the collection and interpretation of political phenomena, entities, or events by making use of non-numeric data.

Qualitative methods are also generally well-suited to projects that aim to provide for thick-description (Geertz 1973, 3–30). According to Geertz, thick-description refers to providing qualitative empirical observation within its social context (Geertz 1973, 3–30). As noted in Chapter 2, thick-description is also a key component of good process-tracing. Most qualitative PIR research projects aim to provide thick-description of a particular political phenomenon and, therefore, we need tools to help us be better observers of the social world.

## Why Use Qualitative Methods?

Some scholars focus exclusively on positivist comparative case study design of the kind presented in Chapter 6 when discussing qualitative methods (Levy 2002, 131–160). Yet, one of the main advantages of qualitative methods is their versatility. Indeed, qualitative methods encompass a much broader research tradition, spanning **interpretive-ethnographic** (de Carvalho et al. 2019) and **historical-comparative research** (Capoccia and Ziblatt 2010, 931–968).

One obvious reason to turn to qualitative methods is that the availability of a small number of cases constrains a researcher's ability to apply statistical techniques which require a large number of cases. But there are other compelling reasons. One major one is that qualitative analysis allows for more nuanced and in-depth examination of a case. Recall our discussion of ethnic plurality and democracy in the previous chapter. Quantitative methods (discussed in Chapters 9 and 10) necessitate assigning a number ('coding') to a phenomenon such as ethnic plurality, which can never capture the richness of ethnic relations in a particular context. Ethnographic methods and thick-description can do that much better.

Critics of qualitative methods see them as 'highly subjective, pliable to fitting facts to theoretical arguments, nonreplicable, and essentially non-falsifiable' (Levy 2002, 131).

However, good qualitative work should adhere to the same ethical and scientific standards as its quantitative counterpart. This includes standards such as transparency of data and data-gathering techniques. This is true for both positivist and interpretivist designs. Among other scholars, Schwartz-Shea (2015) emphasizes the application of rigorous standards in interpretive research.

Thus, there are many reasons why you might use qualitative methods in your own work. The focus of qualitative research is typically on gathering in-depth data about specific phenomena or events. Because of this, qualitative methods are particularly well-suited to exploratory research, discussed in Chapter 4. Detailed qualitative examination of a single case or a small number of cases, in turn, allows one to map, classify, or uncover new variables, social forces, or actors. Exploratory research can also refer to research projects that aim to uncover new empirical data with the goal of producing generalizable research results, or to build theory (Stebbins 2001). Moreover, exploratory research is usually associated with **grounded theory**, which focuses on generating new theories rather than testing hypotheses derived from existing theories. As such, it is an inductive approach that puts an emphasis on collecting solid empirical data in order to generate explanations based on observation (Glaser and Strauss 1967).

While grounded theory and exploratory research are common research strategies that often rely on qualitative methods, there are also other, **deductive** theory-testing approaches that rely on them as well. To be sure, how we analyze our non-numeric data can range from process-tracing studies that illuminate causal relationships between variables, to studies that focus on exploring emergent causality, to interpretive studies that look for meaning in qualitative empirical data.

## Qualitative Data Collection

Qualitative researchers rely on diverse data collection techniques given their desire to achieve an in-depth understanding of their object of study. While we might assume qualitative methods focus on collecting textual or verbal data (based on interviews), today researchers work with a wide range of social artefacts from visual images and photographs to physical monuments and spaces (Scott and Garner 2013). In the ensuing subsections, we describe some of the most widely used qualitative data collection strategies. These include **archival and document-based research**, interviews, focus groups, **web-based research, and visual methods**. They are summarized in Table 7.1.

## Archival and Document-based Research

Archival or document-based research deals with textual sources. Textual sources come in two forms. Original research often requires us to access **primary sources**, those authored by individuals who had direct access to the information that they are describing, or directly experienced a particular event. Sometimes you might even gain access to primary sources through interviews, particularly if you are conducting oral histories (Gordon 2003, 264). You may think of this as finding 'witness testimony' about an event

**Table 7.1** Qualitative data collection strategies

| Qualitative research data collection in PIR | Examples |
| --- | --- |
| Archival research – primary and secondary source documents | • Personal documents: memoirs, diaries, letters, correspondences, and autobiographies<br>• Official (state) documents: meeting records, legislative debates, legislation, executive orders, official statistics, and other government records<br>• Corporate or business documents<br>• Political party documents and archives<br>• Media reports and articles<br>• Think-tank reports<br>• Internet-based sources<br>• Biographies |
| Interviews | • Structured, semi-structured, and unstructured interviews, one-to-one conversations |
| Focus groups | • Group interviews |
| Internet-based research | • Access to primary or secondary source documents (see Archival research)<br>• Social media |
| Visual methods | • Photographs, images<br>• Films, videos<br>• Physical spaces, monuments |

that you are researching. Primary source documents can also be official documents or pronouncements on the part of an individual, organization, state, or international organization. In some countries, such as Japan, it is routine for organizations to compile their own histories (Gordon 2003, 262).

**Secondary sources** reference, or analyze, primary source documents, or other primary sources. For example, if you cite a campaign press release, you will be engaging with a primary source document. But if you reference a media article which analyzes the contents of this campaign press release, you will be relying on a secondary source. Therefore, secondary sources include a wide range of textual material from media reports to think-tank reports to peer-reviewed articles. For students and novice researchers undertaking qualitative research projects, archival and document-based research focusing on media and other secondary sources is a common data collection strategy. Indeed, most qualitative research agendas include at least some document-based research.

For example, for students with an interest in populist political parties, party programs offer rich textual sources that would help one to understand how populists appeal to voters. Party programs are publicly accessible documents that you can often find on political party websites. For students of international relations, diplomacy is perhaps one of the best-documented practices that one can choose to study. Research projects on diplomacy can benefit from access to treaties, official reports, minutes of meetings, firsthand accounts of diplomatic encounters, memoirs, diplomatic cables, UN Security Council resolutions, policy statements, legislation, and other primary sources.

## Official Document-based Research

Researchers often gather official documents as a source of data. Official documents are published by a state, organization, or business, and provide detailed insight into a particular organization. They come in many different forms, from official transcripts of meetings and correspondences to lengthy analytical reports, policy statements, speech transcripts, budgets, and personnel files. However, in most cases, you will not have unlimited access to an organization's documents, and even if you do, release of the information within them may be forbidden by law due to privacy or security concerns. While most organizations archive their records, access to these archives is often restricted. Usually, we must wait for a certain period of time to have transpired before official records are made accessible to the general public. This is especially true of official government records relating to national security. For example, the Cold War International History Project, hosted by the Woodrow Wilson Center in Washington DC, is a repository of US national security documents from decades ago that have only recently been declassified.

---

### The Cold War International History Project

The Cold War International History Project (CWIHP) is hosted by the Woodrow Wilson International Center for Scholars in Washington, DC. The CWIHP was established in 1991. The Project supports the release of historical materials by governments on all sides of the Cold War. It also aims to accelerate the process of integrating new sources, materials, and perspectives from the former 'Communist bloc' and the non-western world more generally with the historiography of the Cold War, which has been written over the past few decades largely by western scholars reliant on western archival sources. It also seeks to transcend barriers of language, geography, and regional specialization to create new links among scholars interested in Cold War history.

*Source:* www.wilsoncenter.org/about-18

---

For the student of PIR, access to current official documents can pose a challenge. Our interest in electoral politics, social inequality, foreign policy, or other issues salient to our research means that we will be seeking to collect documents from states, political parties, businesses or other organizations that have an interest in not revealing too much of their internal decision-making processes in the context of a world of competitive external actors who might use that information to accrue some form of advantage.

A student wanting to explore the rise of populist parties in western Europe could benefit from publicly available platforms but might also want to access documents that contain important details about internal party deliberations and decision-making processes. For the most part, these documents are unavailable since parties want to protect their internal workings from outside scrutiny. Yet, secondary sources and interviews (described below) might fill in some gaps in knowledge. In other words, the qualitative data we seek may be dispersed across a number of individuals, organizations, media outlets, non-fiction books, and biographies.

Official document-based research requires us to invest time in discovering where to look for sources that may be relevant to our research. At the same time, we should guard against focusing too narrowly on a few documents that could give us a distorted picture of the topic under study. Just as a sample of respondents to a survey might be biased, so could a sample of documents. One way to deal with potential **bias** is to be transparent, clearly defining the scope of documents you set out to collect and those that you have examined versus those that may exist but be inaccessible.

Even when complete access is possible, documents only give you a glimpse into those items that were recorded into an organization's institutional memory. There are many aspects of social interaction that remain invisible to the researcher. For example, even after a thorough document review, you might be left with questions about how a certain outcome came about or how a decision-making process worked. Here, interviews can provide a valuable qualitative data-gathering technique for expanding your knowledge on a given topic.

Finally, you should always question the veracity of what is written in official documents. To do this you need to know the source. You may find that official reports published by a particular governmental agency are historically known to contain unreliable information. In this case, you would want to begin to explore whether or not other sources might have produced more reliable reports. In some cases, consultations with archivists can give you a perspective on their veracity. In sum, the more you know about your document-based sources, the better you will be able to make clear to your readers what kinds of sources you have relied upon for data collection, and how that may, or may not, impact the veracity of your findings.

## Media as a Secondary Source Document

Media reports can constitute a valuable source of empirical data. Today, we have access to a vast media environment, and we see new stories relevant to topics in which we are interested pop up on our Twitter feeds or other social media. The internet gives us access to a dizzying array of media sources from around the globe. Gone are the days when we would have to turn to the international section of a trusted local newspaper to read about events taking place across the world. When using media reports in research, it is important to distinguish between internationally renowned media outlets such as *CNN*, the *BBC*, *The New York Times*, or *The Financial Times*, and sources that have an exclusively local circulation or audience. Alternatively, you should also distinguish between media sources that are independent and those which are effectively state media.

You might find that a news source from which you collected qualitative data is known for promoting a particular perspective on a given issue, and therefore you might want to also expand your search to other national newspapers in order to check the veracity of your collected reports. When relying upon local or unknown media sources, you should consult with experts about whether the sources you are using are focused more on niche audiences or are nationally read. For example, if you are researching Japanese politics, it might be useful to be aware of the fact that the *Asahi* newspaper is generally regarded as a politically left-leaning paper, while the *Sankei* newspaper is seen as right-leaning. But even when relying upon the big international media, you should also familiarize yourself with whether or not your local media sources cater to a particular ideological or political grouping.

Then there are sources which deliberately distort information in the pursuit of political and other agendas. The 2019 Mueller Report documented extensive efforts by the Russian government to sow discord through disinformation so as to influence the 2016 US presidential election. In the best-case scenario, you will be surveying a broad range of media sources, and there are multiple tools available on your university's library website to help you do so (*LexisNexis*, for example, is a powerful database that compiles media reports).

## Interviews

Interview data provide incredibly rich data for qualitative analysis in PIR. Researchers conduct interviews to gain factual data about a particular phenomenon, event or object, or to elicit the perspectives of a primary participant in an important event and to learn about their decisions and behavior (Scott and Garner 2013, 280). The section will present you with three basic interview formats to use in your own research. The format you select will largely depend on the nature of the responses you aim to elicit and the types of data you aim to gather. However, before going on to discuss how to conduct interviews, it is first necessary to say a few words about access.

## Access

One of the first challenges you will encounter in any attempt to gather qualitative data directly from your sources is that of access. One technique that you are likely to make use of, even without being aware that you are doing it, is **snowball sampling**. Jacobson and Landau (2003, 195–196) describe snowball sampling as an access strategy whereby you rely on the first interview participants you meet to introduce you to additional potential participants, who will in turn introduce you to more participants.

Beyond that, in order to secure access to those with whom you would like to conduct interviews you will first need a good understanding of your research context. For example, as Gordon (2003) noted in the case of Japan, securing an affiliation with a local research institution is important. Indeed, in many cultural contexts, a formal introduction or affiliation is key to securing access to interview subjects. In addition to this, Norman and Gordon have both highlighted the need to secure the trust of research participants (Norman 2009; Gordon 2003). This can be achieved in different ways, such as adhering to ethical standards and fully disclosing the purpose of your research and your academic affiliation.

## Three Types of Interviews: Structured, Semi-structured, and Unstructured

Interviews are subdivided into three general categories: structured, semi-structured, and unstructured. The structured interview, based on fixed questions and rigid response categories, often produces quantitative data. Sometimes, it is combined with other qualitative data collection methods, such as focus groups. The semi-structured interview operates with a degree of flexibility but allows the researcher to maintain a basic structure across interview participants. The unstructured interview is less common in PIR, and is essentially an unscripted, free-flowing conversation with the interviewee.

## Structured Interviews

**Structured interviews** are used to obtain quantitative data, and include a predetermined menu of responses. As such, the data that results can be both quantitative and qualitative. A structured interview is essentially a questionnaire that is delivered in a face-to-face interview with research participants, often as part of a larger survey. You will read more about surveys in Chapter 9, on quantitative data collection. One of the benefits of a structured interview compared to other formats is that you can reach a larger number of research participants. Structured interviews are often carried out by teams of interviewers who are provided with a common questionnaire. In order to prevent the introduction of any bias on the part of the researcher into the results of the structured interview, it is important not to deviate from the questions provided in the questionnaire. Another benefit of structured interviewing is that you often do not need to seek permission to make an audio-recording as it is highly scripted. And because you can quickly record responses, there is no lengthy process of generating interview transcripts and trying to tease out what your research participants are trying to tell you.

If a structured interview is essentially a written questionnaire that is delivered face to face, why go through the trouble of a face-to-face interview? Why not just distribute the questionnaire to potential participants and have them complete it on their own? Seale (2011) argues that there are five benefits to conducting structured interviews in person. The first is that the interviewer can explain complex questions to the participant. The second is that written surveys can often take longer than a structured interview and the research participant is less likely to abandon the process halfway through if it is done in person. The third is that there is more scope to ask open and follow-up questions. The fourth is that visual aids, if needed, can be used. And the fifth is that the interviewer has control over the environment in which the interview takes place and can ensure, for instance, that questions are responded to in order (Seale 2011, 183).

## Semi-structured Interviews

In **semi-structured interviews**, you pose a set of open-ended questions, and depending on the response, you may diverge from your planned questions with more specific follow-up ones. Given the flexibility for the researcher to delve into greater depth on particular points raised in the interview, the semi-structured interview is the most common interview format used by researchers in PIR. Semi-structured interviews are particularly valuable because the phenomena that are of interest to scholars in PIR – political developments and events, the foreign policies of states, and the behavior of international organizations, multinational corporations, and civil society organizations – often require us to gain deeper insight into complex social processes. Common interview subjects for semi-structured interviews are often important decision-makers and other experts (see box below). Such conversations are referred to as *elite interviews*.

## Elite Interviews

Who qualifies as an elite when discussing elite interviews? Because the definition of an elite within a particular society is highly subjective, responses to this question often vary. For example, do we use a more restrictive definition, where we focus on those who have a special standing, such as members of Congress or Parliament? Here we use a broader definition that sees elites as anyone who occupies a position of influence or importance within a particular organization that is under study.

For example, if your research project requires you to conduct interviews with representatives of human rights organizations, those activists whom you will interview are considered elites.

In sum, semi-structured interviews permit more in-depth probing on issues of interest to the researcher. Semi-structured interviews thus avoid a pitfall apparent in structured interviews whereby the scope of responses is limited through a pre-selected menu of questions and answers, thereby potentially missing important insights that the interview participant might otherwise offer. Both note-taking and recording are useful in such interviews, and immediate transcription is advised.

## Unstructured Interviews

The **unstructured interview** is often compared to an ordinary conversation that you might have with friends or colleagues. Unstructured interviews are aimed at eliciting the unfiltered perspectives of interview participants. They usually begin with simple, but broad, open-ended questions. For example, if you are trying to understand why an ordinary citizen voted for a populist party in the last election, you might ask: 'Can you tell me about your thinking as you voted in the last election?' Keep in mind that your role as the researcher in an unstructured interview is more like that of a participant in a conversation with your interviewee. Finally, due to the nuanced, complex, and unexpected responses generated during an unstructured interview, they should be recorded either in audio or video form. This, in turn, will necessitate lots of transcription work.

## Conducting Interviews: General Tips and Guidelines

First and foremost, be sure to review ethical guidelines for interviewing. As noted above and in Chapter 3, you must secure the informed consent of interview participants. Securing interviews also involves good communication and etiquette. Contacting elites with busy schedules who might not see the utility in talking to a student researcher requires time and persistence. Your interview request should be polite, formal, and indicate maximum flexibility on your part. It should be very brief in its description of your project, and avoid any academic jargon. It should, moreover, indicate how the subject will contribute to your research. In arranging the appointment, be explicit about the amount of time your interview will require, and calibrate your questions appropriately. It is generally polite to ask for an hour, and if you are lucky, the conversation will be longer. Finally, either in advance or on the day of your appointment, you should agree on the terms of the interview, and whether it will be *on the record* (the information can be used with no caveats, quoting the source by name), *off the record* (the information cannot be used for publication, but it can inform your research indirectly and perhaps verify facts or correct any misconceptions) or on *deep background* (the information can be used but without any attribution whatsoever, even anonymously). The interview consent form presented at the end of this chapter will help you establish the ground rules prior to the conversation.

Once someone has agreed to an interview, there are a few things you should always do to prepare. The first is to make sure you have thoroughly researched the interviewee and the institution they represent. If the participant has any kind of public profile, they will have likely made statements or granted interviews to the media, authored reports or opinion pieces, and delivered testimony before an official body. It is essential that you are familiar with what your interview participant has said on your topic in the past so as to show that you have done your 'homework' and, more importantly, so you can avoid wasting time asking the interviewee about their views on topics that are already in the public domain. Instead, you can make use of the interview to solicit novel insights and triangulate (or corroborate) data with what you have garnered from other sources.

Harvey (2011) highlights the importance of being well prepared and well informed when discussing his own experience conducting interviews, and how this can lead to unexpected payoffs:

> In one notable instance, I expected to conduct an interview with a CEO on his experiences of moving to and working in the US, but found myself being the interviewee. Although this interview did not directly lead to any valuable data for my research at the time, it did lead to me interviewing at least 50 senior executives as a result of the recommendation of this CEO. (Harvey 2011, 434)

In this instance, an ability to demonstrate a deep knowledge on a particular topic convinced one interviewee to open doors for the researcher.

At the interview itself, you should maintain a professional demeanor. As noted in Chapter 3, as researchers we should always strive for transparency about the purpose of our research in our communications with research participants. This includes how you intend to use the interview data, and whether or not you can protect the confidentiality of the research participant. If you use a thorough **interview consent form**, you will likely have provided this information to the interviewee at the time you delivered the form.

## Crafting Your Interview Consent Form

Interview consent forms offer interview participants the option of anonymity; however, the promise of anonymity can also harm our ability to present our research findings to colleagues in a transparent manner. For example, when attempting to process-trace a decision-making process, it makes a difference if you are able to speak with the relevant decision-maker on a given issue. However, if you were able to interview this decision-maker, but you are unable to reference this person by name, the strength and validity of your findings may appear weaker.

In order to still provide maximum transparency in the research process, and cope with the weakening of our arguments presented in published research when interview subjects decline to be identified by name, interview consent forms often provide participants with a sliding scale of anonymity. Below is an example of a menu of choices that can be offered to interview participants:

- Consent to the use of my name, position, and affiliation in published research (example: John Smith, Leader of Political Party A)
- Consent to the use of only my position and affiliation in published research (example: Leader of Political Party A)
- Consent to the use of only my affiliation in published research (example: an official from Political Party A)
- I do not consent to the use of either my name or affiliation in published research (example: a confidential informant)

---

Also, try not to give verbal or non-verbal cues to your interview participants that suggest approval or disapproval. Doing this could be either off-putting to your research participants or lead them to alter their responses to you. An additional word of advice is to make sure that you carefully document your interview. There is nothing more frustrating than getting great insights in an interview only to realize that your notes are insufficient, or that you have not recorded the conversation. In the best-case scenario, your subject will allow for an audio recording of your interview. If so, be sure to check that any technical equipment that you are using to record the interview is properly working before the interview.

New communications technologies are changing how researchers conduct interviews. In the past, doing research far from our own homes was cost-prohibitive as it would require fieldwork visits to foreign countries. Today, these trips can be supplemented via internet-based videoconferencing platforms such as Skype. This provides an easy and inexpensive way to conduct an initial or follow-up interview. As remote communications technology continues to improve in quality, we can expect more interviews to be conducted in this virtual sphere. However, just because we are not conducting a face-to-face interview does not mean that any of the ethical standards described above are more relaxed. In fact, we should ensure that when using data gathered from social media, or when interviewing research participants via internet communications software, we have secured their informed consent. As communications technology evolves, so does the capacity of authoritarian states to monitor those who use them. Anything you do digitally is not anonymous and could be subject to recording by third parties. Potential interview subjects may be reluctant to be interviewed via Skype precisely for this reason.

Once the interview is completed, send an email to the participant thanking them for their time. It will help to open the door to potential follow-up interviews that you might want to conduct. Sometimes, we end up building long-term professional relationships with interviewees, and the best way to do this is to remain in touch with them after the interview. If the interview was on the record, you will send the interviewee any quotes that you want to use in published research in order to verify that he or she is not being misquoted on a particular issue. Some interviewees will agree to be quoted on the record only after seeing how you plan to use their contribution. Finally, once your work is published, it is also good practice to alert your interview participants.

In sum, interviews are a vital tool for qualitative research and an important window into the political world, providing us with unique insights into how individuals perceive specific phenomena, events, or objects, and invaluable data on how processes played out and decisions were made. Just as we acquire knowledge about the world around us through daily conversations, interviews can impart a tremendous amount of insight that we cannot find in official documents or media reports alone. On the other hand, we must always be aware of the need to triangulate interview data with other sources. Interviews reflect the biased perceptions of our interview subjects, and thus we should be careful when using data gleaned from interviews alone as statements of fact.

## Focus Groups

Focus groups are a form of collective interviewing. They generally entail bringing together groups of six to 10 research subjects in order to discuss a particular topic or question in-depth (Bryman 2008, 479). Usually more than one focus group is used as the researcher aims to gather information on how people perceive certain information in the context of social interaction. Bryman notes that while the number of focus groups used in studies ranges from 8 to 52, generally most research studies that make use of focus groups use between 10 and 15 groups. All focus groups are led by a moderator, who has a list of issues to explore, or questions to ask. The moderator can choose to be more or less interventionist. Focus groups are rarely used by individual student researchers because of the time-intensive nature and costs associated with gathering participants together and facilitating discussions across multiple groups. Instead, focus group research is done in the context of larger funded projects that allow the researcher to hire companies that specialize in the task.

## Internet- and Social Media-Based Research

More and more, your first point of access for qualitative data is likely to be the internet. We use the internet to access media reports, primary documents, journal articles, and books; often we also harness its vast resources to gather data. As with any other source, we should always check the veracity of the internet source we are using. This is becoming increasingly difficult as an industry has emerged around creating news items with fake or highly biased content. Often, these webpages are designed to look like authoritative news sites. When it comes to data on the internet, it is helpful to always remember that webpages and their content can be created by anyone. Even community-based information resources such as news stories circulated on social media are open to manipulation. There are no gatekeepers to guard against malicious or false content for those who publish online.

Social media as a tool to gather qualitative data also has its limitations and risks. Although the costs of using Facebook or other platforms as an interface to reach research participants may be low, online surveys, or surveys that you circulate through social media, have significant limitations and you need to be clear about this in how you present your research. The proliferation of social media has also resulted in large amounts of data being generated by individuals. On the one hand, this has created a rich reserve of potential data. Among other things, we can read the perspectives of activists in the country we might be studying by simply 'friending' them on Facebook or 'following' them on Twitter. On the other hand, it is difficult to assess whether or not these perspectives reflect the views of a broad range of people, or the extent to which the views or social media profiles we are following are genuine at all. For example, in 2019 Brookings Institution researchers Grewal, Kilavuz, and Kubinec published a report on the attitudes of Algerian military personnel by using Facebook to target individuals whose profiles listed military affiliation. This report was criticized by Porter (2019), who argued that targeting individuals on the basis of their Facebook profiles is not sufficient to determine whether the respondents were actually members of the Algerian military.

Online encyclopedias such as Wikipedia contain a wealth of information on places, individuals, events, theories, and concepts and have grown in popularity in recent years. Wikipedia is a source you probably access if you hear about a name, place, or topic with which you are not familiar. However, given that Wikipedia relies upon users to generate content, information can be added that is intentionally false or misleading. It is therefore not advisable to rely upon a Wikipedia entry as a source for qualitative data to be used in a PIR essay or thesis. Yet, that is not to say Wikipedia cannot be helpful. Wikipedia can still function as a useful starting point from which you can access other sources.

Governmental websites give us instant access to a wide range of data as well. With a move towards 'e-government,' more countries are providing access to an ever-greater number of official documents, statistical data, legislation, official reports, and policy memoranda. Many states now publish their national security strategy documents on the web. Some provide detailed web-based resources on foreign and domestic policies. For example, if you are interested in US foreign policy, a visit to the US State Department website (www.state.gov) can provide you with access to official statements on Washington's policy toward a specific country, region, or even issue area. Meanwhile, the United Kingdom's Foreign and Commonwealth Office also maintains a webpage that provides access to similar information on UK foreign policy (www.gov.uk/government/organisations/foreign-commonwealth-office).

Moreover, all major international organizations maintain detailed websites and online archives that can provide you with direct access to a wide range of useful research data. The United Nations maintains a website that can provide you with a wealth of information on the UN and its subsidiary bodies (www.un.org). If you are interested in international justice, the International Criminal Court provides you with easy access to legal documents, cases, and situations under examination by the Court (www.icc-cpi.int). For those interested in the work of *ad hoc* international criminal tribunals, such as the former International Tribunal for the Former Yugoslavia (ICTY), which now operates under the name International Residual Mechanism for Criminal Tribunals (IRMCT), the archived ICTY website can still provide you with instant access to a vast archive of legal documents and trial testimony in its online archive, which you can access upon completion of a short registration process (http://icr.icty.org).


## Data Collection for Visual Methods in Qualitative Research

Recently, there has been a move among some scholars of PIR to embrace the qualitative analysis of visual data in PIR research (Bleiker 2018). How do images, such as war photographs, frame our understanding of events in world politics, such as war crimes and atrocities (Petrović 2015, 367–385)? How do physical monuments and public spaces shape narratives of memory (Pavlaković and Perak 2017, 268–304)? These questions, posed by scholars, have demonstrated that our quest to understand the political world may lead us beyond the realm of gathering textual or verbal data. How do we engage with this body of social artefacts that are non-verbal? As Bleiker writes, 'No matter how diverse and complex visual images and artefacts are, they all have one thing in common: they work differently from words. That is their very nature. They are of a non-verbal nature, but we as scholars need words to assess their political significance. Something inevitably gets lost in this process' (2018, 24).

It is this gap between the political significance and the emotion that visual images – whether video recordings, photographs, monuments, or architecture – represent that researchers seek to bridge. Much like textual data, when setting out to collect visual data, you will need to select what types of image you are looking for. Images are defined by Scott and Garner as 'a conveyer of information' (2013, 328). Images can include both static photographs, pictures, or paintings, and film and video (2013, 328). In order to carry out your own visual research project, you can start by selecting a particular image or film, or set of images or films.

You might, as in the case of Petrović (2015), select an iconic image from a conflict and set about investigating the circumstances in which the photograph was taken, and then examine the meanings that the photograph communicated (2015, 367–385). Alternatively, you may look for specific monuments, or physical spaces, that commemorate a particular event and attempt to interpret the feelings that these monuments evoke through their physical characteristics (Pavlaković and Perak 2017, 268–304). As with textual artefacts, you will set out to examine your visual artefact on the basis of what you know about the intended purpose of the subject. What perceptions or emotions did the photographer, or publisher, aim to evoke through a particular image? Or what feelings or impact was a monument or film designed to communicate? In addition, you may look at how these visual artefacts were received by audiences. What impact did a photograph have on a viewing public? How did it achieve this impact?

While your collection strategy for visual data will not diverge too much from what you would do if you were looking for textual sources, you might find yourself needing to visit a physical space, such as a building or a monument, in order to get a better sense of your object of study. More on how to analyze what you find will be presented in the next chapter.

## Chapter Summary

Qualitative methods are widely used in PIR and allow for detailed, nuanced examination of empirical cases and processes. While qualitative methods are sometimes perceived to be less 'rigorous' than their quantitative counterparts, in fact nearly all the same ethical and scientific standards apply. As we have seen in this chapter, there are many ways to collect qualitative data: reading primary and secondary documents, interviews, and the internet, to mention just a few. While the focus of qualitative data is on the non-numerical, this does not mean that it is exclusively focused on texts. There are qualitative PIR projects that focus on the arts, physical spaces, and performance, and sources and tools associated with qualitative methods can help us generate quantitative data. We are now ready to explore some common tools for qualitative data analysis, the subject of the next chapter.

## Suggested Further Reading

Bestor, Theodore C., Steinhoff, Patricia G., and Bestor, Victoria Lyon. 2003. *Doing Fieldwork in Japan*. Honolulu, HI: University of Hawai'i Press.
This edited volume brings to you the first-hand experiences of a number of scholars who carried out their fieldwork in Japan. While the text is Japan-specific, many of the challenges faced during the course of fieldwork are also relevant to projects carried out elsewhere.

Scott, Greg, and Garner, Roberta. 2013. *Doing Qualitative Research: Designs, Methods, and Techniques*. New York: Pearson.
Scott and Garner's book is not specifically tailored to students of PIR, but it does provide further guidance on how to carry out qualitative research. In particular, Part 4 of this book will be most relevant in relation to data collection as it contains chapters on participant observation, interviewing, focus groups, and visual methods.

Sriram, Chandra Lekha, King, John C., Mertus, Julie A., Martin-Ortega, Olga, and Herman, Johanna (eds.). 2009. *Surviving Field Research: Working in Violent and Difficult Situations*. London: Routledge.
This edited volume is essential reading for students of PIR who will undertake fieldwork in violent or difficult contexts. It provides students with a broad overview of the many practical challenges they might face during their fieldwork along with ethical considerations that students should take into account before going into the field.

# 8

# Tools and Strategies for Qualitative Analysis

━━━━━━━ Learning Objectives ━━━━━━━

- To learn the advantages and logic of of qualitative analysis;
- To understand various concepts, tools, and strategies of qualitative analysis, such as Historical Institutionalism (HI) and process-tracing;
- To become familiar with how to carry out Qualitative Comparative Analysis (QCA) and discourse, content, and visual analysis.

You have collected your qualitative (i.e. non-numerical) data. Now, it is time to interpret and analyze it. You need to make sense of what your data is telling you. Although you may already have a strong sense of the story your data will tell, it is still important to keep an open mind when sifting through them. You may find unexpected revelations which you had not considered at the outset of your study. For example, you might have thought that the data would affirm a particular hypothesis while in fact your data negated it. This chapter explores a number of qualitative data analysis strategies, tools, concepts, and methods upon which you can draw to help make sense of your data.

Qualitative analysis allows you to take a deep dive into the richness of your non-numerical data and cases in order to tease out causal stories, challenge taken-for-granted ideas, or bring to the table new perspectives, voices, or insights. After a period in which quantitative approaches dominated, qualitative methods made a comeback. As Mahoney observes, since the 1990s 'the field of comparative politics [has seen] an unprecedented wave of publications concerning qualitative and small-N methods' (2007, 122).

Before you do anything else, you will need to think about what you want from the qualitative data you collected and your overall logic of inquiry, as described in previous chapters. Do you want to explain divergent or shared outcomes among your cases? Do you want to account for causality by describing a process? Or, are you mapping the genealogy of a particular practice or discourse? As you can tell, these questions recall a recurring theme in this book: the difference between positivist and interpretivist research. You will also choose a method of qualitative analysis based on the source of your data. As we discussed in the previous chapter, qualitative data can be collected from a number of different sources, from interviews to newspaper archives, from personal correspondence to physical monuments, and from government documents to works of art.

We begin the chapter with a discussion of causality and qualitative methods, noting that one main advantage of qualitative tools is their ability to specify causal processes with greater precision than quantitative ones. Interpretivists, as we know, have different aims than positivists, but they also use qualitative methods to meet these goals, as we will discuss. We then go on to discuss a series of strategies and tools for qualitative analysis. If you have asked a research question that is positivist and want to focus on causal depth in particular, you are likely to draw upon **Historical Institutionalism (HI)** (Capoccia and Ziblatt 2010, 931–968) and associated concepts such as **critical junctures** and **path dependence.** Or, if you really want to dig into how a causal process unfolds, you may choose to use **process-tracing**. We also present **Qualitative Comparative Analysis (QCA)**, a method which expands on the comparative case study design presented in Chapter 6 and helps us to uncover potential causal relationships for a small number of cases. On the other hand, you may have adopted an interpretivist epistemological perspective whereby you do not consider yourself to be detached from the qualitative data that you have been gathering; rather, you are aware of your own positionality and biases. In this case, **discourse analysis, content analysis,** or **visual analysis** are tools that can illuminate meaning derived from sources such as texts, images, films, or even physical spaces.

## Qualitative Analysis and Causality

Debates over how social scientists can specify causality have long been a central point of contestation for methodologists. Below, we present qualitative approaches that have causality as their goal (HI, process-tracing and QCA) and others that may or may not seek to uncover causality (discourse and content analysis and visual methods). For positivists, one of the advantages of qualitative research is that it allows one to specify causal processes with some precision. By contrast, as you will see in Chapters 9 and 10, quantitative work is often only able to tell us that two variables are related, but not whether one is causing the other. Even if we can specify a causal relationship using qualitative methods, we may not understand the underlying casual processes. Qualitative methods can detail the **causal mechanisms**, or specific conditions or pathways that link a causal variable to an outcome.

Mahoney points out that the fact that qualitative methods cultivate an in-depth knowledge of our cases allows us to make more complex causal arguments that rely on concepts such as path dependence (described below), and that such complex causality is rare in quantitative studies (Mahoney 2007, 130). Tilly provides a number of examples of such mechanisms in a survey of scholarship on democratization. For example, Tilly highlights Yashar's work on explaining divergent outcomes in Costa Rica and Guatemala (Tilly 2001, 21–41). Yashar argued that it was the dynamics of coalition building in Costa Rica, contrasted with the absence of such dynamics in Guatemala, which account for Costa Rica's move toward a non-militarized civilian form of governance and Guatemala's slide into military-led authoritarianism (Tilly 2001; Yashar 1997).

Another example relates to our ongoing consideration of how human rights matter in the policies of western states. Risse, Ropp, and Sikkink (1999) propose a theoretical model to account for how international norms impact domestic politics. Building upon IR constructivism, Risse, Ropp, and Sikkink use a series of case studies that include both 'successes' and 'hard cases' to look for variation of norm effects across states. Importantly, they identify and describe the underlying causal mechanisms that account for change (1999, 1–38).

However, interpretivists see immense value in qualitative methods as well. They may even use qualitative methods to understand causal processes, but in a different way than positivists. Interpretivists argue that **efficient causality**, whereby we know in advance the universe of potential **explanatory variables** and the outcome, is ill-suited to making sense of complex social phenomena. Basically, they contest the assumption of positivist researchers that the dependent variable is knowable at the outset of a causal process.

Connolly (2004, 2005), whose work we encountered in Chapter 6, proposes an alternative way to study causality. He advocates emergent causality, which assumes that outcomes are unknowable at the outset because a change in a particular social practice will catalyze further changes that will in turn feed back and alter the social variables that are under study, thereby creating new opportunities that open up new (hitherto unknowable) possibilities for action. Projects relying on emergent causality thus do not engage in hypothesis testing or search for a conjectured causal relationship between variables.

---

## Efficient Causality versus Emergent Causality

**Efficient causality:** Efficient causality assumes we already know potential outcomes (dependent variables) at the point a causal phenomenon emerges. Examples include positivist research questions that aim to identify a singular cause of an already-known effect. The aim of research is to causally link the dependent variable back to an independent variable.

**Emergent causality:** Emergent causality assumes that outcomes are unknowable at the outset because of complex social processes that are generated through social practices. These social practices feed back and alter the social variables under study, and create new possibilities for action. As a result, emergent causality sees causality as an emergent condition that opens up possibilities for action. Examples include interpretive research questions that explore causal relationships.

---

## Historical Institutionalism and the Study of Politics

Historical Institutionalism (HI) is a qualitative research method that examines political, economic, and social change in social institutions over periods of time. Historical institutionalists are sometimes said to be more structuralist than voluntarist. The **agent–structure debate** is about the extent to which outcomes are predetermined by factors such as institutions and socio-economic structures or whether they are shaped by the choices of individual decision-makers. While rational choice theory emphasizes the role of decision-making agency, historical institutionalists focus on the role of sociological and cultural factors as conditioning outcomes. Hay and Wincott (1998) write that from a historical institutional perspective:

> Actors cannot simply be assumed to have a fixed (and immutable) preference set, to be blessed with extensive (often perfect) information and foresight and to be self-interested and self-serving utility maximizers. (Hay and Wincott 1998, 954)

HI's commitment to examining how historic developments and legacies influence current political outcomes requires researchers to develop deep contextual knowledge about their cases and to carefully link events that happened one hundred years ago to the present. HI often relies on a case study research design and is associated with the work of Charles Tilly (2001). HI was also used in Lipset and Rokkan's seminal work that traced the historical origins of West European party system cleavages, arguing that contemporary party system cleavages are the result of three critical junctures (Lipset and Rokkan 1967).

More recently, authors such as Bunce (2005) have connected pre-communist political developments (such as imperial legacies) to post-communist politics. HI lends itself to what Tilly (1989) has called 'big structures, large processes, and huge comparisons.' It is thus strong on causal depth.

For adherents of HI, institutions – whether political, economic, or social – act as a powerful constraining force on decision-making, and therefore politics is often characterized as going through long periods of path dependency. **Path dependence** refers to a period of time where the choices available to decision-makers are constrained by the choices made in the past. In this sense, path dependency can act to explain long-term institutional stability or resilience. On the other hand, periods where institutions do not exert strong constraints on decision-makers are referred to as **critical junctures**, where key choices can set in place new institutions that in turn will constrain the choices of future decision-makers.

Let us now see how the concepts associated with HI can help us understand a real-world case, that of Algeria. In 2011, while a wave of protests removed autocratic leaders in Tunisia, Egypt, and Libya, Algeria's authoritarian system under President Abdelaziz Bouteflika was seemingly able to ride out the revolutionary transformations of the 'Arab Spring.' Why was this? In order to respond to such a question, in-depth knowledge of your case's historical, political, economic, and cultural past is essential.

Some scholars have used the tools of historical institutional analysis to analyze how the Algerian state was able to maintain its 'stranglehold over civil society' when other autocratic states in North Africa witnessed their autocratic leaders fall under the pressure of sustained protest (Entelis 2011, 653). Algeria experienced a prolonged period of authoritarian rule from independence in 1962. The victory of the nationalist FLN (Front de Liberation National) in Algeria's national liberation struggle and France's recognition of Algerian independence can be seen as a critical juncture where Algerian elites had a number of choices, such as crafting a new post-independence constitutional order that would constrain the choices of future generations of elites. This new order put in place a strong and dominant ruling party, strong armed forces, and a strong internal security apparatus. These strong institutions then constrained the choices of future generations of elites. However, faced with economic crisis and growing demands for political pluralism, Algerian president Chadli enacted a series of reforms that led to another critical juncture: multiparty elections in 1990 and 1991. Those elections had the potential to open up a wide range of possibilities for political change, but that possibility was closed when the military, frightened by the strong showing of Islamists at the polls, cancelled the election results, which in turn led to the outbreak of an eight-year-long civil war in which hundreds of thousands of Algerians died. The memories of that war, in turn, are often cited as another reason that Algerians were unwilling to protest against the authoritarian regime in 2011 (though they did eight years later, in 2019, and forced Bouteflika, the longtime ruler, to resign). Thus, HI and the concepts of critical junctures and path dependency can help us to account for Algeria's trajectory since independence in a way that quantitative methods cannot.

## Process-tracing

Why was Tunisia's transition to democracy largely successful, while Egypt fell back into the grip of authoritarianism? Why did the United States intervene militarily to support revolutionaries in Libya, but not in Syria? How did refugees come to be seen across Europe as a security issue rather than a humanitarian one? You probably have noticed that the first two questions are causal, while the third one is interpretive. But all three questions share one feature: they will require you to explore the processes, either material or discursive, that brought about an outcome.

For example, in the case of the first question on transitions to democracy, you will be writing about the multiple and complex events that took place after the Arab Spring uprisings of 2011, documenting how they led to divergent outcomes – democracy in Tunisia, authoritarianism in Egypt. Post-2011 transitions in both of these countries involved a series of decisions made by key actors. In early 2011, for instance, the Muslim Brotherhood made the decision to work with the interim military government rather than join the secular democratic activists, which led to early parliamentary elections (Hellyer 2017). Each step did not irreversibly determine the next, but did shape the trajectory of transition in a particular way.

There are a number of strategies that researchers use in PIR to help bring such processes into focus for the reader. One is process-tracing. You have already been introduced to process-tracing in the context of research design in Chapter 6. You will recall that process-tracing is the attempt to link possible causes with observed outcomes by carefully describing sequences of events or decisions. David Collier notes the following advantages of process-tracing:

a    identifying novel political and social phenomena and systematically describing them;
b    evaluating prior explanatory hypotheses, discovering new hypotheses, and assessing these new causal claims;
c    gaining insight into causal mechanisms; and
d    providing an alternative means of addressing problems posed by statistical approaches to causal inference (Collier 2011, 824).

Process-tracing can also complement quantitative analysis tools. Collier writes that process-tracing 'can add leverage in quantitative analysis' and 'strengthen causal inference in small-N designs based on the matching and contrasting of cases – designs which have great value, but whose contribution to causal inference urgently needs to be supplemented by within-case analysis' (2011, 824). Collier further observes:

As a tool of causal inference, process-tracing focuses on the unfolding of events or situations over time. Yet grasping this unfolding is impossible if one cannot adequately describe an event or situation at one point in time. Hence, the descriptive component of process-tracing begins not with observing change or sequence, but rather with taking good snapshots at a series of specific moments. To characterize a process, we must be able to characterize key steps in the process, which in turn permits good analysis of change and sequence. (Collier 2011, 824)

The value of process-tracing is that it enables a compelling narrative to be told about causal processes in real-world cases. But the downside to process-tracing is that it is not possible to generalize from a causal story told about a single case. To generalize beyond your case, you need to supplement process-tracing with comparative research designs and other methods and tools, described in other chapters.

## How to Use Process-tracing

There is by now a rather large scholarly literature on process-tracing in PIR and other social science disciplines. We reference some of these works in the 'Suggested Further Reading' list at the end of this chapter. Among them is a 2011 article by David Collier which contains valuable examples and exercises for students (2011, 823–830). Here, we present some basic features of the technique, but if you plan to use it in your thesis or paper, it would be useful to read more about it.

Process-tracing, as we noted above, is about telling an empirical story in a systematic way that highlights causal processes. The first step is knowing where to start your story. If you want to explain the US decision to intervene in Libya in 2011, you would probably start your story with the outbreak of demonstrations in the city of Benghazi in February 2011. Though this event was distant from decision-making in Washington, the way it was understood by US foreign policy-makers will be key to your causal story. The challenge is to find a convincing starting point. It is always possible to think of reasons why you might want to push your starting date back. Take as another example an essay that aims to explain the outbreak of war in the former Yugoslavia in 1991. One could start, as many popular accounts often do, with the rise to power of Serbian leader Slobodan Milošević in 1987. But the case could also be made that it was the revoking of Kosovo's autonomy in 1989 that triggered violence in Serbia's southern province that made it possible for Milošević to foment nationalism in the first place. Alternatively, one could look at the founding of the Yugoslav state in the aftermath of the Second World War and the failure to fully confront the legacy of fascist atrocities and partisan revenge killings. But at times it is also not helpful to go too far back, unless you can identify a critical juncture, as discussed earlier. The focus of our analysis in PIR is on explaining a particular political event, and while it may be helpful to provide historical and contextual background, our process stories will more often than not start closer in time to the event that we are trying to explain lest they become too long and complex. In other words, going too far back risks making your process story impossible to tell within the scope of a research paper or thesis.

In addition to knowing where to start, the other difficult part to process-tracing is marshalling the evidence needed to show that a particular event or decision was the cause of an outcome. Some of this evidence will inevitably come from data gathered using techniques described in Chapter 7, such as interviewing or document analysis. When reading your interview transcripts or poring over primary documents, you might find that respondents have provided you with data that either supports or contradicts a proposed causal process story. When evaluating this data, you will find that evidence that supports one causal process story over alternative stories provides greater weight. This is also true for data that you are collecting from textual sources, such as media sources or primary source documents.

## Qualitative Comparative Analysis

The scholar Charles Ragin (2008) developed Qualitative Comparative Analysis (QCA), an approach to small-N research design that formalizes and strengthens the MSS (most similar systems) and MDS (most different systems) research designs described in Chapter 6.

QCA assumes the inherent complexity of social phenomena: that multiple causal variables may also interact with each other to produce outcomes. It is not possible to explain QCA fully here, but it is worth outlining its main principles since it has gained wide popularity in PIR and other social sciences (Toshkov 2016, 269–282).

Let's look at a simple example based on fictional data. Let's say you are interested in explaining why some peace settlements hold while others don't, instead giving way to a renewal of violent conflict. You have reviewed the literature on conflict and conflict resolution and decided to focus on two explanatory variables: (1) whether the peace settlement was guaranteed by an outside power; and (2) whether the peace settlement included a transitional justice mechanism. Now you want to learn whether either of these factors, independently or together, can explain why peace was maintained in a particular state over a determined period of time. Let's say that you have six observations, or cases, and you examine them in terms of these two variables, as presented in Table 8.1.

**Table 8.1**   Conditions for a lasting peace settlement

| Case | Outside guarantor | Transitional justice mechanism | Lasting peace? |
|------|-------------------|-------------------------------|----------------|
| A | No | No | No |
| B | Yes | No | No |
| C | Yes | No | No |
| D | No | Yes | No |
| E | No | Yes | No |
| F | Yes | Yes | Yes |

A possible conclusion is immediately evident: when peace settlements include both outside guarantors and transitional justice mechanisms, peace seems to hold. But with QCA you can also take the next step of constructing a 'truth table,' which lists possible combinations of variables and the number of associated outcomes for each combination, as demonstrated in Table 8.2.

**Table 8.2**   Truth table for cases in Table 8.1

| Outside guarantor | Transitional justice | Lasting peace | No lasting peace | Total cases |
|-------------------|---------------------|---------------|------------------|-------------|
| No | No | 0 | 1 | 1 (A) |
| No | Yes | 0 | 2 | 2 (D, E) |
| Yes | No | 0 | 2 | 2 (B, C) |
| Yes | Yes | 1 | 0 | 1 (F) |

Now let's say you want to understand how the two variables are related to the lack of a lasting peace. There are several different paths to a failed settlement observed for these six cases: the top three rows of Table 8.2, to be exact. We might say, then, that failed peace settlements occur when there is no outside guarantor and no transitional justice, no out-side guarantor and transitional justice, and an outside guarantor but no transitional justice.

Furthermore, it seems that the presence of an outside guarantor is associated with a failed settlement both when there is transitional justice (Case F) and when there isn't (Cases B and C). Therefore, transitional justice is unlikely to make a difference in the ulti-mate failure of a peace settlement when there is an outside guarantor. Make sense?

Similarly, transitional justice is associated with a failed settlement both when there is an outside guarantor (Case F) and when there isn't (Cases D and E). So the coupling of a transitional justice provision in a peace agreement with an outside guarantor does not automatically overcome the challenges to peace.

We can conclude, in the end, that peace agreements can fail when there is transitional justice or when there is an outside guarantor. Put differently, each of these conditions seems to be *unnecessary but sufficient* for failure. But Table 8.2 also indicates that the combination of transitional justice and an outside guarantor leads to a lasting peace, but individually neither of them can produce such an outcome.

This is a very simple example, and many researchers use a more complex small-*N* design that considers more variables will rely on computer applications to analyze truth tables. For example, if we added another condition to the tables above – another binary such as high or low income inequality – as an additional potential determinant of the success of peace settlements, in addition to two more cases, the scenario would become much more complex. For one, the truth table would have twice as many rows: the addition of even a single added binary doubles the number of possible combinations.

There is another challenge associated with using QCA. Sometimes QCA forces you to deal with missing observations. Perhaps none of the cases exhibit the combination of low income inequality, transitional justice, and an outside guarantor. Maybe there are no such cases, or maybe you have not been able to collect data on them. In such cases, you must resort to theorizing or making assumptions.

The problem of missing observations in complex QCA designs leads us back to the issue of case selection discussed in Chapter 6. Sometimes, you will be working with all the cases available. Let's say you want to look at militarization in post-Soviet states. There is a fixed number of cases to examine – 15 to be exact. In other kinds of projects you will have to pick cases, and as we point out in Chapter 6, the goal is to choose based on adequate variance in both the dependent and independent variables. But the cases should also be similar enough so as to eliminate some possible explanatory variables.

In QCA, it is possible to envision a scenario in which you choose only cases with the same outcome – to use the earlier example, let's say five cases in all of which peace agreements fell apart. Using the logic of MSS design presented in Chapter 6, you might conclude that the absence of a hypothesized cause (let's say high income inequality) in one proves that this variable is not necessary to the outcome. But you can't say anything about sufficiency. Conversely, if you choose cases that all exhibit a hypothesized causal factor, you can establish sufficiency, but not a necessity. Therefore, variation is important.

Here are two final notes about QCA. First, the examples we have looked at in this section all used binary coding, known in QCA as 'crisp sets.' It is also possible to use non-binary measures, known as 'fuzzy sets,' which Rihoux and Ragin elaborate upon extensively in their work (2009). Second, in a perfect world, you would include all the hypothesized causal factors that are possible in your QCA model. In the real world of PIR research, this is hard to do. Including too many variables can mean that unnecessary conditions are included, skewing the results, while including too few variables means that you might be missing a confounding variable. As we noted in Chapter 6, small-$N$ research design, in the end, is an art. (So is the interpretation of quantitative analysis results, as we argue in Chapters 9 and 10.)

## Other Tools for Qualitative Data Analysis

When looking over your interview transcripts, official documents, web-based resources, or photograph images, you will no doubt realize that qualitative data lends itself to many different interpretations and means of analysis. A commonly used qualitative analytical technique used in PIR to analyze the data you collect from such sources is discourse analysis. A related technique is content analysis, which is sometimes described as being purely quantitative (Lowe 2004, 25–27). This is not the case. As Berg and Lune point out, 'content analysis is not inherently either quantitative or qualitative' (2012, 354). Content and discourse analysis can assume many different forms. We can look at language to explain the world around us (positivist), or we can use language to understand how language constitutes or produces the social world (interpretive). Bryman makes an additional distinction between discourse analysis and critical discourse analysis, with the latter being informed by Michel Foucault's work on power and discourse (2008, 499–511). The next two subsections will address content analysis and discourse analysis and provide some practical guidance on how to apply these two qualitative methods of data analysis.

## Content Analysis

Because some scholars view content analysis as the breaking down of textual data into numeric form, or some sort of counting exercise, they see content analysis as a quantitative method. This is because content analysis allows researchers to examine large amounts of data through categorization and coding. However, as noted above, content analysis is neither purely quantitative nor qualitative. Content analysis is best defined as an activity in which 'researchers examine artifacts of social communication' (Berg and Lune 2012, 353). As such, it can include textual data, photographs, television programs, films, and other forms of art (Berg and Lune 2012, 353).

In order to conduct a content analysis, you must first specify its scope. Often, qualitative research projects will require us to gather large amounts of textual data. Content analysis is useful in qualitative research because it allows us to analyze such textual datasets. In order to do this, content analysis necessitates the use of techniques such as **coding**, or isolating particular terms to which we assign a particular value in order to make sense of vast amounts of textual information.

For example, let us assume you are interested in a content analysis of news coverage of the 2016 Brexit referendum. Perhaps you want to contrast coverage by distinct media outlets in the United Kingdom. Given that the number of media outlets that detailed the referendum is far too large for you to systemically analyze, you may do this by choosing a couple of representative news outlets (a form of case selection). You need to establish some criteria for selecting your news outlets, such as major national networks with international coverage and readership. As an example, you could settle upon *The Daily Telegraph* and *The Guardian*, which both maintain extensive websites, and are in the English language. However, even after narrowing your scope to two manageable sources, you also need to create a timeframe, such as a period of two months leading up to the 2016 Brexit referendum. You would then be able to create a catalogue of news stories from both websites or newspaper archives. However, at this point, you still need to categorize the news story content. If you are doing a primarily textual analysis on the basis of news stories published electronically (almost always the case unless you are looking at historical archives), there are a number of software packages available (potentially through your university) that can assist with content analysis, such as *SPSSTextSmart*.

**Categorization** can be a complex task and can be approached in two different ways. The first, a deductive approach, would involve creating categories on the basis of your pre-existing knowledge and expectations. Given the political polarization surrounding debates on the European Union, one could expect the news coverage to privilege a particular narrative or perspective. Thus, we could create two categories, which reflect the narratives that we expect to find (such as stories about mass migration and its effect on local employment and wages versus the economic and cultural benefits migrants bring), and perhaps a third, neutral, category for such stories.

Alternatively, we could take an inductive approach to generating categories by diving straight into the news content so as to identify the kind of content that we discover during the course of our research. You might find, after reading a number of news stories, that there are many more nuanced themes that you were not necessarily aware of at the outset of your study.

Once we have generated our categories, either inductively or deductively, we have to code keywords in the text. Coding for content analysis is essentially the process of pinpointing words that represent a particular concept or category. For example, we could code terms related to sovereignty, such as 'borders,' 'regulation,' or 'migration.' Content analysis software will allow you to code such terms. However, in many cases students also use basic software packages to conduct basic keyword searchers, which can be done using Microsoft Word or most web browsers. Alternatively, you can generate a word cloud on several websites.

Keyword counting is perhaps the most basic form of content analysis. Many different elements within texts can lend themselves to counting. For example, we might want to count references to *he* or *she* in order to get a sense of gender. Alternatively, we can focus on themes, which convey a particular message in sentence form. Other elements that can be coded include characters or individuals who appear in documents; paragraphs (in the event that each paragraph covers a particular idea or claim); concepts (in the event that words can be grouped into particular clusters); and semantics (how strong or weak a word is in relation to other words) (Berg and Lune 2012, 359–360).

Once you begin coding your textual data into categories and counting words, you might be able to distinguish the emergence of specific trends or patterns. The more you have thought about your categories, the better your analysis will be. At this point, you will have generated a large amount of coded data, which you can use descriptively in your analysis, or you can attempt to discern correlations or relationships using quantitative statistical tests, which will be introduced in Chapters 9 and 10. In short, the principle aim of content analysis is to look for patterns in communication.

## Discourse Analysis

Discourse analysis is a qualitative method that focuses on the interpretation of linguistic forms of communication. The communication you analyze can be either spoken or written and can include both official and unofficial texts. Scholars of PIR who rely on discourse analysis see politics as constituted by actors whose identities are formed through **inter-subjective** understanding, meaning that language plays a key role in constructing the meanings of the objects under study. Researchers' principal interest is to understand how and why particular discourses emerge, become dominant, and are used by political actors.

Hardy, Harley, and Phillips define discourse analysis as 'a methodology for analyzing social phenomena that is qualitative, interpretive and constructivist' (2004, 19). They argue that discourse analysis is more than just a technique for understanding the content of texts, but also brings with it a set of assumptions about how the world is constructed through language (Hardy, Harley, and Phillips 2004, 19). However, discourse as a source of data is not exclusively interpretivist in usage, as we can point to language as a source for discerning actor motivation, thereby also highlighting **causal mechanisms** at work (and thus making it amenable to positivist projects, too).

In order to illustrate this, let's go back to our example of how human rights matters in western foreign policy. Perhaps you want to understand how foreign policy actors use rhetoric and your focus is on the United States. To conduct a discourse analysis, as with content analysis you will first need to specify the scope of what you will be examining. You will need to identify a specific timeframe. Then you will need to settle on what primary source documents you will draw. What particular speeches, statements, or declarations will you examine, and why? What is it that you are looking for or attempting to understand? Are you analyzing the uses of terrorism in US foreign policy discourse? Remember, discourse analysis does not normally rely upon just a single text, speech, or official document, so you will need to attempt to gather those statements which are the most prominent or canonical. However, unlike content analysis, where you can code entire sets of documents, such as US State Department daily briefings over a longer period of time, discourse analyses rely on fewer representative texts. When reflecting upon official discourses, it is important that these texts are authoritative, or come from official sources that are authorized to speak on behalf of the organization under study.

To conduct your discourse analysis, you need to justify your selection of texts (or cases). This case justification is important because you will be making an argument as to the representativeness of the texts for a broader discourse that serves to constitute and produce something of interest in PIR. After you have identified and justified your textual dataset, the processes will depart from content analysis, because now you will not be interested in categorizing data into specific coded typologies. Rather, you will attempt to discern why and how actors resorted to a particular discourse.

Let's say that you are conducting a discourse analysis of political messaging on the part of populist political parties in Europe. Who is a populist? What exactly constitutes populist rhetoric? For example, is the word 'populism' being applied to a broader set of discourses that go beyond traditional definitions of populism? Does the use of this discourse legitimize a certain course of action? These are questions that would be of interest in a discourse analysis, and your task would be to identify key pieces of discourse that have helped to shape popular understanding of a phenomenon like populism. Or, perhaps, as mentioned above, you would seek to understand how populist discourse has turned migration into a security rather than a humanitarian issue.

In short, despite criticisms of discourse analysis being 'unscientific', it is a useful tool for illuminating the world around us. The focus of discourse analysis is on understanding how language constitutes and produces the world around us: how it creates categories, how it limits our choices, or how it creates new choices.

## Visual Analysis

More recently, a growing body of research in PIR has engaged with non-textual and non-verbal social artefacts. The power of images is a topic that is increasingly discussed both in PIR scholarship and in the media (Bleiker 2018). For example, you might recall the controversy surrounding the use of images of refugees in the 2016 Brexit campaign by populist political parties that sought to advance an anti-migrant, or anti-refugee, position. This was done in part through posters, such as that commissioned by populist figure Nigel Farage, which juxtaposed a photograph of migrants against slogans suggesting the need for the United Kingdom to take back control of its national borders. This generated a significant amount of controversy and comparisons to how similar images were used in other contexts to incite a strong emotional response (Stewart and Mason 2016). When undertaking visual analysis, you are trying to understand the emotional response that the creator or publisher of an image seeks to achieve, and the response that such images elicit.

There are a number of qualitative research designs that have been employed in visual analysis in PIR, such as zeroing in on a single iconic image as your object of study, and attempting to deconstruct this image (for example, Petrović 2015). Alternatively, you may look at a set of images, such as that in David Shim's study of how everyday photography and satellite imagery play a decisive role in shaping knowledge about North Korea (Shim 2013). Whichever strategy you employ, you will need to set out a clear question to guide your analysis and justify your choice of imagery. You will then go about researching how a particular image came to occupy an iconic place in the public sphere, and what kind of response the authors of the image sought to evoke, or the response that the image stimulated among the viewing public.

---

## Key Terms in Qualitative Research

**Process-tracing:** Telling the process story of how a change in one variable is linked to a change in another variable. For interpretivist research, process-tracing can also be used to trace the genealogy of a particular idea or concept.

*(Continued)*

**Causal mechanisms:** Specific conditions or pathways that link a causal variable to an outcome.

**Critical junctures:** Periods of time where the constraints exerted by institutions are lessened, and elite choices can put in place new institutions that will in turn constrain the choices of future elites.

**Path dependency:** The proposition that past decisions, or events, constrain the policy options available to decision-makers.

**Efficient causality:** Efficient causality assumes that a known dependent variable can be causally linked back to an independent variable.

**Emergent causality:** Rather than focusing on grand theoretical claims through making claims to direct causality between variables, emergent causality sees causality as an emergent condition that opens up possibilities for action.

## Chapter Summary

Qualitative methods include a broad range of data collection and analysis techniques that provide researchers with deep insight into the political world. Among the advantages of qualitative methods is their ability to specify causality and causal processes with greater precision than quantitative methods. This is in part because qualitative methods are ideally suited to specifying historical and cultural nuance. This chapter also highlighted some key concepts and strategies for qualitative analysis. Some, like Historical Institutionalism (HI) and process-tracing, are well suited to demonstrating causal linkages and processes, while content analysis, discourse analysis, and visual analysis are well suited to interpretive projects seeking to show how meanings are constructed. We also illustrated how Qualitative Comparative Analysis (QCA) works as a way to strengthen causal inference in a comparative case study design. In the two chapters that follow, we turn to quantitative data collection and analysis.

## Suggested Further Reading

Bennett, Andrew, and Checkel, Jeffrey T. Eds. 2015. *Process Tracing: From Metaphor to Analytical Tool*. Cambridge: Cambridge University Press.
Bennett and Checkel's edited volume on process-tracing provides ten essays that discuss how process-tracing has been used in PIR research.

Capoccia, Giovanni, and Kelemen, R. Daniel. 2007. The Study of Critical Junctures: Theory, Narrative and Counterfactuals in Historical Institutionalism. *World Politics*, 59(3), 341-369.
Capoccia and Kelemen introduce how the concept of critical junctures has contributed to Historical Institutional research in comparative politics.

Capoccia, Giovanni, and Ziblatt, Daniel. 2010. The Historical Turn in Democratization Studies: A New Research Agenda for Europe and Beyond. *Comparative Political Studies*, 43(8/9), 931-968.
Capoccia and Ziblatt provide a methodological justification for a historical-comparative approach to the study of democratization.

Checkel, Jeffrey T. 2006. Tracing Causal Mechanisms. *International Studies Review*, 8(2), 362–370.
Checkel's essay provides a concise introduction using process tracing in PIR research.

Hardy, Cynthia, Harley, Bill, and Phillips, Nelson. 2004. Discourse Analysis and Content Analysis:
Two Solitudes? *Qualitative Methods*, 2(1), 19–22.
Hardy, Harley, and Philips provide an accessible overview of discourse and content analysis.

Mosley, Lana, ed. 2013. *Interview Research in Political Science*. Ithaca: Cornell University Press.
Scholars offer advice on interviewing for undergraduate and graduate students.

Tilly, Charles. 2001. Mechanisms in Political Processes. *Annual Review of Political Science*, 4,
21–41.
Tilly focuses on how research on causal mechanisms contributes to our understanding of complex
processes in PIR.

# 9

# Collecting and Preparing Data for Quantitative Methods

━━━━━━━━━━ Learning Objectives ━━━━━━━━━━

- To define quantitative methods and consider their advantages and disadvantages;
- To learn how to operationalize, measure, and code concepts so they can be used in quantitative analysis, while considering levels of measurement;
- To identify ways to gather quantitative data through existing datasets, surveys, and content analysis;
- To understand the importance of quantitative data quality and related concepts such as the validity and reliability of data;
- To become familiar with basic principles of creating and carrying out a survey, such as sampling and bias.

If your research design consists of a large number of cases, it may be well suited to quantitative methods. Quantitative methods are deeply rooted in North American PIR in particular. Browsing a prestigious PIR journal such as the *American Political Science Review*, you will see that its contents are dominated by research articles using various kinds of quantitative methods. While quantitative approaches are popular among many scholars of PIR, the presence of numbers may scare some students away from the discipline. In fact, you may have chosen to study PIR precisely to avoid mathematics. But in contrast to mathematics as a field of study, which can often be abstract, the mathematics you will need to know to carry out quantitative analysis in PIR is applied and more practical. Moreover, as a social scientist, or even as an informed citizen, you cannot avoid engaging with numbers. Media reports confront us on a daily basis with information, and arguments, in numeric form. It is hard to imagine making sense of the world around us without an understanding of **descriptive statistics** (numbers used to summarize and describe data). Immigration figures, economic trends, crime rates, and rising average temperatures are all descriptive statistics with which we come into contact in daily life.

Learning to gather and analyze quantitative data in the service of research can be exciting and fulfilling. In fact, many students of PIR who learn to use statistics report high levels of satisfaction with their newfound ability to think more concretely and precisely about social phenomena, in contrast to the abstraction of their more theoretically-oriented classes in the field. At the very least, it is useful to become a thoughtful consumer of quantitative methods in PIR research, and both this and the next chapter should help in that regard. This chapter introduces quantitative methods and how to collect quantitative data. It begins with an overview of quantitative methods, discussing their advantages and disadvantages. It then describes how to define concepts in such a way that they can be turned into numerical form, a process known as **operationalization.** Finally, it covers several ways to collect quantitative data: surveys, content analysis, and the use of existing databases.

## Overview of Quantitative Methods in PIR

In the next chapter, you will become familiar with two primary tools of quantitative analysis: statistical methods and formal models. Statistical methods are most often used to answer positivist research questions that seek to explain a relationship in a generalizable way. However, before you decide to use statistical methods, you need to: (1) ensure that your number of cases is sufficient to make a statistical analysis valid; (2) have the appropriate training in statistics, including the use of a statistical software package; and (3) identify the **level of measurement** of the data you will be using (explained later in this chapter). You also have to decide on the general contours of your quantitative design. For instance, will you deploy a **cross-sectional design**, comparing a number of cases at a single point in time? A survey or poll is an example. Or, will you use a **time-series design**, collecting data at regular intervals for each case and then comparing the results over time? Time-series designs become especially useful when we want to understand how relationships change over a longer period of time: for example, how attitudes toward immigration might vary with fluctuations in the economy.

For practical reasons, certain research questions simply lend themselves to quantitative analysis. Let's say you are trying to understand why populist parties have done so well in elections in recent years. And that you want to test the effect of variables such as unemployment and levels of immigration on the support for populism. Here, a case-oriented research design would be both impractical and unlikely to generate generalizable conclusions. Yes, you could profile some voters, and they may have interesting stories to tell, but your paper would read more like a piece of journalism than a PIR research product. However, by analyzing a dataset consisting of a large number of voters, you can make some generalizable conclusions about what causes and doesn't cause populists to do well in elections.

And yet, quantitative methods in PIR go beyond statistics. Scholars of PIR also use mathematics in **formal models** (an example of which is **game theory**) to understand, explain, and predict strategic choices. The key difference between formal models and statistical methods is that formal models purport to describe and predict behavior based on certain assumptions about human rationality and strategic behavior, while statistical analysis attempts to find relationships among variables based on a large number of observations. This makes formal models highly deductive (which starts with a premise), in contrast to statistical methods, which are inductive (which moves from specfics instances to more generalized conclusions).

## Advantages and Limitations of Quantitative Methods

From the positivist perspective, one main advantage of quantitative methods is that they can, in principle, better identify, estimate, and predict the strength of causal relationships than qualitative ones. To be sure, the strength of the causal relationships will depend on the size, nature, and quality of our **dataset** (a collection of numerical information about a set of cases). Even when all aspects of research design are all perfectly executed, and the proper statistical tests are applied, we can only come up with *partial* and *probabilistic* conclusions about causality using statistical tests. And yet, even then statistical methods are useful because they can help us eliminate some categories of explanations (by 'controlling' for certain variables) while highlighting others, thereby encouraging us to delve more deeply into a particular causal relationship using other methods. Quantitative methods can also help to overcome the problem of **spurious relationships**: two variables that appear to have a relationship, though in fact a third factor accounts for it.

Consider the question of what determines populist party success. You may observe that populists do well in towns and cities where there is no opera house. Of course, it is not the lack of opera houses that conditions support for populism, but the fact that a lack of certain cultural institutions may be reflective of economic marginalization, which in turn may explain high levels of support for populist parties. Statistical tools can deal with such spuriousness, though not always perfectly.

Another advantage of quantitative methods is that they offer **transparency** and **replicability**, both of which are characteristics of all good research. The transparency associated with quantitative methods stems from the fact that they often require us to translate our argument into a common statistical language, and thus to be explicit and precise about our concepts, methods, and findings (Braumoeller and Sartori 2004, 129–151). Meanwhile, scholars who use formal models lay out their proofs line by line, for all to see. The need to precisely measure concepts in numerical form and the ethical responsibility researchers assume in terms of sharing their datasets also means that others should be able to test and hopefully replicate their findings. In other words, in contrast to qualitative methods, the transparency and replicability associated with quantitative methods make it easier for other scholars to inspect your work, challenge it, build upon it, or confirm it. Think about it: if your empirical evidence and arguments are based upon obscure documents or interviews you have conducted, how can others be sure that you stand on solid ground? How do they know you did not exclude important documents, or leave out interviews with key people? As one scholar has put it, quantitative methods help 'make cumulative knowledge possible' and 'put the science in political science' (Howard 2017, 171).

However, quantitative approaches, like qualitative ones, have limitations. Many quantitative approaches require a large-$N$ sample, or a large number of cases. You may simply not have enough observations to apply statistical techniques. Moreover, it is not possible to quantify every concept which might be of interest to PIR research. For example, complex beliefs or emotions are difficult to represent numerically. As noted in Chapter 6, while we may be able to assign a number to a concept such as ethnic pluralism (by looking at the percentage of minorities in a given state or region), it may be that the content and history of ethnic relations is more important than the level of homogeneity or heterogeneity in a given society. Moreover, there is deep contention among scholars over how to measure and quantify even foundational PIR concepts such as democracy (Collier and Levitsky 1997). In light of such debates, how can we know that a quantitative index of democratization, such as that compiled yearly by *Freedom House*, is valid? It might exclude a key dimension of democracy some scholars see as vital to its conceptual definition, such as gender equality. This is why scholars using a quantitative measure of a 'big' concept like democracy often rely on several indices, either combining them or trying each one separately in statistical tests and seeing whether the result is the same. And even when and where scholars agree on how to define and operationalize a concept, they might disagree on its appropriate level of measurement (explained later in this chapter).

Gathering quantitative data is also subject to **error** and **bias**. For example, survey instruments, described below, are vulnerable to errors such as mistakes in **measurement** and flawed sampling techniques. Perhaps this is why the American writer, Mark Twain quipped that there are 'three kinds of lies: lies, damn lies, and statistics.' There are many tricks that those using statistical tests can do to 'beat' what they want out of the data

(Howard 2017, 173). Interpretation of statistical results is often a judgment call. Moreover, some of the techniques used in journals such as *American Political Science Review* are so sophisticated and esoteric that it is hard for someone without advanced training in mathematics to understand them, much less attempt to replicate them. Thus, with quantitative analysis, as with qualitative methods, there are certain limits to full transparency. As for formal models, while they can help us to understand political outcomes by modeling decision-making and other kinds of strategic behavior, they are based on a set of what some see as overly-rigid assumptions about rationality that do not always reflect how human beings act in the real world.

Many kinds of quantitative analysis are inaccessible to students who lack in-depth training in statistics and formal models. Such training is beyond the scope of this and the next chapter, which are intended as an overview of quantitative data collection and analysis. However, in addition to statistics courses available at universities, today's generation of students is lucky to have access to a wide variety of free, online courses and training in using statistical methods, as well as access to free, open source statistical software such as *R*. Some of these resources are listed in Table 10.1 in the following chapter. However, before we deploy statistical tests, formal models, or other forms of quantitative analysis, we have to understand how quantitative data is defined, measured, and gathered.

## From Conceptual Definition to Operational Definition to Measure

Quantitative analysis requires that concepts, variables, and social data be translated into numerically measurable form. In other words, to use quantitative tools, you must move away from natural languages, such as English, toward *formal* language, or that of mathematics. To do so, a concept must be translated from a **conceptual definition** into an **operational definition**. Conceptual definitions are general in nature and outline the main dimensions of a phenomenon, while operational definitions specify how the concept will be measured numerically. A number of operational definitions may be possible for any given concept and social scientists invest much energy in formulating and debating the most appropriate one. This is especially true for 'big' concepts such as democracy, or more abstract ones such as 'populist power.' For instance, one conceptual definition of democracy might be 'the degree of freedom in a given society,' while the operational definition might be 'the number of freedoms guaranteed to individuals in the constitution of a given country.' A conceptual definition of populist power could be 'the influence of populist parties in parliament,' while an operational definition could be 'pieces of legislation passed with strong populist support per month.' Of course, all of the above conceptual and operational definitions are subject to debate, and the choices you make about which to use can profoundly affect your results. Let's think about this more.

Take a concept such as 'inequality,' which one may hypothesize to be a determinant of populist party success. One possible operational definition for inequality is 'the percentage of the population which controls a certain proportion of the total resources and wealth in a given country.' This operational definition, in turn, needs to be measured quantitatively. For example, you could use a popular indicator of inequality, such as the **Gini coefficient**, which measures the degree of concentration in a country's income distribution.

The coefficient can run from 0 to 100. When its value is 0, it indicates 0 percent concentration in a country's income distribution. A country with a Gini coefficient of 0 would be an (obviously fictional) country in which everyone receives exactly the same income. By contrast, a Gini coefficient of 100 means that one person receives all of a country's or region's income while everyone else gets nothing, another rather unrealistic scenario. Most countries have Gini coefficients in between these two values, indicating that no society is completely equal.

The important point here is that the Gini coefficient is an example of how to measure a particular operational definition of inequality. In order to carry out quantitative research, you similarly will need to translate your key concepts into identifiable and measurable entities. Operationalization affects how we measure key variables, which in turn can impact the results of our study. Your operationalization and measurement strategy should (1) develop a precise schema to account for the values each variable of interest can take and (2) methodically assign each unit under study a value for each variable of interest. For example, if you think religiosity somehow affects support for populism, and you have gathered data on levels of religiosity in a survey, you now have to think through how to assign numerical values to each individual in your survey based on their declared level of religiosity. This is known as coding. In PIR research, some concepts are easily operationalized, measured, and coded. As an example, for a concept like 'wealth,' we can use **per capita GDP**, or the **Human Development Index (HDI)** (UNDP 2018). But other concepts, such as 'political polarization,' or 'values in foreign policy,' require careful reflection in order to make them usable in a quantitative analysis. However, as noted above, not every concept can be easily quantified.

One of the easiest ways for you to operationalize, measure, and code concepts is to simply follow the lead of scholars who have thought about such issues for a long time. It is perfectly fine to use operationalization and measurement strategies gleaned from others so long as you give them credit through proper citation. For example, let's say you want to test if gender equality has something to do with populism. The Variety of Democracies (also known as V-Dem) project at the University of Gothenburg in Sweden has a concept and accompanying operational definition for gender equality that you may find useful. V-Dem has even carried out a survey to measure it. To maximize its reliability and validity as a measure (validity and reliability are defined below), V-Dem has asked thousands of coders to apply their expertise on gender equality in hundreds of countries around the world by coding its various dimensions. V-Dem's concept is called the 'Women civil liberties index' and is defined as: women having 'the ability to make meaningful decisions in key areas of their lives,' which is 'understood to include freedom of domestic movement, the right to private property, freedom from forced labor, and access to justice' (Varieties of Democracy 2019). The V-Dem data, and accompanying operational definitions, are readily available – and free – on the organization's website. To cite an alternate example, Table 9.1 provides an example of an operationalization and measurement strategy in the context of research on how the media influenced the 2011 Arab Spring (Baglione 2020, 174). Here, the concept, definition, and numerical values are from Freedom House, a non-governmental organization whose data, like those of V-Dem, are publicly available. The idea here is to turn a hypothesized determinant of the Arab Spring uprisings – media exposure – into an operational definition that can then be measured and coded for use in a quantitative analysis.

**Table 9.1** Quantitative data – from concept to coding

| Conceptual definition | Operational definition | Measure | Coding guide |
|---|---|---|---|
| Access to the media | Degree of media freedom in a given country | Freedom House ranking of media freedom | Scale: 1 = full media freedom; 100 = no media freedom |

## The Quality of Quantitative Data: Validity, Reliability, and Measurement Error

In the preceding examples, organizations such as V-Dem and Freedom House have done the work of collecting quantitative data for you through surveys. However, whether you are using a publicly available dataset or collecting your own data, it is important to consider its **validity** and **reliability**. Validity means that the measures you use accurately reflect reality, whereas reliability refers to the ability to repeatedly achieve the same measure of a variable, regardless of who is doing the measuring. A measure that is valid should also be reliable, but reliable measures are not necessarily valid.

Let's think about this in terms of some real-world examples. In the run-up to the US invasion of Iraq in 2003, intelligence officials were relying on a small number of informants who told them that Saddam Hussein's weapons of mass destruction (WMD) program remained active. The data was *reliable* in the sense that the informants kept relaying the same information over time. But it was not *valid* in that what they said did not reflect reality. In fact, Saddam Hussein did not have WMD, as the world found out after the invasion.

Consider a scandal from the high-tech world which speaks directly to the importance of collecting high-quality data. Young inventor Elizabeth Holmes founded a company called *Theranos* that quickly attracted hundreds of millions of dollars in capital from top investors (Carreyrou 2018). Holmes claimed that her company had developed a small medical device that was capable of performing hundreds of tests from just a drop of blood that could be extracted, relatively harmlessly, from just a prick of one's finger. However, it eventually emerged that the company's claims were fraudulent. How was it that Holmes could fool so many for a number of years (including a major chain of American pharmacies, Walgreens)? The Theranos story is in part a cautionary tale of how emotions and good marketing strategies can lead even the savviest individuals to neglect the importance of solid data. But it is also a useful lesson about validity and reliability. At times, it turns out that Theranos was delivering patients some valid, if not reliable, results. But it was doing so not because its signature device worked, but because it was 'outsourcing' the blood samples to conventional, third-party blood analyzers.

When we rely on a well-regarded source, such as Freedom House, we can assume that the data we find on their websites is reliable and valid. That does not mean we should not question and qualify our results based on Freedom House's data collection methods, and scholars have done just that (as investors should have questioned Theranos's claims). In fact, the V-Dem project is in part premised on the notion that Freedom House's data collection approach has certain limitations.

How can we test for validity and reliability in data? PIR researchers sometimes use **inter-rater** or **inter-coder reliability** to ensure the accuracy of data. One way to do this is to assign a group of researchers to code the same phenomenon (after being trained on the measurement strategy). Then, their results are compared. The **test-retest method**, meanwhile, tests for reliability by examining if the same measure results at different moments in time. Validity can also be tested using **face validity**, which simply means asking if the data appears accurate based on what we know.

More rigorous validity tests include **content validity**, which breaks concepts down into their major attributes and measures each one. The concept of democracy can be operationalized and measured in a number of different ways, from minimalist to maximalist ones. For example, using a maximalist measurement, we might include economic inequality in the operational definition. But what if levels of economic inequality are somehow related to democratization? If they are, we cannot test for the effect of inequality on democracy, lowering our content validity. But content validity will also be lowered for an operationalization and measurement strategy for democracy that is not sufficiently broad.

Because quantitative data – whether collected by you or someone else – is frequently subject to **measurement error**, scholars often rely on several indices, either combining them or testing each one separately in statistical tests and observing whether the result is the same. Or, they may try more than one operational definition of a concept and see if they come up with the same result. As an example, let's return to our running example of a research project on the determinants of populist party success in the context of a large-N quantitative study. Let's say you are including educational attainment among the hypothesized independent variables. The theory underlying this variable is that those with less education possess fewer critical thinking skills and thus will be more receptive to populist appeals. Now, you have to decide how to operationalize 'educational attainment' (and also what level of measurement to use – a topic we cover below). One measure you might use is number of school years completed. An alternative might be to simply ask whether or not an individual completed secondary school. If you find that one measure produces a statistically significant result while the other doesn't, you will have to grapple with why this is the case. Ideally, as researchers we should measure our variables in more than one way and demonstrate that they lead to the same result. This is known as **triangulation** of quantitative evidence.

## Variables, Units of Analysis, and Levels of Measurement

A **variable** is a measurable characteristic or feature that varies for a particular case. Needless to say, you need to have more than one value to work with if you wish to carry out any kind of project whose goal is causal inference. After you have decided upon conceptual and operational definitions for your key variables, you must identify the **unit of analysis**, the entity to which the concept being quantified applies. If our concept is populist support, our unit of analysis may be an individual's response as recorded in a survey or exit poll. If the concept we are considering is human rights content in a western country's foreign policy, then the unit of analysis becomes a state, since we are talking about national-level policy. Some concepts can apply to more than one level of analysis, which is why it is important to specify. Think of a concept such as tolerance for homosexuality. We could examine individual attitudes toward same-sex marriage (in which case the unit of analysis is an individual) or the amount and content of legislation that aim to expand (or restrict) the rights of LGBTQ persons (now the unit of analysis becomes a law). Of course, even when our unit of analysis is the individual, we are still interested in aggregate results. Therefore, if we are looking at support for populism, we may rely upon a Europe-wide survey, and then aggregate results by country, region, and so on. Or we may aggregate them by gender, income level, or ethnicity. In other words, we survey individuals so we can say something about the group to which they belong.

In preparing our data for quantitative analysis, we have thus moved from concept to conceptual definition to operational definition to measurement and finally to unit of analysis. There is one last step you will need to undertake so that your data is ready to be used in a statistical analysis: you must think about the level of measurement of the data you will be using. This is critical, because, as we will see, not all statistical tests lend themselves to all levels of measurement. We also need to think about levels of measurement as we collect data in a survey, as discussed below.

**Nominal data** is the most basic level of measurement. Nominal data is not presented in any particular order, nor does it indicate the amount of the thing being measured. When coded, the numbers chosen are arbitrary. For example, if we list the regions of Asia as Northeast, South, Southeast, and West, we are not aiming to indicate the amount of 'regionness' each possesses, nor listing them in any order. We may code these regions as '1,' '2,' '3,' and '4' respectively, but this is merely so that we can include them in a statistical analysis. In this case, numerical values are simply useful labels for mutually exclusive categories. Religion is another example: someone can be Muslim, Jewish, Protestant, Catholic, Buddhist, or Atheist, for example. Indicators of race and ethnicity are usually also measured with nominal values.

**Ordinal data** is listed in order, or ranked, and while it is more precise than nominal measures, categories remain mutually exclusive. For example, countries can be ranked in order of the size of their economies, from lowest to highest, or vice versa. Alternatively, respondents in a survey may be asked to identify their political philosophy as being 'very liberal,' 'liberal,' 'moderate,' 'conservative,' or 'very conservative,' creating a scale rank-ordered from most liberal to most conservative. However, with ordinal data we cannot assume that the values are evenly spaced. In other words, the difference between 'very liberal' and 'liberal' is not necessarily equal to the difference between 'moderate' and 'conservative.' Above, we characterized religion as a nominal variable, but we could also conceive it as ordinal if we think of a related concept, such as religiosity, and measure it according to categories of the importance religion plays in an individual's life (i.e., not important, somewhat important, very important, etc.).

The most precise levels of measurement are **interval** and **ratio data**, which have uniform 'distance' between individual values. A classic example of interval data is temperature scales: the difference in temperature between 20 degrees Celsius and 25 degrees Celsius is the same as that between 5 degrees and 10 degrees. Ratio measures are more common than interval ones. Any concept that can be operationalized and measured in terms of percentages or currency figures can be used as ratio data. Unlike in interval data, 0 does indicate the absence of a phenomenon. The number of times that the United Nations Security Council votes for a human rights-related resolution is ratio data. So is the number of human rights treaties signed. Ratio data allow us to compare different values for each measure with absolute precision. Fifteen abstentions by a UN Security Council member state in one time period compared to 10 abstentions in an earlier period is a 50 percent increase. By contrast, ordinal measures limit us to comparisons of 'more' or 'less.'

The 'higher' the level of measurement of a variable, the more powerful are the statistical techniques that can be used to analyze it. On the other hand (and we will not go into the technical details here), if you use a statistical technique that assumes a higher level of measurement than is appropriate for your data, you risk getting findings that mean little. If you use a technique that fails to take advantage of a higher level of measurement, you risk overlooking important things about your data. When you take a course on statistics, you will learn that certain statistical techniques also require your data to have other features.

The chosen level of measurement will depend on the concept being measured. For example, does what you are measuring (such as receptivity to populism) indicate two distinct categories (e.g., for or against), or do we think of it as a spectrum? Researchers frequently debate appropriate levels of measurement. The American National Election Study for many years has used 'feeling thermometers' (American National Elections Study 2019). Respondents are asked to locate a presidential candidate or a party on a scale ranging from 0 to 100, with higher numbers representing warmer feelings toward the person or group. Some researchers have treated this as interval data, while others have asked if the difference between 60 and 70 is really the same as that between 90 and 100 (Howard 2017, 86). Because of their utility in more advanced and accurate statistical techniques, PIR researchers planning to use quantitative methods are usually keen to gather ratio or interval data, or operationalize and measure their concepts such that they become ratio or interval data.

## Identifying and Collecting Data for Statistical Analysis

Where do the numbers used in quantitative analysis come from? Whereas formal models do not require datasets, in order to run statistical tests, we either need to gather our own data through surveys or questionnaires, or make use of pre-existing datasets. For most students, as suggested above, existing datasets are the practical choice. Some examples of publicly available datasets are presented in Table 9.2, but this is far from a comprehensive list. As we have also emphasized earlier, before relying on a dataset that someone else has put together, it is vital to evaluate its quality. The list in Table 9.2 includes reputable sources of data, but even these are not immune from criticism. Other possible sources of data include official government-collected figures, such as census or economic data. Such numbers are sometimes fed into the datasets of international organizations such as the World Bank, or the International Monetary Fund (IMF), or various agencies of the United Nations. But the quality of government-collected statistics will vary. Some governments have a political interest in skewing the truth on economic data. One example was Argentina, which deliberately underreported its inflation rate for many years, leading the IMF to stop relying on official Argentinian government figures (Howard 2017, 122). Meanwhile, academic studies have found that some authoritarian governments inflate growth rates to try to justify their repressive rule. You certainly would not want to rely on official government indices to measure a phenomenon such as corruption. What government would freely admit that it is corrupt? That is why we have non-governmental organizations like Transparency International, which compiles an annual index of corruption *perceptions* for most countries in the world (see transparency.org).

**Table 9.2**  Examples of where you can find publicly available datasets

Correlates of War: www.correlatesofwar.org

Environmental Treaties and Resource Indicators: http://sedac.ciesin.org/entri/

Varieties of Democracy: www.v-dem.net/en/

Peace Research Institute, Oslo: www.prio.org/Data/

Stockholm International Peace Research Institute: www.sipri.org/databases

World Bank: http://data.worldbank.org

OECD: www.oecd.org/statistics

However, in the event you are researching a topic for which there is no pre-existing dataset, you will be confronted with the task of generating your own data. While creating a new dataset on a topic of interest in PIR may be an option, data gathering requires a tremendous amount of time and resources. Surveying and coding are labor-intensive tasks, even with the assistance of new electronic tools. Nevertheless, it is important to understand the basic principles of survey research even if you are to be merely a consumer of survey-generated data.

## Survey Design for Generating Quantitative Data

Balnaves and Caputi (2001) define **surveys** as 'a method of collecting data from people about who they are (education, finances, etc.), how they think (motivations, beliefs, etc.), and what they do (behavior)' (Balnaves and Caputi 2001, 76). Designing and carrying out a survey is exciting because it may lead you to uncover information that no one else has. In survey research, considerable attention is paid to the issue of **sampling**, or the manner in which we select survey respondents. Survey researchers have a strong preference for large **random samples** because they provide the most accurate estimates of what is true in the larger population.

Beyond this, almost anything goes in PIR survey research. Surveys can be long or short. They can be conducted in person, by telephone, through the mail, or over the internet. They can cover voting intentions, political attitudes, identity, or anything else that it is possible to ask people about and receive meaningful answers. Although survey data are most frequently analyzed using statistics, there are also survey questions that lend themselves to qualitative analysis.

When designing and carrying out a survey instrument, you must be conscious of **bias** in the sample. A prominent recent example of a biased survey sample is the voters' preference polls carried out prior to the 2016 US presidential election, most of which failed to predict the victory of Donald J. Trump. Sample sizes were reportedly too small, thereby undercounting the number of white, working-class and older voters who were enthusiastically pro-Trump. In order to better understand the distorting effect that a biased sample can have on research findings, try to imagine a population from which you want to draw a sample. Let's say you wanted to investigate support for populist parties in your municipality. Think about how you would go about distributing your survey. Would you distribute it at the gates of a university campus? Probably not, unless you wanted to investigate a population of students. Perhaps there may be specific locations where you can find a broader cross-section of the population you wish to sample, such as the train station. For well-resourced research projects, you would contract with a professional survey firm to generate a random sample within your population. In the best-case scenario, the firm would come up with a **probability sample**, by which all persons in the target population have an equal chance of being selected for the survey. For example, in a telephone survey based on **random digit dialing (RDD) sampling**, researchers know the chance that a particular telephone number will be selected.

Let's return briefly to the earlier discussion of existing datasets as sources for quantitative analysis in the context of our discussion of sampling. Some of these datasets are based on surveys carried out by organizations with massive resources. The US Census is an example. Others, however, such as the V-Dem project mentioned earlier, are based on targeted surveys of experts on the countries included in the database. So, for example, dozens of local and foreign experts on a country such as Nepal are surveyed on questions about that country's democratic development, providing a broad but simultaneously informed target group. In other words, surveys do not always aim for the broadest representative sample; sometimes, we want to focus on an 'elite' or narrower group.

Thoughtful design of survey content and questions is key to getting meaningful results. It is important that you carefully think about how you will pose your question and what kinds of responses, and by extension what kind of data, you aim to collect. Here, as previewed earlier, you will need to consider levels of analysis. Depending on how you formulated your questions and possible responses, you might collect nominal, ordinal, interval, or ratio data. These levels of analysis have corresponding question types attached to them, as described in Table 9.3. In all cases, questions must be written carefully so as not to confuse, mislead, or suggest an answer. While formulating your questions, for example, you should avoid **leading questions**, which imply or encourage a certain answer. Such questions are undesirable as they produce inaccurate information. As discussed in Chapter 3 on research ethics, surveys (like interviews) require the informed consent of your research participants.

**Table 9.3** Common types of survey question and scales

---

**Nominal Questions**: Nominal questions generate responses that are categorical. Generally, these are closed-ended questions with a menu of categories provided for the respondent to choose from.

*Example*: What is your gender? Male/Female

**Interval Questions**: Interval questions ask respondents to place themselves in a particular class of responses.

*Example*: What is your average score?

\_\_\_ Less than 60%
\_\_\_ 60%–69%
\_\_\_ 70%–79%
\_\_\_ 80%–89%
\_\_\_ 90%–100%

**Scales**: Scales allow researchers to determine the intensity of preference among respondents. The most common form of scale question is the Likert scale, which asks respondents to indicate their level of agreement or disagreement with a given statement.

*Example*: Armed humanitarian intervention should be allowed to take place even in the absence of a United Nations Security Council resolution authorizing the use of force.

(1) Strongly disagree, (2) Disagree, (3) Agree, (4) Strongly agree

---

## Data Collection for Content Analysis

You may assume that the interpretivist approach to PIR research referred to throughout this book is antithetical to the use of quantitative methods. It's actually not. Here is an example. Let's say you are interested in human rights and foreign policy. Specifically, you want to pursue an identity-focused explanation (related to the constructivist paradigm in IR) for US humanitarian interventions, which might necessitate the study of discourse around such interventions. Studying discourse would provide clues into how Americans see themselves and their role in the world: perhaps as noble, well-intentioned protectors or defenders of human rights. In such a study, you might want to analyze primary documents such as the speeches of top US officials, or the writings of prominent opinion-makers.

In Chapter 8, we introduced you to discourse analysis and content analysis. Content analysis in particular is a tool of *both* quantitative and qualitative research which is applied to determine the frequency and meaning of concepts, terms, or words in recorded communication. This systematic and replicable technique allows one to compress many words of text-specific content categories based on explicit rules of coding which in turn allows the researchers to make inferences about the producer of the text (individuals, groups, organizations, or institutions), and simultaneously, about the larger political, social, economic, and cultural context in which the words were written or spoken. Given its focus on analyzing language, it is well suited to interpretive research questions exploring the social construction of political phenomena.

As discussed in Chapters 7 and 8, there are numerous powerful tools, some of them free and available online, to locate and analyze the content of documents, media reports, and other texts. Returning to the example of American discourse around humanitarian intervention, these tools would allow you to quickly locate words and concepts, such as 'duty' and 'mission' and 'exceptional,' across thousands of pages of text so that soon you have a large number of observations which you can present as descriptive statistics, or in a graphic form such as a 'word cloud.' Perhaps, in addition to your interpretive analysis, you can also think of running a statistical test. For example, maybe you want to examine whether certain kinds of rhetoric around US humanitarian intervention are more likely under Democratic than Republican administrations, all else taken equal.

As noted in previous chapters, news articles, magazines, advertisements, laws, speeches, press releases, social media, and much more are equally rich sources of data for quantitative analysis. The volume of available text, in fact, has exploded in the digital age. The easiest way to acquire text in this form is from online databases such as *Lexis-Nexis* and *ProQuest*, which are available through your university's library website. Text data stored on websites can also be extracted with automated 'scraping' methods. These days, it is also possible to use character recognition technology to convert the text found in archives and hardcopy books into computer-readable texts.

However, it is extremely time-consuming, expensive, and in many cases impossible to read each and every document related to one's research. Provalis Research text analytics software (*QDA Miner* and *WordStat*) makes it possible to systematically import and analyze very large volumes of text documents without spending vast sums on hiring coders. The software gives researchers the flexibility of manual and advanced computer-assisted qualitative coding of documents and images. It can dramatically assist you in your research by identifying keywords, key phrases, themes, topics, images, speakers, and sentiments.

You might want to use content analysis to gather quantitative data from documentary sources for your project on the determinants of populism. Let's say that you have a hunch that negative stereotypes of migrants in the media are fueling a rise in populism. You could select five major media outlets and identify every article related to migration published in those newspapers over a certain period of time. You would then operationalize, measure, and code the tone of the articles and the message of any accompanying data (on crime, for instance) or images (masses of people streaming across borders, for example). Combined with survey data that includes questions on media consumption, you might find interesting relationships between media content and attitudes toward migration, which in turn are associated with populist support.

## Chapter Summary

Quantitative methods aim, through numerical measurement and formalization, to provide greater precision to a field of study that explicitly takes on the task of improving our understanding of a world defined by uncertainty. They provide specificity, transparency, and the ability to more accurately make causal inferences. Quantitative methods thus offer unique advantages to your research design, though they also come with some disadvantages, as this chapter has outlined. Not every concept in PIR is easy to quantify, and statistical results are far from conclusive.

The first step in quantitative analysis is operationalizing your concepts in such a way that they can be represented in numerical form. Next, you must collect your data. Students today have access to an ever-increasing number of datasets that chart PIR phenomena from human rights treaties to armed conflict. Content analysis is an example of a data collection technique that is suited to both quantitative and qualitative and positivist and interpretivist research designs. You can also gather quantitative data through surveys. The construction of a survey instrument requires careful attention to a number of principles, from sampling to how we ask questions. In the process of quantitative data collection, operationalization, and measurement, we must also consider factors such as the validity and reliability of our measures and data. Finally, decisions about units of analysis and levels of measurement will help to determine the statistical tools we can use to analyze our data. We delve into the logic and techniques of statistical analysis and formal models in the next chapter.

═══════ Suggested Further Reading ═══════

Adcock, R., and Collier, D. 2001. Measurement Validity: A Shared Standard for Qualitative and Quantitative Research. *American Political Science Review*, 95(3), 529-546.
An important work on measurement validity.

Axinn, William G., and Pearce, Lisa D. 2006. *Mixed Method Data Collection Strategies*. Cambridge, UK: Cambridge University Press.
Data collection strategies for mixed method research designs.

Braumoeller, Bear F., and Sartori, Anne E. 2004. The Promise and Perils of Statistics in International Relations. In Detleft F. Sprinz and Yael Wolinsky-Nahmias (eds.), *Cases, Numbers, Models: International Relations Research Methods*. Ann Arbor, MI: University of Michigan Press, pp. 129–151.
IR scholars present the downside of quantitative methods.

Collier, David, and Levitsky, Steven. 1997. Democracy with Adjectives: Conceptual Innovation in Comparative Research. *World Politics*, 49(3), 430–451.
A highly influential article by two top political scientists on defining and measuring concepts.

Collier, David, LaPorte, Jody, and Seawright, Jason. 2012. Putting Typologies to Work: Concept Formation, Measurement, and Analytic Rigor. *Political Research Quarterly*, 65(1), 217–232.
Another important contribution on concept formation and measurement.

Merritt, Richard L., and Rokkan, Stein. 1968. Comparing Nations: The Use of Quantitative Data in Cross-National Research. *International Conference on the Use of Quantitative Political, Social, and Cultural Data in Cross-National Comparison*. New Haven, CT: Yale University Press.
A classic piece of research on using cross-national quantitative data.

Monroe, Burt L., et al. 2015. No! Formal Theory, Causal Inference, and Big Data are Not Contradictory Trends in Political Science. *PS: Political Science & Politics*, 48(1), 71–74.
An article on emerging quantitative trends in PIR.

Rossi, Peter H., Wright, James D., and Anderson, Andy B. (eds.). 2013. *Handbook of Survey Research*. London: Academic Press.
A guide to designing and carrying out surveys.

# 10

# Tools and Strategies for Quantitative Analysis

━━━━━━━━━━ Learning Objectives ━━━━━━━━━━

- To distinguish between descriptive and inferential statistics;
- To use measures of central tendency to characterize a single variable;
- To become familiar with some bivariate statistical tests;
- To describe how statistical regression allows us to measure the nature and strength of relationships among variables and interpret the results of a statistical regression;
- To understand how formal models can help us describe and interpret strategic interactions.

Now that you have operationalized, measured, and coded your key concepts and variables, determined your units of analysis and levels of measurement, and collected quantitative data through surveys or content analysis (or decided to use an existing dataset), you can apply one or more tools of quantitative analysis to interpret your data and test hypotheses. Perhaps the most common tools of **statistical analysis** used to test for causality in PIR are **correlation** and **statistical regression**, to which you were briefly introduced in the previous chapter. With the help of a software package such as SPSS, Stata, or R, statistical regression allows us to examine the relationship between two or more phenomena, predicting the value of a **dependent variable** based on the value of an **independent variable**. Alternatively, some researchers use another form of quantitative analysis, **formal modeling**, to represent and predict the strategic behavior of individuals, organizations, or states.

We open the chapter with the topic of **univariate analysis**, introducing various descriptive statistics, which are often used to describe the basic features of a single variable. We then move on to **inferential statistics** (which are used to extrapolate or generalize to a larger population), identifying key concepts and techniques, such as statistical significance and the chi-squared test. We then describe the logic of correlation and regression, describing how to interpret the results of each.

It is nearly impossible to understand and appreciate PIR research output today without some background in statistics. At the very least, it is important to be an educated consumer of statistical data as presented in PIR journal articles. While we provide only an introduction to quantitative methods here, we highly encourage students to take a course in statistics at their university or to avail themselves of one of the many free training programs that are available on the internet. Some of the online resources are listed in Table 10.1.

However, even if you receive advanced training in how to use statistical software packages, you can't just plug a bunch of numbers into a program and expect to get a result from which you can make decisive conclusions moments later. Working with statistics entails much trial and error, attempting different statistical tests depending on the nature of your data and the relationships you want to understand. Moreover, interpreting statistical results is also an art – two PIR researchers may see the same results of a statistical test completely differently. Using statistics is also a bit like learning a language or a musical instrument. In other words, you have to practice regularly, and there is always room for improvement, as well as new techniques to learn.

**Table 10.1**  Free online courses in statistical analysis

| Provider | Website URL |
| --- | --- |
| Coursera | coursera.org |
| Stanford Online | online.stanford.edu |
| Khan Academy | khanacademy.org |
| Udacity | udacity.com |

## Univariate Statistical Analysis

Though statistical methods are often used to determine the relationship between two or more variables, there are times when you might want to investigate one variable in depth. Univariate analysis focuses on the quantitative analysis of a single variable. Looking at the numerical characteristics of a single variable might be useful when you are engaging in case selection (Chapter 6) as a way to identify a 'typical' case, or an exceptional case, also known as an outlier. With univariate analysis, you will also be able to determine the distribution of the data (see below), which could influence the kind of inferential statistical tools you choose to apply later on.

Here is an example from the research project on populist parties. Let's say you have conducted a survey in which you asked four questions about income, education level, religiosity, and views on immigration. You have hypothesized that all of these are independent variables likely to influence one's support for populist parties. An analysis of the responses to any one of these questions, such as religiosity, would be a univariate analysis. Using a statistical software package (or a straightforward formula), you could begin by calculating the **margin of error** (also known as the **confidence interval**) for one of the variables. The smaller the margin of error, the more confidence you can have that your results reflect the actual population. The bigger the margin of error, the further your results are from the characteristics of the total population.

If your survey involved drawing a sample of 1,000 people, and you find that 34 percent report attending religious services often (a way to operationalize religiosity), it is quite unlikely that the proportion of the actual population who attend religious services is exactly that. If you calculate the margin of error, you might find that it is 3%, and thus that the actual proportion of respondents attending a religious service often is likely between 31 and 37 percent. If you were to conduct the survey again in two months (also drawing on a sample of 1,000 people) and find that the percentage reporting regular attendance at religious functions is down to 32 percent, there may be a decline in religiosity, but it is also entirely possible that, given the margin of error, there has been no change at all. The margin of error depends on our desired confidence level and the size of our sample, with larger samples more likely to reflect the actual population characteristics, and vice versa. Certain surveys, such as a census, aim to measure the *entire* population and theoretically have no margin of error. The important point here is that we have to be realistic about the precision of our results.

## Measures of Central Tendency

In describing the characteristics of a single variable, you might also want to provide **measures of central tendency**, or their 'typical' values. Measures of central tendency are examples of descriptive statistics. They are distinct from inferential statistics, which are used to extrapolate or generalize to a larger population. Key measures of central tendency you can calculate on your own (or better yet, have a statistical software package do it for you) are the **mode** (the most frequently occurring value), the **median** (the value that falls at the center of a distribution), and the **mean** (also known as the average). The statistic you decide to use will be in part related to your level of measurement (Chapter 9). For instance, the mode works well for nominal variables, the median for ordinal variables, and the mean for ratio measures. The mode religion in much of southern Europe is Roman Catholicism (with religious identity measured by nominal categories – Protestant, Catholic, Jewish, Muslim, etc.). In Spain, Portugal, and Italy, since most people are self-described Catholics, this is also the **majority** religion. In Bosnia and Herzegovina, over 40 percent of people describe themselves as Muslim, and because the other two major religions (Orthodox and Catholic) have smaller proportions of adherents, Islam is the mode religion. But notice that it is not the majority religion since Bosnians who identify as Muslims make up less than 50 percent of the population. In fact, there is no majority religious group in Bosnia and Herzegovina.

We cannot, however, calculate the median value for a set of nominal data. If we want to use the median as a measure of central tendency, we need, at the very least, a set of ordinally-measured data. Returning to the example survey mentioned above, the variable 'religiosity' might be measured using an ordinal survey question in which respondents can say if they attend religious services 'never,' 'sometimes,' or 'often.' If 20 percent of your respondents (let's say a sample from an electoral district in Ireland) say that they never attend, 60 percent say 'sometimes' and 20 percent say 'often,' then the median, with half of the responses below and half above, would be somewhere in the group who answered 'sometimes.'

When your variables are measured with interval or ratio data, you can quickly compute the arithmetic mean, or average. It's easy (think primary school mathematics class): you add up all the values and divide by the total number of cases. Both education level (measured by years of school completed) and income are likely to be ratio measures. Adding up all the years of school completed and dividing by 1,000 cases (the number of respondents in the survey above), you might find that the average number of years of schooling in your sample is 12. And, if your country is a developed European one, you might find that average yearly household income for your sample is US$32,000. This does not necessarily mean, of course, that any single respondent to the survey had a yearly household income of exactly that amount. Measures of central tendency do not have to represent an actual value in the dataset.

## Distributions of Data

All of these measures of central tendency can be distorting if not understood in the context of the **distribution** of a variable, or how its numbers are distributed around the typical value. Three kinds of distributions are shown in Figure 10.1. A **normal distribution** has a peak in the middle and symmetrically distributed values on both sides. The mean, median, and mode are the same. Or the distribution may be skewed. A **Skewed distribution** with a significant 'tail' on the left is said to be **negatively skewed** and if the 'tail' is on the right it is **positively skewed**. For negatively skewed data, the mode is usually greater than the median, while the mean is smaller. The opposite is true for positively skewed data. A given set of data for a single variable may also have a **bimodal distribution**, in which most values are clustered around two peaks. Such a distribution may exist in survey data recording feelings toward a highly polarizing political leader, with most people either loving or hating him or her, and few in the middle.

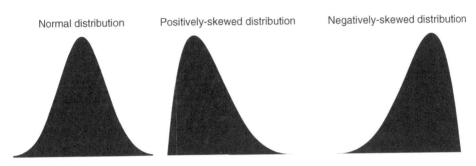

**Figure 10.1**   Types of distribution in univariate analysis

   As noted above, characterizing the distribution of your data will help put your measures of central tendency in context. This helps to capture reality while avoiding descriptions of data that are influenced by the extremes (like a few very wealthy people). If the mean yearly household income of your sample is US$32,000 per year, but the distribution of incomes in the sample is highly skewed in one direction (i.e., a small number of people have a very high income while most others are destitute), the likelihood is that mean income as a measure of central tendency is of limited value in understanding how most people in your population actually live. One way to begin to visualize the distribution of your data is to create bar charts, histograms, box plots, and other graphics.
   But if you are working with ordinal or ratio data, you can also measure its distribution using various *ranges*, such as the interquartile range, which describes the middle 50 percent of a distribution, between the 25th and 75th percentiles (you may have seen exam results reported using interquartile ranges). Your statistical software package will also allow you to calculate the **standard deviation** and **skewness** of the data, both of which describe the average distances between every observation and the mean (but also require ratio or ordinal data to be applied). Standard deviation works mainly for normal distributions, while skewness is better suited to less normal ones. If the data follows a normal distribution, then about two-thirds of the values will be within one standard deviation of the mean, while 95 percent will be within two standard deviations. The skewness measure, as its name suggests, works best for skewed distributions. It can be positive or negative, with a positive figure indicating a skew to the right (the third graph in Figure 10.1) and a negative figure indicating a skew to the left (the second graph in Figure 10.1).

In sum, how you describe your data using univariate analysis will depend in part on its distribution. The mean is a good measure of 'typicality' if your data is distributed normally. But if your distribution is skewed in some way, such as household income in an unequal society (let's say Brazil, or the United States), perhaps the mode or median would better capture the typical financial situation of an ordinary family and the resources available to them. For example, in the United States, mean income is substantially higher than median income because of the presence of a small number of very wealthy people who skew the distribution and move the mean figure in an upward direction. Thus, the choices you make about univariate analysis will depend both on the data and the question you are asking. As you see, this is not a linear process. Indeed, as we noted at the outset of this chapter, working with quantitative data and statistical tools often entails trial and error.

## Bivariate Statistical Analysis

**Bivariate analysis** focuses on two variables to determine if a relationship exists between them. First, however, you will need to determine whether a possible relationship is **statistically significant**. Simply put, if you can describe a relationship as statistically significant, you can say with some confidence that it really exists. Furthermore, you must be quite confident about statistical significance before you can make any causal inferences from your data. To be exact, the probability that the **null hypothesis** (which states that there is no relationship between the variables) is true has to be less than 5 percent for a relationship between two variables to be declared statistically significant. This percentage is called a '$p$-value.' In other words, being only 90 percent sure that a relationship exists is not good enough. We want to be 95 percent sure ($p > .05$). If our calculation (performed either manually or using a statistical software package) tells us that there is no statistical significance, you can pretty much move on to other variables and tests. However, if you find statistical significance of some strength, that does not mean that you have a substantively important relationship, or causality. More work needs to be done to determine causality. Moreover, if you are working with non-nominal variables, you might also want to look at the **direction of the relationship**: is income positively or inversely related to support for populism?

There is more than one way to test for the nature of bivariate relationships. In what follows, we describe a cross-tabulation and a chi-squared test, sometimes also known as the Pearson chi-squared test, which measures the statistical significance of a relationship between two categorical (nominal or ordinal) variables. We then briefly describe the commonly-used Pearson correlation coefficient, which is used to test the relationship between two interval or ratio variables.

## Cross-tabulation

As always, in deciding on a particular statistical technique, we first need to determine the level of analysis of our variables. If we find that the two variables whose relationship we want to test are measured nominally or ordinally, we can use a **cross-tabulation** (or cross-tab), which you may encounter in studies of public opinion and voting behavior. This means that it is also ideally suited to our running example, the determinants of populist party support. The first step in cross-tabulation is to generate a table like Table 10.2 (some-times called a **contingency** or **frequency table**) with values across the top and down the side. Let's say you are starting with the following hypothesis:

*Opponents of permissive immigration policies are more likely to back populist parties and candidates.*

Now, let's assume you have access to a dataset from a survey of 8,000 eligible voters in a given European country. To evaluate the above hypothesis, you would need to put survey respondents into categories that reflect both their views on immigration and their support for certain political parties. You would be interested in two nominal survey questions in particular. The first gauges how respondents feel about current immigration policies (the **independent variable**) by asking whether they want immigration to be (1) decreased, (2) increased, or (3) kept at the existing level. The second asks respondents what political party they will support in the next election (the **dependent variable**), with a choice of (1) Populists, (2) Centrists, or (3) Liberals. The results are presented in Table 10.2.

**Table 10.2**   Party support and attitudes toward immigration

|  | Populists | Centrists | Liberals | Total |
|---|---|---|---|---|
| Immigration should be decreased | 1800 | 800 | 800 | 3400 |
| Immigration should be increased | 400 | 200 | 1600 | 2200 |
| Immigration should be kept at existing levels | 800 | 1000 | 600 | 2400 |
| Total | 3000 | 2000 | 3000 | 8000 |

Looking at the contingency table, we can begin to search for patterns. We might calcu-late the percentage of pro-populists who want immigration to be decreased versus those who want it to be kept at existing levels, for example. If negative attitudes toward immi-gration affect party support, as we hypothesized, we would expect many supporters of a reduction in immigration levels to be concentrated in the upper-left row, which they are. Given today's polarization on the issue of immigration, we would also expect most supporters of big increases or decreases to identify with one of the ideologically-oriented parties (Populists and Liberals). Thus, it is possible to observe clear patterns simply by look-ing at the above contingency table. However, if we want to specify the relationships and their strength more precisely, we must turn to statistical tests.

## Bivariate Statistical Tests: The Chi-squared Test

One simple statistical test you could perform straight away is to calculate the **Pearson chi-squared statistic** (an inferential statistic). The chi-squared test works best for evaluating relationships between variables that come in categories, as we have meas-ured our two variables above (i.e., what party a voter supports, or the attitude toward immigration as measured by three discrete categories). In this case, the null hypothesis is that there is no relationship between attitudes toward immigration and support for populism. The chi-squared statistic allows us to determine at what **confidence level** or **probability level** we can uphold the hypothesis. In this sense, the actual value of the statistic is less important than its *p*-value, which tells us the probability that we would see the observed relationship between the two variables in our sample data if there were truly no relationship between them in the unobserved population (the null hypothesis). For example, if your chi-squared statistic holds at the .01 confidence (*p*) level, you can be 99 percent sure that the results you found (i.e., opponents of immigration support the Populists) did not occur simply by chance.

Statistical software packages like those mentioned early in the chapter can be used to perform the chi-squared test. If you were to run it for the data in Table 10.2, you would find an extremely robust relationship between attitudes toward immigration and support for certain parties. Moreover, this relationship is significant at greater than the .001 level, implying that 99.9 percent of the time attitude toward immigration policy is a powerful predictor of party support. However, if we imagine survey results in which differences between attitudes toward immigration do not seem to line up with preferred parties, the chi-squared statistic might indicate a confidence level of .10, meaning that we are now less than 90 percent sure that one's beliefs about immigration help determine what party one chooses. We would likely discount a causal relationship between the two variables.

## Pearson Correlation Coefficient

If you have two ordinal or ratio variables, your statistical software package can also calculate the **Pearson correlation coefficient**, for which the notation is *r*. R can range from −1 to +1, with positive numbers indicating a positive relationship (as one variable goes up, so does the other), and vice versa. The farther *r* is from 0, the stronger the relationship. Let's say you are measuring the effect of income on support of conservative parties. You would gather individual data in a survey, and both variables would be measured as a ratio. You would generate a graph with income on the *x*-axis and warmth toward conservatives on the *y*-axis. Each respondent would have one point on the graph, with an income level and a corresponding feeling toward conservatives. If all these points formed a perfectly straight line sloping from low to high from the left, *r* would be 1. In other words, higher incomes are associated with more support for conservative parties.

This statistical test, however, only tells us about the correlation between two variables, and not **causation**. One should not confuse the two. A rainy day may be strongly correlated with a certain electoral outcome in a developing country, but it is obviously not the rain itself that is causing the result. The relationship between rain and the outcome is probably spurious. More than likely, the rain is preventing poorer people from certain neighborhoods who are likely to vote for a certain party from getting to the polls.

## Statistical Regression

While bivariate analysis is often sufficient for many undergraduate research projects, many PIR researchers are interested in analyzing the relationship among three or more variables.

This is often where the most interesting results are found, and where the results are more reflective of the complex reality of real phenomena in PIR. Returning yet again to our example of a research project on the determinants of populism, let's say that you are testing a hypothesis which posits that populist parties get the most votes when and where economic inequality has increased at the highest rate in the past decade. The theory behind it is that growing economic inequality tends to generate resentment among ordinary people, and populist parties are adept at addressing such frustrations by appealing to anti-elite or anti-immigrant sentiment, for example. A logical interpretation of the above hypothesis is that *we should not expect populist parties to do well in districts and countries where levels of economic inequality are low.*

What if we find a case, like an electoral district in Country X, where a populist party did poorly in the last election *despite high levels of inequality*? In principle, we could discount our hypothesis – after all, we have found a case that disproves it. But we could only discount it assuming that the theory behind our hypothesis is **deterministic**: that is, if the theory maintains that economic inequality is a necessary and sufficient condition of populism. Rarely, however, do we understand theory to be quite so deterministic. Rather, we would usually propose that economic inequality is but one cause, among others, of support for populism and that it increases support for populism only when some other conditions, such as rapidly changing demographics due to high levels of immigration, are also present. In other words, if this district in Country X had experienced a massive influx of migrants in recent years, there may be voters whose awareness of and frustration with growing inequality did not necessarily translate into populist support until it was triggered by a parallel consciousness of a new population of migrants who were benefitting from extensive social services and exercising downward pressure on wages. This is a plausible and nuanced description of the relationship between inequality and levels of support for populism, but it would be difficult to test such a multifaceted causal argument with a single case or even a handful of cases and come up with generalizable results.

If you are working with continuous or interval data (which spans a continuum), you will likely turn to regression analysis, which comes in several forms. For many undergraduate projects in PIR, **bivariate linear regression** is often sufficient. The central premise of statistical regression is that even if the outcome of any single case may not be full determined, a distribution of outcomes over a large number of cases can reveal certain patterns, and thus be **generalizable**. If you have the ambition and training, you may want to try your hand at a **multivariate regression analysis**, and even if you don't, you are likely to come across multivariate regression in published PIR work. Therefore, even if you will not use multivariate regression in your own project, it is useful to know what is going on when you see regression results in a journal article.

Regression of a larger dataset and multiple variables helps to increase the likelihood of uncovering statistically significant relationships between variables. Returning to the example above, using regression, we can be more certain that it is indeed a combination of inequality and immigration that explains populist success, rather than another variable such as pre-existing political attitudes or political culture, as long as we include a large number of observations across geographical space and time in our sample. We can put this yet another way: even if there are individual cases in which inequality and immigration are not associated with the strength of populist parties, by analyzing a large number of cases over time we can still expect that there would be more instances of populist success under conditions of inequality and immigration, thereby lending weight to the theory.

Let's say you have only two independent variables, income (I) and religiosity (R), and one dependent variable, populist support (PS). A multivariate regression model will allow you to estimate the relationship between I and PS while controlling for R. In other words, you can examine whether income influences support for populism independent of religiosity. Or we can estimate the relationship between R and PS while controlling for I. The model can also help us identify statistical significance, as well as the direction and strength of the relationship. Moreover, multivariate regression analysis can provide insight into whether or not our **bivariate regression analysis** produced a spurious relationship. A spurious relationship is when two variables appear to be related to each other, but the relationship is actually caused by a third, or intervening variable.

To further illustrate regression analysis, let's return to the example of human rights and foreign policy and work with the following hypothesis:

*The greater the media coverage of human rights abuses, the more likely western states will respond.*

Here your approach to operationalization and measurement will be critical. Media exposure (the independent variable) can be operationalized and measured in a fairly straightforward way. You can use a media database to determine the number of headlines devoted to a specific issue in a particular timeframe. For the dependent variable, western responses, there are many possibilities depending on how you conceptualize what exactly a government 'response' entails. You can look at the number of mentions of the human rights issue in official statements, or you can count parliamentary laws or resolutions devoted to the issue. Whatever your operationalization strategy, you have to justify it and explain how the data was gathered. The important thing is that the data for both are measured using continuous (interval or ratio) variables.

Besides the independent variable for which you are testing (media exposure), you will also put other independent variables into the model to control for various factors: for instance, if you are looking at the determinants of US government responses to human rights crises, besides media exposure you may want to consider the effect of variables such as the domestic economic situation, public opinion, political polarization, and other potential explanatory factors. Then you will use a statistical package to perform the regression. Regression analysis will attempt to fit a line through all the data points. It does so not by connecting the dots, but rather by capturing the trend of the direction and the slope of the data. The software will come up with a statistic called $R$-squared (in mathematical notation, $R^2$), which measures how close this line conforms to the data. The two scatterplots in Figure 10.2 illustrate two different distributions of data with resultantly different $R^2$ values.

When $R^2$ is 1, the calculated line fits the data points perfectly, which means that the independent variable explains all of the variation in the dependent variable. However, as the value of $R^2$ goes down, the explanatory power of the independent variables also decreases. The closer $R^2$ is to 0, the worse the fit of the line, which means that the points are scattered around the graph with no apparent pattern to them.

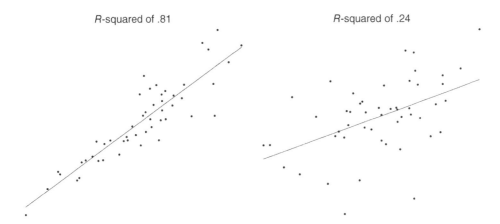

R-squared of .81                                    R-squared of .24

**Figure 10.2** Example scatter plots

An $R^2$ of .81 (the scatterplot on the left in Figure 10.2) means that 81 percent of the variation in the dependent variable is explained by our hypothesized determinant. In the context of our example, 81 percent of the variation in western responses to human rights abuses are explained by the level of media exposure. In the scatterplot on the right, only 24 percent of the variation is explained by the independent variable, suggesting a rather weak relationship between the two variables. Other factors explain the remainder of the variation. Perhaps the better fit of the line on the left is owing to the fact that we used a better model – controlling for more potential causal factors.

Interpreting regression results is an art. We just said that the .24 $R^2$ value does not indicate a particularly robust relationship. And yet some PIR scholars would be satisfied with even less, as long as some of the independent variables are statistically significant (Howard 2017, 175). They might say that PIR phenomena are complicated, and even if we can grasp a bit of a relationship, that is a good thing. Other scholars might argue that the .24 result means little substantively. Whatever side you fall on, a good research paper or thesis will not take results at face value, simply concluding, for instance, that the .24 $R^2$ value means that there is no relationship and the matter is finished. Instead, you should engage with issues such as the validity or reliability of your operationalization and measurement scheme, or consider what other, more sophisticated, statistical tests might better capture the relationship.

You also have to consider the **standard error**. A regression coefficient is always accompanied by a standard error, which tells us how certain you can be about the formula itself. The larger the standard error, the less certain the regression line. However, the standard error is not a quantity of interest by itself. It depends on the relationship with the regression coefficient. Regression results will also often include 'p-values,' or levels of statistical significance, discussed earlier. A p-value of '.01' indicates the highest level of confidence in our results, a p-value of .10 indicates a low level of confidence, while a p-value of .05 falls in the middle. Often, these levels of statistical significance are indicated with asterisks, with three asterisks (***) indicating the highest level of confidence.

Finally, it is important to remember that whenever you work with regression analysis, whether bivariate or multivariate, *correlation is not causation*. It may be easy to say that increased media exposure to certain human rights abuses is related to more western government activity around these abuses. The regression analysis may show that they are indeed related. But it is an entirely different thing to say that media exposure *caused* the response. This is where regression analysis needs to be complemented by additional, qualitative approaches to data collection and analysis, such as interviews and process-tracing. In other words, you may have to go out and talk to government officials and understand what motivated them to respond (or not) to an instance of human rights abuse. As Chapter 6 noted, multimethod research designs aim to overcome the limitations of a single approach.

## Formal Models in PIR

**Formal models** are used to represent complex reality in a stylized form, often using mathematics. They are rooted in the field of economics. Formal models are particularly well suited to understanding how states interact in the international system, but we also see formal models used in scholarship on issues from electoral and legislative behavior to ethnic conflict and humanitarian intervention to political transitions (McCarty and Meirowitz 2007, 1; Morrow 1994; Williams and Zeagev 2004, 233–254). Like statistical analysis, formal models require a degree of training that is beyond the scope of this book. However, just as in the case of statistical analysis, it is certainly worth understanding the principles of formal models so you can be a more informed consumer of PIR literature. If you are interested in actually applying formal models in your own paper or thesis, you should probably take a course on formal models and consult with your advisor or supervisor.

Formal models were born of real-world concerns about war and peace. An urgent need to understand high-stakes strategic choices that confronted policy-makers during the height of the Cold War between the US and the Soviet Union led both decision-makers and scholars to seek increased certainty in formal models so as to prevent a nuclear exchange between the rival superpowers. They have also been applied to conflict management in the context of intra-state wars (Fearon 2004), with scholars attempting to model the conditions under which belligerent parties are likely to acquiesce to a peace agreement (Walter 2002). Formal models are based on the principles of rational choice theory, which assumes that an individual (or state) will act in their self-interest and make decisions among a range of options based on utility-maximizing motives. As such, formal models have been closely tied to the realist tradition within IR (Kahler 1998).

One foundation of formal models is that actors (individuals, states, or groups) have the ability to strategically consider a number of policy options. A second foundation is that these actors are rational and utility-maximizing when making choices among these options. Consider a classic 'game', the so-called 'Prisoner's Dilemma'. Two suspects are taken into custody for a crime they allegedly conspired to commit. The police put them in separate interview rooms and attempt to pressure them into confessing. They are each told (but separately) that if they confess, they will get a lighter sentence. If the other suspect doesn't confess, they will be set free. However, if they don't confess and the other suspect does, then they will get a heavier sentence. The Prisoner's Dilemma, like all formal models, depends on a set of assumptions:

- the prisoners cannot communicate with each other;
- the prisoners know what their payoffs will be and can make comparisons between the payoffs;
- the prisoners are rational and intelligent; they seek to maximize their *utility* (which is a way of saying they are looking for the best deal for themselves);
- the prisoners are only facing this situation once (the game does not repeat).

This strategic interaction is presented in Table 10.3.

**Table 10.3**  The Prisoner's Dilemma

|  | Prisoner 2 stays silent (cooperates) | Prisoner 2 betrays Prisoner 1 (defects) |
|---|---|---|
| **Prisoner 1 stays silent (cooperates)** | Both serve a lighter sentence | Prisoner 1 serves heaviest sentence while Prisoner 2 goes free |
| **Prisoner 1 betrays Prisoner 2 (defects)** | Prisoner 1 goes free while Prisoner 2 serves longest sentence | Both serve a medium sentence |

Based on our understanding of this 'game,' we might predict that both prisoners would 'confess.' Though cooperating with each other would lead to a lesser prison sentence, it is clear that given the uncertainty surrounding their partner's actions, a prisoner would still rather confess. If one prisoner doesn't confess and his counterpart doesn't confess either, then the first has missed an opportunity to go free. If the second does confess, then the first is still better off confessing because otherwise they would spend more time in prison. When both players have *dominant* strategies such that they have no rational reason to change their decision, then the result is known as a **Nash equilibrium**.

In the Prisoner's Dilemma, given that betrayal always leads to a better payoff for both prisoners, it is considered a dominant strategy. Strategic dominance is simply when one strategy is better than another for one actor, no matter how the opponent plays. Here, since both players have a dominant strategy, the Prisoner's Dilemma has only one unique Nash equilibrium. Though there are other non-equilibrium outcomes that would be better for both players, the Nash equilibrium occurs when both players 'sell out' the other. Thus, pursuing utility-maximizing rational behavior logically leads both prisoners to betrayal. If both of them remained silent and cooperated, then they would get a better reward – less time in prison. However, this is not the likely outcome because the choice to cooperate would be *irrational*.

The Prisoner's Dilemma has been used as a metaphor for understanding a range of PIR phenomena, from cooperation on arms control to coordination on environmental issues. Researchers often manipulate the payoffs to make the game more interesting and reflective of various real-world phenomena. One of the central insights of the Prisoner's Dilemma, and formal models more generally, is that two actors with rational goals might nonetheless make choices that lead to a less-than-optimum outcome. In the context of IR, this often means armed conflict.

The eminent formal modeler James Fearon (1995) wrote a famous paper called 'Rationalist Explanations for War,' in which he argues that 'the central puzzle about war, and also the main reason why we study it, is that wars are costly but nonetheless wars recur' (1995, 379). Fearon asks why this is the case. After all, wars are costly and unpopular. Using the principles of formal modeling, Fearon argues that there are two main reasons why wars break out. First, players have secret information that the other side does not know about, and incentives to misrepresent that information. Second, the players have commitment problems.

In a more recent application of formal models to the ongoing hostilities between the United States and North Korea over the latter's nuclear program, Fearon (2017) warns of a 'spiral of hostility' that might lead to war between the two countries, especially a preventive or pre-emptive war in which one state thinks it needs to act against the other before it is too late. Both North Korea and the US prefer the status quo to a military conflict. But the problem is that while each side knows that *it* prefers the status quo, it doesn't know that the opponent does too. (One of the key assumptions in formal models is the unavailability of perfect information.) This lack of information about the other side's intentions is compounded by the lack of trust engendered by decades of acrimonious relations. So North Korea might build or deploy more weapons, or undertake other hostile acts, to try to make itself more secure in case Washington undertakes its own aggressive policies. One of the things that Pyongyang most fears is that the real intention of the United States is to change the North Korean regime. And a primary interest of any regime is survival (an interest we would build into any formal model). The United States, for its part, does prefer the status quo (no war), but sees the North Korean nuclear development program or its launch of intercontinental ballistic missiles over Japan as a threat, even though the North Korean regime's behavior is really just motivated by fear that the United States wants to overthrow it. The US then takes further actions (sanctions, military exercises with South Korea), and North Korea retaliates with more provocative behavior. Perhaps one of its rockets inadvertently hits a civilian target in Japan or South Korea. You get the point: things can escalate quickly, even though neither side wants war.

Formal models can help us understand such outcomes, and the processes by which they come about, using **decision trees**, a tree-like chart of key decision points and their possible consequences. For these reasons, formal models are a favored analytical tool used by intelligence analysts to inform policy-makers about their choices, and the consequences of these choices. But formal models' rigid assumptions about rationality have also attracted no shortage of criticism. Humans are 'rational' in different ways. The idea that humans act entirely rationally, for example, negates the importance of emotions. Moreover, the utility and rewards associated with certain choices may vary from person to person. As such, formal models as a tool of quantitative analysis have many detractors. Yes, one can deploy them to come up with elegant models, but the messy real world of PIR may not be suited to such elegance. Even some economists, who first popularized the use of formal modeling, have rejected the assumptions of formal theory and instead turned to experimental and other research designs which better reflect the complex ways in which humans actually make decisions and interact with each other.

## Chapter Summary

A large body of research in PIR relies on quantitative analysis, which allows us to describe relationships among variables with precision, transparency, and replicability. Some of the items in the quantitative researcher's toolbox that have been explored here include various ways to characterize a single variable (univariate analysis) and tools to analyze two or more variables, including statistical regression. We also briefly covered formal models as an alternative way to model and understand strategic interactions and the way they shape outcomes.

We have aimed to provide you with a snapshot of the underlying logic of quantitative analysis, which, besides assisting you in your own data analysis, will also help you to make sense of the quantitative research designs you will encounter in the PIR literature during the course of your own research. We have also presented some of the techniques in quantitative research that you may choose to apply in your research paper or thesis. Carrying out your own quantitative research project might require you to delve into large datasets and apply some of these techniques. There is a wide range of statistical software packages that you can make use of in order to carry out your project. In addition to helping you analyze your dataset, statistical software packages can generate figures and graphs, thereby allowing you to visualize quantitative data in ways that are easily accessible to readers.

While quantitative analysis is one way to work toward the goal of causal inference when we pose positivist research questions, we also need to be modest about what we can actually conclude about causality based on statisitical analysis when dealing with complex PIR phenomena. It is usually safer to say that your variables are somehow correlated than to go out on a limb and say that one is *causing* another. To say that with any confidence, we often have to supplement our statistical models with experimental methods or careful qualitative case studies that allow us to establish causality with more certainty. Interpretivist approaches may help put the entire enterprise in a broader perspective, or even lead us to question the search for causality. In other words, as we have emphasized throughout this book, *plurality* in methods is a good thing in PIR research.

## Suggested Further Reading

Achen, C. 1982. *Interpreting and Using Regression.* Thousand Oaks, CA: Sage.
A useful introduction to regression analysis.

Barnes, Tiffany D., and Burchard, Stephanie M. 2013. 'Engendering' Politics: The Impact of Descriptive Representation on Women's Political Engagement in Sub-Saharan Africa. *Comparative Political Studies*, 46(7), 767-790.
An example of a multimethod design.

Blaydes, Lisa, and Chaney, Eric. 2013. The Feudal Revolution and Europe's Rise: Political Divergence of the Christian West and the Muslim World before 1500 CE. *American Political Science Review*, 107(1), 16-34.
An extremely innovative quantitative approach to analyzing historical trends.

Cohen, Dara Kay. 2013. Explaining Rape during Civil War: Cross-national Evidence (1980-2009). *American Political Science Review*, 107(3), 461-477.
Cited in Chapter 6, this article uses multiple methods in an innovative way.

Fish, M. Steven. 2002. Islam and Authoritarianism. *World Politics*, 55(1), October, 4-37.
A creative example of how statistical regression can be used to look at a timely research topic.

Friedman, Jeffrey. (ed.). 1996. *The Rational Choice Controversy: Economic Models of Politics Reconsidered*, Vols 1-2. New Haven, CT: Yale University Press.
Critically engages with rational choice and formal theory in PIR.

Horowitz, Michael C., and Stam, Allan C. 2014. How Prior Military Experience Influences the Future Militarized Behavior of Leaders. *International Organization*, 68(3), 527-559.
An article that uses time series analysis, among other quantitative tools.

Inglehart, Ronald, and Welzel, Christian. 2010. Changing Mass Priorities: The Link between Modernization and Democracy. *Perspectives on Politics*, 8(2), June, 551-567.
A fascinating look at the connection between economic growth, values, and democratization based on survey data.

Jacobson, Gary C. 2015. It's Nothing Personal: The Decline of the Incumbency Advantage in US House Elections. *Journal of Politics*, 77(3), July, 861-873.
Quantitative analysis is often used in the study of American politics, in part because of the availability of solid data.

Johnson, James. 2019. Formal Models in Political Science: Conceptual, Not Empirical. *The Journal of Politics*, 81(1), e6-e10.
An advanced look at formal models.

Mansfield, Edward D., Mutz, Diana C., and Silver, Laura R. 2015. Men, Women, Trade, and Free Markets. *International Studies Quarterly*, 59(2), June, 303-315.
Uses statistical tools in creative ways to explain how gender affects attitudes toward free trade.

Margalit, Yotam. 2013. Explaining Social Policy Preferences: Evidence from the Great Recession. *American Political Science Review*, 107(1), 80-103.
An interesting article based on surveys and statistical methods.

McCarty, Nolan, and Meirowitz, Adam. 2007. *Political Game Theory: An Introduction*. Cambridge, UK: Cambridge University Press.
Like the Osborne volume below, a primer in formal models.

McLaren, Lauren. 2012. Immigration and Trust in Politics in Britain. *British Journal of Political Science*, 42(1), 163-185.
A research article using statistical tests.

Morrow, James, D. 1994. Game Theory for Political Scientists. Princeton, NJ: Princeton University Press.
A well-known and well-regarded work on how to use game theory.

Osborne, Martin J. 2004. *An Introduction to Game Theory.* New York: Oxford University Press.
As the title suggests, this is a general introduction to using formal game models.

Pearl, Judea. 2009. Causal Inference in Statistics: An Overview. *Statistics Surveys*, 3, 96–146.
An overview of causal inference and statistics.

Peterson, Erik. 2016. The Rich are Different: The Effect of Wealth Partisanship. *Political Behavior*, 38(1), 33–54.
An interesting example of real-world, relevant research based on statistical regression.

Sarsons, Heather. 2015. Rainfall and Conflict: A Cautionary Tale. *Journal of Development Economics*, 115, 62–72.
The perils of statistics in social science.

Walt, Stephen M. 1999. Rigor or Rigor Mortis? Rational Choice and Security Studies. *International Security*, 23(4), 5–48.
Deals with some issues related to formal models in IR.

# 11

# Writing Up Your Paper

━━━━━━━━ Learning Objectives ━━━━━━━━

- To become familiar with the basic structure of a PIR research paper;
- To learn how to write a good title and abstract that capture the essence of your research and attract readers;
- To concisely and clearly formulate your main argument based on your findings;
- To understand the core features of an effective introduction, data analysis section, and conclusion;
- To know how to use different conventions for citing others' work and creating bibliographic entries for them;
- To think about how your academic writing style helps you communicate your results.

Like a long hike or run, the last stretch of the research process – writing your thesis or paper – is often the most challenging (Baglione 2020, 217). You know you are almost there, and yet, you are tired, and have to summon all your willpower to finish. But you also want to finish strong, lest you have wasted substantial time and energy for nothing. By the time you get to the 'writing up' stage of your paper or thesis, you may feel fatigue with your topic. You may be close to graduation, and, to use an Americanism, even have a little 'senioritis.' But it would be regrettable to both your efforts and to the potential contributions of your research to PIR not to to write a final product that clearly communicates your argument and findings. Since, as we noted in Chapter 3 on research ethics, PIR research is inherently about human activity and thus seeks to deal with real-world issues and sometimes even affect change, the need to communicate your results clearly is even more important.

While writing up may seem like a daunting task, in fact things are not so bad considering all the work you have already done. You have come up with a research question and identified a related body of scholarship to engage with. You have written a literature review and selected a research design, choosing cases and variables to observe, operationalize, and measure. You have gathered the needed data and analyzed it. What is left is to write an introduction, articulate your main argument, summarize your data analysis, present your main findings, and put together a conclusion, all while citing the work and materials you have consulted. You need to make sure that your final product is cogent and clear, and flows clearly between sections or chapters. You will also need a title and a bibliography or works cited section that deploys a chosen or assigned reference style. And perhaps an abstract. Many theses also contain a preface and an acknowledgments section in which you describe the intellectual trajectory of your research and thank your advisor(s), family, friends, and perhaps others for their support. This chapter provides some strategies, and practical advice, on how to approach the writing-up stage of the research process.

## The Structure and Contents of a PIR Research Paper

Table 11.1 presents the basic structure and contents of a PIR research paper. While there are many variants on this structure, the core elements listed in Table 11.1 usually appear in most PIR research write-ups. In a longer document, such as a thesis, the literature review and methodology might merit their own sections or chapters. In a shorter paper or essay, they might be subsumed in the introduction. While in principle there is flexibility in how to structure your paper, be sure to consult your research supervisor for guidelines: she or he may have specific expectations.

**Table 11.1**  Sample structure and contents of a research paper in PIR

Title

Table of Contents

Abstract

Preface and Acknowledgments

I  Introduction

    a  Statement of research question and its importance to PIR scholarship and policy
    b  Summary of argument and how it contributes to the existing literature
    c  Case selection and justification
    d  Methodology: what is your epistemology and why? How did you gather and analyze the data?
    e  Outline of the paper or thesis

II  Literature Review

    a  Review of how existing scholarship and associated theories have answered your question or similar questions
    b  Hypotheses that emerge from existing scholarship and their respective utility and limits
    c  Your argument and how it advances, confirms, and/or challenges existing scholarship

III  Data/Empirical Analysis of Cases

    a  This may be one or more sections or chapters depending on how you decide to organize it
    b  This is where you systematically apply your methods, whether positivist or interpretivist, to your data and report your findings

IV  Conclusions

    a  Summary of findings
    b  Implications for PIR and policy
    c  Challenges and paths forward

V  Bibliography/References/Works Cited

    a  Depending on the citation method you are using, this will contain either all the works you cited in the text using parenthetical citations or a list of additional works you did not directly cite in footnotes/endnotes but consulted in the course of your research.

Before we get to the details of each section, it merits repeating that in the real world of PIR research, you may find yourself moving back and forth between data collection and writing, and among the various sections, as you stumble upon gaps in your work. This is quite normal. Academic writing, reflecting the social phenomena that we study, is not a linear process. You may have already written segments of your paper even as you were still gathering data. Once you get to the stage where you are exclusively or primarily writing, the important thing is to make daily progress. Successful writers often set daily or weekly word goals for themselves. They find the time that they are most effective, position themselves in the right atmosphere, and write until they have met that goal, often putting aside things like citations and proofreading for later.

## The Title and Abstract

We have placed this section first, but you may not come up with your final *title* until last. You may have already proposed working titles earlier in the research process, but it is only after you have your findings and have written a compelling introduction and conclusion that you will be ready to formulate a title that:

- Captures a potential reader's attention;
- Identifies the research topic and cases;
- Hints at the argument and contribution of your research.

In other words, in your title, you want to communicate key information in an appealing way. Table 11.2 contains examples of recent PIR article titles that received awards from the American Political Science Association (APSA). You will see that some of them employ humor or various literary devices (such as repeating the same consonant sound, e.g., 'Status, Security and Socialization') as a way to capture a potential reader's attention. Usually, the first part of the title is creative and clever (and sometimes even provocative), while the part that comes after the colon contains the details on cases and contribution (e.g., 'From Trinidad to Taiwan: The Neighborhood Basis of Patronage Politics'). One fun way to select a title is to make a list of a number of potential candidates, and then ask your classmates or friends to vote for their favorite, either in person or using social media.

**Table 11.2**  Recent titles of APSA award-winning books and articles

| |
|---|
| The Death Camp Eldorado: Political and Economic Effects of Mass Violence |
| King Makers: Local Leaders and Ethnic Politics in West Africa |
| Mobilizing without the Masses: Control and Contention in China |
| Quitting Work but Not the Job: Liberty and the Right to Strike |
| Structural Domination and Structural Freedom: A Feminist Perspective |
| Status, Security and Socialization: Conditions for China's Cautious Compliance in International Security Institutions |

During the course of your research, you have probably relied upon **abstracts** to determine whether you wanted to delve deeper into an article or book. While your professor may not explicitly require an abstract for your paper or thesis, writing one is an extremely useful exercise as it forces you to formulate an 'elevator briefing' version of your paper. In an abstract, you must distill your question, argument, methodology, findings, and contributions of your research into a short paragraph of usually about 200 words. If you ever want to participate in an academic conference, you will be required to submit an abstract as part of your application – which is another reason why it is good to practice writing one.

An abstract can also serve as a marketing strategy for your research. Maybe you have also relied on an abstract to summarize the contents of a book or an article so that you can cite it (that's OK, even seasoned PIR researchers do that!). We provide an example of an abstract in Table 11.3 from the prestigious international relations journal *International Security* by the scholar Aisha Ahmed (Ahmed 2019). You will see that it starts by contextualizing the research in real-world issues (jihadist behavior), and then goes on to pose a research question and define a puzzle (how do jihadist norms change, considering their rigid adherence to rules and ideologies?). The abstract then notes the cases examined (Nigeria and Pakistan) and summarizes the findings and main argument.

**Table 11.3**   A sample abstract from *International Security*

*In recent years, jihadists across the world have transformed their gendered violence, shocking the world by breaking from prior taboos and even celebrating abuses that they had previously prohibited. This behavior is surprising because jihadists represent a class of insurgents that are deeply bound by rules and norms. For jihadists, deviating from established Islamist doctrines is no easy feat. What then explains these sudden transformations in the rules and norms governing jihadist violence? An inductive investigation of contemporary jihadist violence in Pakistan and Nigeria reveals a new theory of jihadist normative evolution. Data from these cases show that dramatic changes in jihadist violence occur when an external trigger creates an expanded political space for jihadist entrepreneurs to do away with normative constraints on socially prohibited types of violence. As these jihadist leaders capitalize on the triggers, they are able to encourage a re-socialization process within their ranks, resulting in the erosion of previously held taboos, the adoption of proscribed behaviors, and the emergence of toxic new norms.*

*Source*: Ahmed, Aisha. 2019. 'We Have Captured Your Women': Explaining Jihadist Norm Change. *International Security* 44(1), 80–116.

## The Introduction

The introduction is a critical part of your thesis or paper, so if you find yourself rewriting it multiple times, that is not a bad thing. In fact, like the title and abstract, you may also want to save the task of writing an introduction for last, once you are sure of the contents of the paper and have formulated an argument. In the introduction, you will present the research question and explain why it is important and interesting. When we say important and interesting, of course we mean it should be *intrinsically* so, but you also have to explain why it is important and interesting in the world of PIR. In other words, how does it advance PIR scholarship? The introduction should also state the relevance of your research question to the larger world, and to multiple audiences in that larger world. Put differently, in the introduction you want to whet the reader's appetite, so that they continue on and read your entire product.

Also in the introduction, you will summarize your main argument (discussed below) and findings. The main argument should be succinct and clear. You might even want to put it in italics, an indented block quote, or other distinguishing format (or even its own subsection). Then, you will want to introduce your cases and explain to the reader why you have chosen them. Here, you may need to get into issues of research design, especially when it comes to small-*N* designs, since, as we explained in Chapter 6, case selection can impact your findings. But you may also discuss these issues in a separate methodological section, depending on the length of your paper. Finally, the introduction often provides a 'map' of the entire product, section by section or chapter by chapter.

## Introducing your Methodology

In the introduction, or a separate section on methodology, you will lay out your research design and explain your epistemological assumptions. Is your work a positivist essay focused on providing an explanation for a particular event? Is it an interpretivist project focused on the meanings of political phenomena and concepts and how they are constructed?

As you discuss your methodology, you should state the insights you hope to gain from deploying your selected approach, and its potential limitations. The methodology section or subsection will allow other researchers to trace (and perhaps replicate) what you have done in terms of data collection, a topic discussed in previous chapters. If you are employing quantitative methods, the discussion of methodology might specify data sources, **operationalization**, and **measurement** strategies, and provide a justification for the statistical technique(s) you have chosen to use (Bryman 2008, 670). You should always be explicit about which datasets you are using for your quantitative analysis. Where are they found? Who collected the data? How was it collected? If you are generating your own data through surveys, questionnaires, or content analysis, you should describe how you did this to your reader in the introduction. In the event that you have carried out surveys or questionnaires, you should also specify your sampling procedures (Bryman 2008, 270). If these procedures were particularly complicated, you can provide even more details in an appendix to your paper. You will often see such appendices in journals with articles that employ quantitative approaches. Finally, the introduction should contain one paragraph which contains a 'map' of the remainder of your thesis or paper, specifying the logic of its organization. What should the reader expect? What comes next? Use this as another opportunity to further whet the reader's appetite.

## The Literature Review

We have covered the process of writing a literature review in Chapter 5, so let this serve as a summary of that chapter's more detailed contents. The literature review:

- provides a categorical and analytical summary of existing scholarly work on your topic;
- informs the reader of major points of disagreements in scholarship regarding your topic;
- informs the reader of how your research question relates to existing work and analytical frameworks;
- hones in on your approach and answer to the research question while situating it in the existing literature.

To remind you, the body of a literature review is often organized around competing epistemologies or approaches to answering a particular question. For each, you will analyze the approach, evaluate its utility and limits, and then examine how your research topic or question relates to it. Your literature review is hopefully written such that it builds up to your **main argument,** which you have already summarized in the introduction. At this final stage, the literature review considers how your arguments contribute to or challenge any of the existing perspectives.

## The Thesis or Main Argument

The main argument of your research paper is also sometimes called a thesis. We refer to it as a 'main argument' to avoid confusion with the other meaning of 'thesis,' an extended research paper. Perhaps it is even more accurate to call this the *statement* of your main argument, since you will actually be referring to and substantiating your argument throughout the paper. You can summarize the main argument in the introduction, and at the end of the literature review you might repeat it in expanded form. You can even put it in its own section.

You may already have had a good sense of what your main argument will be, even at an early stage of the research process. Or perhaps you have just had a hunch. As we have emphasized throughout the book, the research process is not linear. It is normal to revise your argument over time as evidence comes to light and as your thinking evolves. So more than likely, you will be honing your argument until the very end. But at some point, you have to articulate it, at several different points in the paper (and in the abstract).

You have seen arguments in the academic articles you gathered for your literature review, and you have also probably seen them in op-eds and heard them in speeches. The main argument is an overarching answer to the research question you have asked, based on the evidence you have gathered. For a positivist research question, it summarizes the causal claim you are making. For an interpretivist project, it will be a summary of your narrative. It should be clear and concise, but also not trivial or obvious (Baglione 2020, 110). While not all arguments can be counterintuitive or controversial, some of the best ones are. Like the entire essay, the argument should show how you are breaking some new ground.

Being concise does not mean that your main argument has to be limited to one or two sentences. In fact, some arguments have to be written out in an entire paragraph in virtue of their logic. Consider an example from our project on when western states include human rights in their foreign policies. Let's say you are looking at the United States as a case study, and examining a number of cases in which Washington either has or hasn't intervened to deal with an unfolding or impending atrocity. Here is a sample argument that you might arrive at based on the results of your small-*N*, comparative research design:

- While many existing accounts have focused exclusively on strategic, internal US government deliberations around humanitarian interventions, this paper demonstrates that a number of external political factors – public opinion, media, and pressure groups – powerfully influence the thinking of presidents when they are making the decision of whether or not to use the US military for humanitarian intervention.
- Additionally, I show that presidents are most influenced by outside pressures when their domestic approval ratings are low, and tend to ignore these pressures when they are more popular.
- Hence, I make a domestic politics-focused argument about US humanitarian interventions.

Note that the sentence in the first part refers to the uniqueness of your argument and how it builds upon or challenges existing work. In this manner, your main argument references the literature review. Notice also that the argument contains both conceptual claims and a summary of your findings. For projects employing hypothesis-testing through statistical analysis, the argument will summarize your findings even more explicitly: for example, the nature and strength of the relationship between two or more variables. Here is a sample argument from our project on the determinants of populist party support:

- This essay finds that economic inequality, educational attainment, and views on immigration are all robust explainers of support for populism.
- However, the intensity of the effects of each of these three variables is not the same. My statistical analysis suggests that the most powerful determinant of populist support is views on immigration, which itself is strongly associated with perceptions of the economic situation.

The argument for an interpretivist essay is likely to be different. You will recall that PIR researchers employing an interpretive epistemology believe that political life consists of actions laden with meanings. Those meanings can be uncovered through the study of words and discourses, rather than merely actions or stated beliefs and reasons. So, if you were doing a project on the prospects for Iraqi national reconciliation among Sunnis, Shia, and Kurds, you might want to analyze the discourse around Iraqi nationalism, what it means, and how it is understood and interpreted by various Iraqi groups. More specifically, you might want to look at political groups in Iraq that wrap themselves in the Iraqi flag, and examine the way in which they express Iraqi national identity in their public discourse, banners, and other messaging. Your main argument might be articulated as such:

- Tracing the discourse of Iraqi Shia political groups in recent years, I demonstrate that the appeals these organizations make to Iraqi nationalism do not alter the meanings that non-Shia Iraqis attribute to these groups.
- In short, Sunnis and Kurds perceive the Shia nationalist narrative as a thin cover for Shia claims to exclusive ownership over the Iraqi state, and their perceived intention to use this claim to marginalize and repress other groups (Boduszynski and Lamont 2017).

You will return to the main argument and hone it further as you work on the sections below. And you should – the main argument, after all, must be razor-sharp!

## Data/Empirical Analysis

The data analysis section of your thesis or paper is the beating heart of your research, and as such is the longest one. It is the section that will make or break the argument. It should not only present the data, but also tell a story based upon that data. While certain methodologies, especially interpretivist ones, may be more conducive to writing a compelling narrative, any research method should allow you to tell a story.

Beyond this, the data and empirical analysis sections will vary significantly from paper to paper in terms of organization. There are, however, a few principles that you should keep in mind regardless of methodology and approach. The first is *consistency in structure*.

You should try to follow a similar structure for every section and case within your data analysis so as to allow the reader to more easily follow the logic of your research process, your findings, and your arguments. Let's say you are examining how economic status, as filtered through views on immigration, contributes to populist party support across three European cases. If your approach is qualitative, for each case you will use a consistent strategy to link the independent variables to outcomes in populist party support. For example, you may show how populist parties emphasized immigration in their messaging strategies targeting lower-income voters. Process-tracing, described in Chapter 8, might be a a a useful tool. Even if your quantitative findings are based on statistically significant relationships, you need to be explicit about possible causal pathways.

To achieve consistency, you may want to have common subsections for each case, and parallel diagrams, charts, or other graphics, and then, at the end, a section that compares all the cases. It is extremely important to 'flag' your main argument by peppering the data analysis with 'signposts' that will remind the reader of how the analysis relates to the literature review you outlined earlier in the paper. In our experience, one of the most frequent failings of undergraduate papers is that students tend to get lost in their empirical narrative while neglecting to remind the reader of why particular facts or events matter and relate to the overall argument. It is perfectly fine to stop and remind readers at the end of a paragraph of why a point you are making is significant to the analytical strategy and argument. If this seems a little repetitive at times, that is OK. Reminders and reinforcement may be awkward in a novel or work of journalistic nonfiction, but they are appreciated in a complex PIR analysis. In other words, it is vital that the reader consistently sees how the analysis fits into the larger goals of the paper or thesis.

## The Conclusion

In reading PIR research – articles, books, conference papers, and so on – you have undoubtedly seen that conclusions come in different forms. Some are drawn out, summarizing the argument of an article thoroughly and suggesting avenues for further research. Others, by contrast, are quite pithy, providing only a basic recap of the main findings. Yet, there are a few elements that all good conclusions should contain. They should:

- Tie the entire product together;
- Remind your reader of what you argued and why it is important;
- Summarize and interpret the key findings;
- Allow you to step back from your results: what did you learn, what does it mean for PIR, for other cases, and for the wider world;
- Consider any challenges and limitations of your research, and discuss how further research could advance your goals.

In some ways, the conclusion performs functions similar to the introduction by summarizing the key contributions of the paper. The conclusion, however, is also an opportunity to broaden the discussion to related issues, cases, and findings. To what extent do your findings enlighten us on other cases? If you found that views on immigration determine support for populism in Europe, to what extent does this apply to other advanced industrialized democracies? If it doesn't, why or why not? Moreover, in the conclusion you want to create *confidence* in your findings while also being open about their limitations. What other methods could you have applied if you had more resources or time at your disposal, or what other cases could you introduce to strengthen your confidence in the results? Finally, while we have emphasized that you should leave the normative issues out of research questions, discussions around normative concerns are welcome in the conclusion. What *should* policy-makers do based on your findings? For example, one normative implication of the finding that attitudes toward immigration shape support for populism is that progressive parties should pay more attention to voters' anxieties about this subject if they want to succeed.

Your conclusion should elegantly tie together all your hard work, but it does not have to be definitive. Conclusions, in spite of what the name suggests, do not have to be entirely conclusive. An honest evaluation of what you have found is important. Research in PIR is by its very nature a messy enterprise, and there are seldom findings that can be neatly packaged in a box. Thus, when writing about complex issues, such as the causes of conflict, it is perfectly fine and expected to express a healthy dose of humility about your ability as a researcher to have figured it all out. Nobody has.

## Citing and Referencing the Work of Others

Transparency and academic honesty, as noted in Chapter 3, are two of the principle norms associated with PIR research. An essential practice associated with both of these norms is using **citations** and **referencing**, or acknowledging your debt to the sources of data, research, and ideas upon which you have drawn. The process of citing and referencing can be an extremely stressful and time-consuming enterprise if you are not systematic and organized when gathering materials and taking notes on them. Whenever you read or research material for your writing, make sure that you include in your notes the full publication details of each relevant text that you consulted. If you are not meticulous about this early on, you will find yourself in the frustrating and time-consuming situation of locating lost references. Some attention to this early on will save you a lot of time, and grief, later. These details should include:

- Surname(s) and initial(s) of the author(s);
- The date of publication;
- The title of the text;
- If it is an article, the title of the journal and volume number;
- If it is a chapter of an edited book, the book's title and editor(s);
- The publisher and place of publication;
- The first and last page numbers if it is a journal article or a chapter in an edited book;
- For particularly important points, or for parts of texts that you might wish to quote verbatim, also include the specific page reference.

## When and How to Use Citations

You should acknowledge your source every time you make a point that is substantially someone else's. If this sounds vague, it is. Knowing when to cite requires practice. The best way to develop good practice in citing others is to ask for advice and to pay close attention to how experienced researchers cite the work of others. Most PIR research papers will contain citations throughout. For obvious reasons, the literature review is likely to have lots of citations. By contrast, other sections, such as the introduction and the conclusion, are likely to have more of your own ideas, and thus comparatively fewer citations.

Below we introduce different kinds of reference conventions, but here it is worth saying a few words about how to actually refer to the work of others, a subject which is related to our discussion of writing style a bit later in this chapter. One overall guideline is to vary how you do this. Your writing will not be smooth if every citation reads, 'As Author X argues…'. There are many other ways to introduce others' work: varying the place in the sentence where you mention the author's name, for instance, or sometimes summarizing their argument and only naming them in the parenthetical citation or footnote/endnote (see below). You do not need to specify the author's title, institutional background, or affiliation (i.e., 'Professor X of Oxford University maintains that…') except in very specific cases. Whether you use first names is a matter of stylistic choice. If you do choose to note first names, it should only be in the first mention of that author in your paper. As with the issue of when to cite, how to introduce citations in your writing is a skill that you will develop through practice writing and by extensive reading of published scholarly work in PIR and other disciplines.

## Reference Styles

It is helpful to know what **reference style** you will use early in the research process so you will not have to go back later and make cumbersome, time-sapping changes. Reference style refers to two different things. One is whether you will cite work in the actual text using **parenthetical citations** or use **footnotes** or **endnotes**, while the other has to do with the actual bibliographic entry itself. You may not have a choice, as often a certain style is dictated to you by your professor, institution, or publication venue. The American Political Science Association uses a variation of the Chicago Manual of Style citation system, which provides a pragmatic and simple way to reference publications in a variety of formats. You can find the Chicago conventions online at chicagomanualofstyle.org.

The in-text parenthetical citation method has the advantage of allowing the reader to immediately see your source without having to search at the bottom of the page or the end of the section for a footnote or endnote (though electronic versions of articles and books, which often contain hyperlinked footnote/endnote markers, overcome this shortcoming). One disadvantage is that it is less elegant to use in-text citations than it is to deploy a more discrete footnote marker. Another disadvantage is that at times you may want to give additional clarifying information about the reference, in which case you may be forced to insert a footnote or endnote in addition to the in-text citation. As the example below shows, the in-text citation normally includes the surname of the author(s) and the year of the publication. This information usually appears in parentheses at the most appropriate point in the text:

> Some recent studies of voting behavior in Fredonia have suggested a growing anti-elitism in smaller towns (Martinez, 2016).

The fictional text reference above indicates to the reader that a work by Martinez is the example of such a recent study (on voting behavior in Fredonia), which was published in 2016.

The lack of a specific page number suggests that here you are citing an overarching argument or finding of the Martinez study. An alternative way of using in-text citation is in this also (fictional) example:

> A human rights discourse, Munmu and Hanapepe (2018: 244) observe, 'begins to appear in Fredonian foreign policy by the 1990s, but only episodically.'

In this instance, you are not only referencing a very specific point within a book or an article, but also using the author's words verbatim. This allows your reader to find the exact location in their text from which the citation comes, and, if they are interested, permits the reader to further investigate the larger context in which these authors made the point. Moreover, it allows the reader to identify further sources for their own research. Some conventions and publishers allow you to leave out the year of the book after the first mention of it, and just include the page number, assuming that this is the only book or article published by that author or those authors in your paper. If you are referencing several works by the author(s) published the same year, you can use a letter (i.e., Martinez 2016a or Martinez 2016b) to distinguish among them in the text and the works cited. Some electronic versions of books do not contain page numbers, which requires you to figure out some other way of identifying the location of the reference, if at all possible. Notice that the authors' names in this example are outside the parentheses because of the way you introduce the reference.

There are also different conventions for what comes after the authors' names – you will see that in the Martinez example above, the name is followed by a comma. Sometimes there is no such comma. Sometimes, a 'p.' is included before the page number, and sometimes just the page number itself. The important thing is to follow whatever convention is mandated by your professor and publication, and whether there is a mandate or not, to be consistent. When a publication has several authors, it is usual to give the surname of the first author followed by 'et al.' (an abbreviation of the Latin for 'and the others'), although for works with just two authors both names may be given, as in the example above. You may need to cite an unpublished idea or discussion point from an oral presentation, such as a lecture. The in-text citation format would be the same as for a published work and should give the speaker's name and the year of the presentation. Then, this speech will be listed alongside the published materials in your '**works cited**' section. If the idea or information comes from an interview or personal exchange, you could reference the point as shown in this fictional example:

> A party activist in a rural district near the capital expressed his frustration with the permissive stance of national-level party leaders on immigration (Chen, interview).

Then, the interview would be listed in an alphabetically-organized works-cited section among other sources. If you are citing the sources for data in a table or diagram, you would also use the in-text convention followed by a full bibliographic entry in the works cited.

## How to Reference using Footnotes or Endnotes

Some journals (and some of your professors) may prefer footnotes (notes which appear at the foot of the page) or endnotes (notes which appear at the end of the section or work) to reference their writing. Although this method differs in style from the in-text system, its purpose – to acknowledge the source of ideas, data, or quotations without undue interruption to the flow of the writing – is identical. Footnote or endnote markers are a sequential series of numbers (usually Arabic, but sometimes Roman) in superscript above the line of writing or printing, usually in the same place where you would insert the author and in the in-text citation system described above. One difference is that footnote and endnote markers are less frequently used in the middle of a sentence. Here is an fictional example:

> A number of observers have noted that Russia's abstention in 2011 on UN Security Council Resolution 1973, which authorized intervention in Libya, may have had to do with the fact that Dimitry Medvedev then occupied the office of president of the Russian Federation.[1]

Here you will see one advantage of the footnote/endnote method over the in-text one: 'a number of observers' signals more than one author and work, which is far easier to include in a footnote or endnote. Full details of the reference are then given at the bottom of the page or, if endnotes are used, in numerical order at the end of the section, chapter, or paper, according to the reference style you choose (see below). If the same source is referred to several times, on second or subsequent occasions, a shortened reference may be used along with the Latin abbreviation 'op. cit.' as in this fictional example:

> Martinez et al. 2018, op. cit., p. 23.

You can also use footnotes or endnotes to elaborate on a reference, critique it, or propose additional works that deal with the same subject.

## Referencing Websites

Whether the older generation of scholars likes it or not, the internet is widely used as a source of information. But it is hard to cite because information contained within it can change rapidly. Websites and the information on them can disappear or become inaccessible. Some information is behind paywalls. While conventions on citing internet-based sources are evolving, when referencing websites, it is helpful to include details that will help other people follow up the information beyond just providing the URL. One thing you can do is to include the author of the site (whether individual, group, or organization), the date the page was published or last updated (you can find a date at the bottom of many websites), its title, and the date you accessed the site (so that the reader has context in case the information on the site was subsequently modified). Here is an example citation for a (fictional) website:

> Republic of Fredonia Central Bureau of Statistics, Data by Municipality. Last updated January 2017. www.stats.fredonia.gov/municipalities Accessed on September 9, 2019.

## Referencing Styles for Bibliographic Entries and Works Cited

Whichever referencing system you use, you should make sure that:

- You have included in your works cited/bibliography, footnotes, or endnotes full details of all the sources referred to in your text;
- Regardless of the style that you adopt, you have been consistent in your use of punctuation, formatting, and all other elements;
- Each entry has the surnames and forenames or initials of all authors;
- Each entry includes the date of publication;
- Each entry includes a title;
- Each entry has the place of publication (for books);
- Each entry includes the name of the publisher (for books).

The title of a book should be formatted to distinguish it from the other details. If a book title, this usually means italicization, but it could also be in bold font or underlined. Journal, chapter, or report titles should appear in quotation marks. When multi-authored works have been cited, it is important to include the names of all the authors, even when the text reference uses 'et al.' In addition, an entry for a chapter within an edited book should include the editor, the title of the book and the page range for the chapter being referenced. The title of the chapter will be in quotes, while the title of the entire book will be in italics. Here is a fictional example:

> Martinez, Jong-Ick. 2016. 'Populism in Rural Fredonia.' In Q. Smith et al. (eds.), *Europe's New Populisms*. London: The New World Press, pp. 201–243.

Journal articles must also include the name and volume number of the journal and the page numbers of the article, with the article title in quotes and the journal title italicized. The publisher and place of publication are not required for journal entries. Here is an fictional example:

> Martinez, Jong-Ick. 2015. 'Populist Perfectionists: A Learning Model of Populist Party Development in Fredonia.' *Fredonian Journal of Political Science*, 46, pp. 328–348.

Thus far we have discussed the most common types of publication. You may also find yourself citing other types of publication, such as PhD dissertations, think-tank reports, newspaper articles, or legal and historical documents. The same general principles apply to such sources as well, but for specifics you should consult manuals associated with the reference style you decide to use, such as the Chicago Manual of Style mentioned earlier in the chapter.

## Some Notes on Writing in an Academic Style

There are a number of excellent books that offer invaluable advice on writing style. Some of them are in the 'Suggested Further Reading' list at the end of this chapter. Here, we share some key principles for good academic writing, some of them highlighted by Toshkov (2016, 330) and others:

- You are not a lawyer. Do not use rhetorical tricks, emotional appeals, or deliberate omissions to strengthen your argument. Being open about the limitations and uncertainties of your findings is perfectly acceptable. If you are using statistical regression, you will be forced to admit such limitations.
- Academic writing is best when it is expressed in simple and direct language. Long and winding sentences will only turn readers away. So will jargon, though some specialized terms are unavoidable. Keep it simple and keep it clear.
- Avoid the passive voice (though you may see a lot of it in academic papers). Sometimes the passive voice is used to create the impression of impartiality. Usually it makes writing awkward. Avoid the temptation.
- It is perfectly OK to write in the first person (i.e., 'I will argue...' or 'As I stated...'). This is your project. You own it and the ideas within. Be bold! (Disclaimer: there may be some professors who don't like the first person and they may tell you not to use it.)
- Use paragraphs liberally. Make sure that every paragraph has a single topic sentence and captures a single idea. Concise paragraphs are normally four to five sentences long. If you find yourself writing paragraphs that span over a page, double-check to see if the ideas or concepts discussed in the paragraph can be subdivided into smaller paragraphs.
- Don't over-quote or over-cite. Your paper should transmit your own perspective and should be written in your own voice. You should not use the words of others as crutches. Only use direct quotes when absolutely necessary. Every time you use a quote, state the name of the author and make sure the quote flows nicely with your own writing. This is usually done by explaining to the reader the importance of your quote and what you are using the quote to illustrate (Lipson 2005, 153–154).
- Crafting good sentences and paragraphs is an essential part of the writing process. Don't be afraid to use simple sentences in the active voice (while avoiding jargon) and to write in the first person. Being a good writer is certainly based in part on your passion for a topic, but it also requires practice. Authors – whether they are PIR scholars or novelists – go through many drafts and must deal with criticism and sometimes even rejection from editors.

## Chapter Summary

The final stages of the research process entail writing up the key elements of your paper, essay, or thesis: an introduction, main argument, literature review, data analysis, conclusion, abstract, and title. How you write these sections will determine whether your research is accessible, and whether it attracts readers. In other words, you may have come up with the most brilliant research design in the PIR world and collected groundbreaking data, but it is of little value to anyone but yourself if you don't write it up in a cogent research paper.

If you are like most authors, you will have already written some of the sections listed above, and you will also jump among them as you hone what you want to say. The introduction and conclusion 'bookend' your research paper, but they are not identical.

Avoid using the same language in both. Use the introduction to entice the reader and map out the thesis, and the conclusion to summarize, but also to think big about what you have written and what it all means, while also grappling with its limitations and challenges. The data analysis section is the core of the paper: it has to be clear and consistent in its presentation of results and analysis, and refer frequently back to the main argument. After you have written almost everything else, turn to the title and abstract, which are designed to capture the attention of a potential reader, journal editor, or conference organizer.

Finally, you should actively seek out opportunities to share your research. In the next, final chapter, we will discuss ways to publish your research. There is no better way to gain confidence in a topic and your abilities than to present your research to a group and answer questions, which may then improve your work further. In the course of this research, you have become an expert on your topic and should be proud of your efforts.

## Suggested Further Reading

Baglione, Lisa A. 2020. *Writing a Research Paper in Political Science: A Practical Guide to Inquiry, Structure, and Methods*. Thousand Oaks, CA: Sage.
Contains many practical examples of PIR writing geared toward undergraduate students.

Lipson, Charles. 2018. *How to Write a BA Thesis: A Practical Guide from Your First Ideas to Your Finished Paper*. Chicago, IL: University of Chicago Press.
A useful textbook for the undergraduate student.

Strunk, William. 2007. *The Elements of Style*. London: Penguin.
A classic: every student should read it.

The Economist. 2018. *Style Guide*. London: Profile Books Ltd.
A highly useful style guide for all kinds of writing.

# 12

# Final Hurdles and Looking Forward

━━━━━━━━━━━ Learning Objectives ━━━━━━━━━━━

- To be able to resolve common challenges and pitfalls you will encounter during the research and writing processes;
- To understand the general expectations and conventions of academic publishing;
- To be familiar with the general conventions of op-ed and policy paper publishing.

Our final chapter turns to some last words of advice relating to the overall research and writing process. There are several hurdles that all researchers and writers will encounter at some point during a research and writing project. Sometimes these hurdles may slow our progress as we seek to find ways around them, while at other times, they may derail a project all together. Such hurdles can range from the types of challenges that we have specifically addressed in earlier chapters, such as how to find the right articles and books for a literature review, to more fundamental problems such as a simple inability to start or continue writing – a phenomenon known colloquially as **writer's block**.

However, before we begin this discussion, it is important to acknowledge that each of us has a unique way for going about research and writing that best reflects our own work ethic and style. There is no one-size-fits-all approach to addressing the challenges that arise during the research process, and in the end, it will be up to you, through trial and error, to find your own best way forward. This is why effective time management is so important. You need to give yourself enough time to work through any unexpected hurdles that you may encounter. And given that the research and writing process is one that involves constant learning and discovery, it is almost certain that you will encounter unexpected challenges.

In this chapter, following our discussion of some of the challenges you might face in the research and writing process, we will discuss a final important part of the process: assessment, or evaluating the quality of your research output. We will point out that assessment is not the end of a project, but rather an opportunity to gain valuable feedback from your instructors and supervisors on how to become a better researcher and a better writer. Then we will discuss potential pathways forward for your research, such as publishing your research findings either as a short opinion-editorial piece that advocates a policy position based on your findings or as a full-length peer-reviewed article.

## Tips and Advice for the Research Process

First, let us turn to some general obstacles that you may encounter during the research and writing process. One of the challenges that students often cite is that they reach a certain point in the research process and are unable to proceed. In other words, they have hit a roadblock. Sometimes this is because they get lost in the data, or become overwhelmed by the scope of their research question. Often this relates to not being able to fit the data into a theoretical framework. At other times, roadblocks emerge from challenges in data collection or analysis. Other students just get tired, and begin doubting the value of their topic. Don't let any potential roadblocks that arise in the research and writing process keep you from continuing to work on your project. Every researcher, even seasoned ones, arrive at such roadblocks occasionally. What is most important is that you keep working consistently. As we wrote in Chapter 11, research is not a linear process where you must complete each component stage of the process before moving on to the next.

If you find yourself stuck on one issue, try to move on and come back to it once you have thought more about the problem you have encountered. There are many times when you will go back and rethink parts of your project that you already thought were settled. During your literature review, you might discover that your research question needs to be reconsidered as you become more familiar with the literature on your topic. You may revisit your research design if you find that the cases you selected might not be best suited to answering your research question. You may also find that your final written work has departed significantly from what you initially envisioned in your research proposal. There is nothing wrong with this. In fact, the more you rethink your project, the more likely it is that you are applying the concepts and research practices presented in this book in a cogent manner.

As we emphasized in Chapter 11, you should make sure that you devote enough time every day to work on your project. Remember, as you are working on your essay, dissertation, or thesis, that academic research and writing is a continuous work-in-progress type of activity. If something serious does come up, let your supervisor know that it is preventing you from focusing on your research and writing. Do so early. Good communication with your instructor or supervisor will help alert them to any serious problems that might arise during your research early enough for them to be able to provide assistance or guidance.

As we also advised in Chapter 11, save the introduction and conclusion for the very end. Even if you have drafted a tentative introduction early on in your writing, you can expect to rewrite this portion of your text many times before submission. You can expect your project to evolve during the research process, but also remember that you need to maintain its logical consistency from beginning to end. Each section of your essay, or each chapter of your dissertation or thesis, should form one coherent line of argumentation that is traceable throughout. Do not forget to include regular 'signposts' to your main argument. Repetition is OK. If you go back through your draft and find sections or chapters that appear to stand out or do not flow with the preceding or following sections, you may want to go back and see if you can formulate transition sentences between the sections or chapters. If that does not work, you may need to consider whether this particular section is relevant to your overall thesis.

## Try to Visualize Your Argument

We now turn to four general tips that you might find useful in the research and writing process. The first is to visualize your argument, the second is to start writing as early as possible, the third is to always keep research ethics in mind, and the fourth is to become a good time manager.

One major problem with longer writing projects is that you may lose sight of your overall argument. In fact, you may start your essay asking one question, and in the end find yourself answering a completely different question. Alternatively, you may find yourself making arguments that are disjunctured, or lack adequate support, because you have missed key steps along a causal pathway. One way to help make sure that you do not fall into the trap of starting your project with a coherent idea and ending up with a finished project that lacks structure or fails to respond to the research question that you asked, is to map your overall argument. Recall in Chapter 2, where we noted Van Evera's (1997) injunction that good theory should be arrow diagrammable. While not every social process will lend itself to this kind of simple schematic, it can help you map your overall argument. How do different concepts, ideas, or variables relate to each other? What exactly are you trying to say about a particular political phenomenon or issue?

If we go back to the two examples introduced in Chapter 2 – the rise of populism and how human rights matters in the foreign policies of western states – you can try to sketch some causal inferences or logical steps in argumentation to account for both in relation to the different kinds of research questions that were discussed in Chapter 4. For the second issue, you might create a diagram that represents the following argument: increased media exposure→domestic political pressure→foreign policies emphasizing humanitarian action. For the first issue, the rise of populism, you might create a diagram like this: mass migration in electoral districts where inequality is growing→populist success. These examples are simplistic and apply only to positivist projects. Your diagram may be more complex and reflect an interpretivist approach. But having such a schematic in front of you as you write the paper should help keep you focused.

## It's Never Too Early to Start Writing

We sometimes spend too much of our time reading background literature on our topics. After all, on almost any topic of interest in PIR, there is a seemingly endless and ever-growing body of literature. As a result, when it is time to write, we will find it difficult to synthesize the large body of scholarship that we have engaged with into a coherent written work.

In addition, it is also often the case that you will spend weeks or months working on data collection and analysis only to find the task of translating this data into a coherent written work is seemingly insurmountable. One way to avoid encountering writer's block is to make sure that writing is a continuous process that starts from the moment you have formulated a research question.

For example, when reading articles that are relevant to establishing your theoretical framework, write your own short review pieces about them. Try to establish how different perspectives in the literature talk to each other. What are the points of agreement? What are the points of disagreement? By doing this, you will be able to synthesize existing perspectives while also bringing out your own voice. Alternatively, just start writing about what attracted you to the topic in the first place. Maybe it was your experience studying abroad. Maybe it is related to your family history. At the very least, you will have fodder for your preface and introduction. Don't worry if large amounts of this preparatory text do not make it into your final draft. By just trying to put your observations into your own words, you will be helping yourself to better understand the issues, debates, concepts, and frameworks that you will be addressing in your final paper.

## Ethics

As noted in Chapter 3, research and work ethics are something that you should consider throughout the research and writing process. Here it is worth remembering that a good work ethic such as notetaking will help ensure that you do not inadvertently misrepresent data, misrepresent other people's findings, or misrepresent your own findings. Often, those students who get into trouble for failing to attribute someone else's ideas did not intend to commit an act of academic dishonesty, but rather they found themselves in this situation as a result of sloppy research practices. For example, if you are taking notes while reading journal articles, ensure that you make it clear at the top of the page which source you are making notes on. This is easily done by recording the full references of your sources.

Once you get to the end of your project, you should always double- and triple-check the veracity of your findings and claims. If you are using quotes from your interviews, go back and double-check that you have got them right. If you are thinking about publishing your work, you might want to confirm that your interview subjects agree to being named by sending them a short email with the quote that you will be using, and providing some context, such as the paragraph or section in which the quote appears. By taking these extra steps, you will help make sure that your work is not open to accusations of research malpractice on the part of your research participants or your readers.

## Time Management

Throughout the research and writing process, there are a number of challenges that you may encounter that could slow your progress, or may act to impede your ability to write an essay, dissertation, or thesis that reflects your own high standards of research. One common problem is that writing projects often take place over long periods of time. Although some in-class essay assignments will require you to produce a short research essay in a matter of weeks, most thesis projects at either the undergraduate or graduate level will take place over the course of at least one semester, in some cases maybe two or more semesters. As a result, it will be left largely up to you to manage your time during your project. One effective way to do this is to create internal deadlines for yourself, even if your supervisor does not require them. Ideally, working with your supervisor, you will mutually agree on a schedule of deadlines to submit the various parts of the project (topic, research question, literature review, research design, etc.), as well as a schedule of mutually convenient regular meeting times. Yes, some supervisors are more 'hands-off' and laissez-faire, but by being proactive in creating self-imposed deadlines and waystations in the process, you will be helping yourself stay on track. And you will avoid creating a situation where you have left too much to complete for the very end, which in our experience derails many projects which are otherwise well-conceived. A proposed outline for an 8-week schedule is provided in Table 12.1.

**Table 12.1** Sample writing schedule for an in-class essay that is due in two months (an 8-week schedule)

| | |
|---|---|
| **Weeks 1-2** | Background readings on topic for literature review; formulate research question and research design |
| **Weeks 3-4** | Write initial drafts of literature review and theoretical framework sections |
| **Weeks 5-6** | Data collection and data analysis |
| **Weeks 7-8** | Writing up, revising drafts for submission and assessment |

## Assessment and Feedback

When you have completed your essay, thesis, or dissertation, you are ready to submit your writing for assessment. At this point, you will have navigated a number of research choices: (1) selecting your research topic, (2) crafting your research question, (3) drawing up your research design, (4) selecting your strategies for data collection and analysis, and (5) writing up. At the end of this process, you will have most likely gone through many draft versions of your essay or thesis before submission. However, this is not the end of the research process. Rather, a novice researcher in PIR usually still has to face assessment.

Assessment can take on a number of different formats. Most of the time, essays assigned as part of a class will be assessed by your professor. Your feedback will likely be delivered in written form, and sometimes you will also receive a grading rubric with specific evaluation criteria. A grading rubric may be provided to you in your course syllabus or when you are given your assignment (if it hasn't, don't be afraid to ask for one!), and may align with the chapter division of this book. For example, you might have specific assessment criteria that relate to whether or not you have asked a feasible research question, whether or not you have adequately surveyed the literature, whether or not you have adequately justified your methodology and research data, the extent to which you have effectively collected and analyzed your data, and whether or not you adequately responded to your research question. When reviewing your assessment, remember that your actual grade is just an overall indicator of your general performance. Carefully review your instructor's written feedback as this will offer valuable tips for improving your analytical writing for your next assignment.

Sometimes you might find yourself being asked to prepare for an oral defense of a thesis or dissertation. This is sometimes the case for undergraduate and master's theses, and is almost always the case for terminal degrees, such as PhDs. Here, we will focus more on the former as the latter will vary greatly, depending on the country in which you are studying. And also, for a PhD defense, you should receive preparatory guidance from your supervisor, who will be aware of the expectations and norms within your institution.

In case you are asked to prepare a defense for an undergraduate or master's thesis, you should remember that the purpose of this exercise is for you to demonstrate knowledge of your particular topic and effectively justify the choices you have made during the research process. In some European countries, a master's thesis defense is a mere formality that follows the assessment of your thesis and will take place in the context of a graduation ceremony where your supervisor will be present. In other contexts, such as in some master's programs in Japan and other countries, you will be expected to provide an oral justification of your research choices and respond to questions from a second reader. You might think about why you asked your research question in the context of the existing literature and its relevance to the real world. Why have you settled on your particular research design? How have you justified your choices in terms of methodology and methods? Your defense, in other words, is your opportunity to justify your research choices.

## Research and Writing for a Broader Audience: Publishing Your Work

The craft of research will open many doors for you. And, like an artist maintains a portfolio of artistic work, and a journalist maintains a portfolio of articles, your research papers will constitute part of your growing research portfolio, which will serve to demonstrate your mastery of the skills discussed in this textbook.

Once you have completed your assessment and received your feedback, you might feel motivated to say more about your work. If this is the case, let us now turn to a couple of options that you might want to consider to help your research reach a wider audience. Your interest in research means that you most likely want your work to be read by an audience that goes beyond your professors and classroom instructors. To be sure, you likely selected your topic because of some passion for the subject, as well as a strong interest in the field of PIR and a strong desire to contribute to broader scholarly or policy debates. In some cases, you might want to work on publishing your findings in a scholarly journal, or you might want to rework your essay into a research proposal in order to secure funding from a research funding body or to gain admittance to a PhD program. On the other hand, you might be writing on a topic that is both topical and policy relevant. In this case, you might want to consider writing a policy brief or an op-ed. The following sections will walk you through some of the options you might consider in order to help your research reach a wider audience.

## Academic Publishing

Sometimes research papers that start off as in-class essays can inspire you to make a significant enough contribution to a field such that later on your work might be worth considering for publication in an academic journal. When writing a lengthier thesis, we noted that you should look at published peer-reviewed journal articles to get a sense of how to format your own work. The overall thesis structure is generally reflected in peer-reviewed articles, with a few adjustments. For example, if you have divided your thesis into separate chapters, you will need to streamline your submission to a peer-reviewed journal into a single-article format. However, before we turn to how to transform your essay, thesis, or dissertation into a paper that can be submitted to a journal, let us first go step by step through questions you will need to consider before embarking on the path of academic publishing.

The first task you will have before you is selecting a target journal for your submission. In PIR there are a number of journals that specifically solicit papers from students. Examples are *The Undergraduate Journal of Politics and International Affairs* or *The Pi Sigma Alpha Undergraduate Journal of Politics*, or international affairs reviews edited and published by students (see Table 12.2 for more on these journals). Submitting a manuscript early in your career can help you gain valuable experience in the long and rigorous process of academic publishing.

**Table 12.2**  Journals that publish undergraduate research

| Journal title | Types of submission | Website |
|---|---|---|
| *The Undergraduate Journal of Politics and International Affairs* | This open access journal only accepts original single-authored work that received a first-class mark in the UK system, or its equivalent. | www.ujpir-journal.com |
| *The Pi Sigma Alpha Undergraduate Journal of Politics* | Pi Sigma Alpha is a national political science honor society based in the United States. Its undergraduate journal accepts papers written by undergraduates from any major that are of relevance to political science. | www.psajournal.org |

Remember, though, that there are many different journals out there that claim to be scholarly outlets, but as we noted in Chapter 5, not all of them are reputable. A quick look at works published in any journal will help you to evaluate whether the one you are considering is well regarded. When doing your literature review, did you see the journal cited in the works you have cited? In general, this is a good rule of thumb to keep in mind when thinking about academic journals. Another thing you will have to consider is the 'fit' between your paper and the journal. If you aren't speaking to the same debates discussed in the pages of the journal to which you would like to submit, this is a good indicator that your paper might not be a good fit for this particular journal. You might even try and write to the journal's editors to inquire if your article is of interest. You can find names and contact information on the journal's website. But the first step should be consulting with your supervisor, who will likely have experience in academic publishing.

## From Essay, Thesis, or Dissertation to a Peer-reviewed Article

As noted in the section above, if you decide that you want to try to publish your work, you will need to keep in mind the basic structure of the research essay that was presented in Chapter 11. You should make sure that your submission follows this basic structure. Unlike many essays or papers for classes, journal articles will require an abstract. Some journals permit the submission of shorter pieces in the form of either research notes, which are normally concise snapshots of ongoing fieldwork, or policy notes, which are short-form articles that directly engage with public policy debates. Different types of submissions are listed in Table 12.3.

**Table 12.3** Types of submission

| Submission type | Description | Word length |
| --- | --- | --- |
| Research article | Original scholarly research presented in full-length article format. | 8,000-10,000 (see journal for specific guidance) |
| Research notes | Shorter than research articles, can be more policy- or practitioner-focused, focus on the presentation of new fieldwork data, or reflections on personal fieldwork experience. | 5,000 (see journal for specific guidance) |
| Review article/ essay | Usually focuses on presenting readers with the state of the art in a particular field or updates readers on new literature. | 5,000 (see journal for specific guidance; some journals will have maximum word limits that are significantly lower) |
| Responses to articles | Usually responses are written by established scholars as a reply to an article previously published in a journal. Normally response pieces would contest particular arguments put forth in the previously published piece. | 1,000-2,000 (see journal for specific guidance as word limits on responses can vary significantly) |

If your goal is to publish a full-length journal article, you will need to keep in mind that most journals in PIR will consider papers in the range of 8,000–12,000 words in length. If your essay is only 5,000 words, you will need to develop your argument, evidence, or analysis further. On the other hand, if your graduate thesis is 20,000 words, you will have to make choices about what parts will need to be eliminated in order to cut it down to a journal-appropriate length. For non-research article submissions, such as policy or research notes published by think-tanks and other organizations, you may be able to submit a shorter piece. However, be sure to read your journal's submission guidelines closely in order to get a sense of what kinds of submission your journal will consider, if any, for non-research essays. Journal websites will contain detailed instructions, including citation style conventions (to which you should adhere closely).

Once you have submitted your article, your submission will first be reviewed by an editor or an editorial team. If the editor or editorial team decides that your submission is potentially a good fit for the journal and is of high enough quality to send on to peer review, your article will then be reviewed by two or three scholars, who will provide the editors, and you, with written feedback. The reviewers will make recommendations to reject, or to reject but consider a resubmission, or to accept with minor changes, or simply to accept your submission for publication. Often reviews will contain mixed, and at times contradictory, recommendations, and it is up to the journal's editor(s) to point out to you the feedback they consider to be most important and valuable. The review process for academic journals is 'double blind', which means your identity will not be disclosed to the reviewers, nor will you know who has reviewed your work.

## Op-Ed Writing

It is not uncommon for advanced undergraduate or graduate students to want to inform public debates on politically salient issues. Today, there are numerous op-ed outlets for young researchers (see Table 12.4). Some newer outlets aim to publish almost exclusively work by academics, such as *The Conversation* and *The Monkey Cage*, whereas other outlets remain more traditional in their scope, such as major international newspapers that publish op-ed pieces by a wide range of authors. *Foreign Policy* and *Foreign Affairs* are well-regarded venues for commentary on international relations and foreign policy. Other new outlets such as *The International Policy Digest* aim to give voice to writers and points of view whose voices are often not heard, including undergraduate students. While the options in Table 12.4 are just a handful of examples, there are numerous outlets that welcome policy-oriented op-ed submissions.

Like journals, you will find that general readership outlets will have their own specific instructions and guidance for submission, and it is essential that you follow them if you want your piece to be seriously considered. Timing is everything. You should look closely at the news cycle, and pitch a piece when your area of expertise can 'hook' to the latest headlines. When thinking about how to structure an op-ed, remember that you normally have to fit your key arguments into a short 800–1000-word article. This means that you need to make sure that the opening lines of your op-ed both adequately set the stage for your contribution and catch the reader's attention. Make sure that you have distilled your opinion into a single and compelling take-home argument for the reader – a punchline. In 800 words you won't have enough space to make multiple nuanced points on a single issue. Avoid any academic jargon and keep the argument simple.

**Table 12.4**   Policy writing outlets in PIR

| | | |
|---|---|---|
| *The Monkey Cage* | Published by the *Washington Post*, this blog publishes short policy pieces that highlight policy-relevant research in Political Science and International Relations by novice researchers and established scholars alike. | www.washingtonpost.com/news/monkey-cage |
| *War on the Rocks* | This website solicits submissions for short works on conflict- and war-related issues in Political Science and International Relations. This website publishes contributions from scholars and security professionals. | https://warontherocks.com |
| *The Conversation* | This website aims to increase the impact of academic research through the publication of short think pieces for a general audience. | https://theconversation.com |
| *Open Democracy* | This website brings together a mix of investigative journalism, policy pieces by decision-makers, and academics. | www.opendemocracy.net |
| *International Policy Digest* | An op-ed venue that aims to give voice to writers around the world who are often marginalized, including undergraduate students. | https://intpolicydigest.org |
| *Project Syndicate* | The website invites unsolicited contributions across a wide range of fields and expertise from qualified writers. | www.project-syndicate.org |

## Tips for Op-Ed Writing

- Read lots of published op-eds in top media outlets to become familiar with the genre.
- Keep it short.
- Bottom line up front - i.e., make sure that you get to the point, or your main argument, quickly.
- Have a punchline.
- Link your op-ed to the latest headlines.
- Avoid going off on tangential arguments.
- Don't worry too much about the title; often editors will come up with a title for you.

There are a some key differences that you will need to keep in mind when writing for a policy or general audience as opposed to an academic one. One is that when writing for policy audiences, at least some of your readers are ideally decision-makers in your field, and your aim is to demonstrate how your take on a particular issue is the right one. You need to establish this up front. There is no need to take your readers through a survey of existing literature or to emphasize the nuance of your argument. Get to the point in the first few sentences. Another is that your writing style has to be compelling. Unlike academic writing, it does not have to be formal. Don't be afraid to use colorful analogies and metaphors, or literary devices. One well-know opinion writer, Tom Friedman of the *New York Times*, uses such tools liberally. Op-eds do not have the same standards of evidence as academic papers. However, some media venues require substantiation through the use of hyperlinks to various kinds of internet-based sources, from media reports to primary documents. Finally, we have previously emphasized that scholarly PIR research should be devoid of normative claims. By contrast, by design op-eds should be full of them, or at least have one normative claim. In fact, many if not most op-eds take a strong position, or make an explicit policy proposal.

Let's say you want to turn your paper on populist parties into an op-ed. The best opportunity for this would be to time it with some news item related to the subject. Perhaps a populist party has just done well in an election in one country, or a populist president failed in her reelection bid in another. This would be a perfect opportunity to jump in to the public debate with your in-depth knowledge of populism and help interpret these results for a broad public in a compelling, creative, and novel way. You could then make a prediction, or a policy proposal. Many US-based media outlets prefer that submissions be related to US foreign policy concerns. Or, if you want to adhere more closely to your research findings, a venue like *The Monkey Cage* or *The Conversation* may be better.

## Policy Briefs and Policy Papers

Policy briefs and papers are yet another kind of writing, distinct from both op-eds and academic articles. They are meant to provide clear, concise analysis and advice on a particular issue of interest to policymakers. Policy briefs and papers contain a summary of a particular issue, the options to deal with it, and some recommendations on the best options to address it. Like op-eds, policy briefs and papers should be free of academic jargon and theory. They are aimed at government policymakers and others who are interested in formulating or influencing policy, such as members of parliament. Policy briefs and papers can take different formats, but they almost always start with some kind of *executive summary* instead of the more familiar academic abstract. The executive summary highlights the key points, or 'take aways,' allowing someone to quickly understand the bottom line of the longer policy brief. Substantiation for the key points highlighted in the executive summary would follow in the lengthier brief. For examples of policy briefs and guidelines for submission, you can visit the websites of the *European Council on Foreign Relations, Brookings Institution, Cato Institute, Carnegie Endowment for International Peace, US Institute for Peace*, or the *Rand Corporation*, as they all regularly publish updated policy papers on a wide range of topics in PIR. There are a small number of academic journals in the PIR field that specifically solicit policy-focused pieces, which fall somewhere in between an academic article and a policy brief. These include *Global Policy*, which accepts submissions for 'Policy Insight' papers, which 'are critical analyses of developments in policy design, policy making and policy implementation' (Global Policy 2019).

Your paper on why and when western states incorporate human rights into their foreign policy may be a good candidate for submission as a policy brief. You could extract one of your cases and analyze it in depth. Perhaps you have written about the failure of western states to put pressure on the Cambodian regime of Hun Sen over its attacks on democratic freedoms and its dismal record on human rights. Your policy paper could explain why it is not in the interests of Europe and the United States to turn a blind eye to autocracy in Cambodia. Usually, to catch the ear of policymakers, you will want to avoid couching your argument entirely in human rights considerations. The best policy papers relate issues such as human rights to national interest, because, after all, this is what policymakers *have* to care about. So perhaps you can note that Hun Sen's rule is hardly a recipe for long-term stability. Stability is something that all states care about. Notice that, as with op-eds, it is appropriate and encouraged to include normative claims in policy briefs. But, like academic papers, they should be backed up with extensive evidence.

## Chapter Summary

This chapter has provided some general advice for making sure your research and writing process goes as smoothly as possible. But there is no need to worry if you get stuck, or hit a roadblock. We all do at some point, and this is simply a sign that we are thinking critically about our own work, which is a good thing. What is important is that we continue to work through these challenges. You might choose to resolve your problem at a later stage and go on to another part of the research and writing process. You might alternatively need to rethink a decision you thought you had already taken, such as your research design or the scope of your topic and question.

We research PIR because we want to say something about how the world around us works. Your research papers are an expression of your passion for understanding politics and international affairs. As PIR are about choices made by human beings, you might wish to inform these individuals and the choices they make through your research. Certainly you can try to do this through the publication of academic articles, and the careful application of methodology and methods. After all, our research has to be rigorous in order to make an impact. Sometimes academic research – such as Joseph Nye's (2004) elucidation of 'soft power' – makes it into the mainstream. But to communicate your research to a broader audience, you may also consider contributing an op-ed or a policy brief that summarizes the findings of your research and translates them into concrete policy proposals. You could also amplify your research through Twitter and other social media. Indeed, one of the most satisfying things about PIR research is when we help others better understand contentious politics in the complex and rapidly changing world around us.

━━━━━━━━ Suggested Further Reading ━━━━━━━━

Elsevier. n.d. *Publishing with Elsevier: Step-by-Step*. Available at: www.elsevier.com/authors/journal-authors/submit-your-paper
This Web tutorial provides some relevant tips and advice for the journal's selection and submission process, but they are also relevant to other publishers.

Harvard Kennedy School Communications Program. n.d. *How to Write an OpEd or Column.* Available at: https://projects.iq.harvard.edu/files/hks-communications-program/files/new_seglin_how_to_write_an_oped_1_25_17_7.pdf

This concise Web resource provides a summary of what you will need to consider when writing an op-ed, such as elements of style and how to present your research for a general audience.

Lipson, Charles. 2005. *How to Write a BA Thesis: A Practical Guide from your First Ideas to your Finished Paper*. Chicago, IL: University of Chicago Press. See Part V, pp. 233-300.
Part V of Lipson's guide on writing a BA thesis, while addressed primarily to undergraduates enrolled at institutions in the United States, provides a number of tips on how to work efficiently, overcome problems, and manage your time, among other points of advice.

# GLOSSARY

**Abstract** A one-paragraph summary of your research provided at the beginning of a scholarly journal article or dissertation. It justifies the relevance of the work and provides the research question, a brief explanation of the methodology or methods used, and key findings.

**Active citation** The practice of using hyperlinks to an annotated excerpt from the original source.

**Agent–structure debate** A debate revolving around the question of whether or not events are determined by the choices of individual decision-makers or whether they are determined by structural causes, such as institutions or socio-economic factors.

**Annotated bibliography** An organized list of citations to articles, books, and other sources. In addition to the reference entry for the source, it also includes an annotation that evaluates the relevance, accuracy, and quality of the source.

**Anonymization** The process of concealing the identity of research participants in order to protect participants from harm that may result through their identification as research participants.

**Archival research** A type of qualitative data collection which involves seeking and extracting data from archival records. Especially used by historians.

**Attribution** Giving credit to the source of an idea or words; it is done in research through referencing.

**Behavioralism** An approach to Politics and International Relations (PIR) that posits that natural science methods can be imported into the social sciences.

**Bias** A systematic error that affects the outcomes of a study.

**Bimodal distribution** A distribution in which most values are clustered around two peaks.

**Bivariate analysis** Analysis of two variables in order to determine if a relationship exists between them.

**Bivariate regression analysis** A statistical test that allows for researchers to see whether or not a relationship exists between two variables.

**Categorization** Refers to the process of creating categories, which can be either deductive or inductive.

**Case** An individual observation of an empirical phenomenon.

**Case-oriented research design** Research design in which findings or generalizations are drawn from the in-depth examination of cases.

**Case selection** The process (and logic) of choosing observations for a small-N research design.

**Case study method** The strategies used in a **case-oriented research design** and case study research in PIR more broadly.

**Causal effects** The outcomes brought about by a posited causal variable.

**Causal inference** A statement that posits a causal relationship between variables on the basis of observed **causal effects**.

**Causal mechanisms** The conditions or pathways that link a causal variable to an outcome.

**Causation** Causation implies that a change in one variable brings about a change in another.

**Citation** The process of attributing ideas you have borrowed from other scholars.

**Coding** The categorization and quantification of material for analysis. Coding is often used to categorize unstructured data gathered by the researcher for entry into **datasets**.

**Conceptual definition** The precise definition of a term; it is general in nature and out-lines the main dimensions of a phenomenon.

**Confidence interval** A range of values that is likely to include a population value with a certain degree of confidence.

**Confidence level (or probability level)** The probability that can be expected to fall within a specified range of values.

**Confounding factor/variable** An 'extra' variable or extraneous influence that was not accounted for but that affects the outcome of a study.

**Constructivism** This term has been used to describe both a theoretical approach to International Relations and a broader epistemological tradition referred to in this book as intepretivism, which emphasized the need to interrogate social meaning.

**Content analysis** A form of data analysis that allows researchers to examine large amounts of data derived from social communication through their categorization and **coding**.

**Content validity** A way to test for validity where concepts are broken down into their major attributes and each one is measured.

**Continuous variables** Variables that have numerical values and that can be measured along a continuum. They can be interval or ratio variables.

**Correlation** Correlation refers to the co-variance of two variables. Because a change in one variable appears to coincide with the change in another, it is often confused with **causation**.

**Critical juncture** Periods of time where the constraints exerted by institutions are less-ened, and elite choices can put in place new institutions that will in turn constrain the choices of future elites.

**Critical Theory** An approach to studying the social sciences that pays special attention to the role of discourse, power, and ideas. It emerged from a group of scholars known as the Frankfurt School.

**Cross-sectional design** A type of observational research design that allows for compari-sons of different population groups at a single point in time.

**Cross-tabulation (or cross-tab)** A method that quantitatively analyzes the relationship between multiple variables. By grouping variables together, it enables researchers to find trends and patterns between different variables.

**Data** Facts and information collected for analysis.

**Data analysis** The process of systematically applying various methods and techniques to describe and illustrate, condense and recap, and evaluate data.

**Dataset** A collection of numerical information about a set of cases.

**Decision matrix** A chart with values in rows and columns that allows for systematic identification, analysis, and rating of the strength of relationships between datasets.

**Decision tree** A tool of formal models using a flowchart-like diagram to represent decision points and their respective costs and payoffs.

**Deductive reasoning** The testing of theoretical propositions against empirical data.

**Dependent variable** The object that requires explanation or a particular outcome that you wish to explain.

**Descriptive statistics** A form of **statistical analysis** that provides a means to describe our data; it is often used to help present or visualize trends or to collect data.

**Direction of the relationship** The relationship between two variables, describing whether they go up and down together or not. Direction can be positive or negative.

**Discourse analysis** A form of qualitative data analysis that focuses on the interpretation of linguistic forms of communication.

**Distribution** How a dataset is distributed or dispersed around the typical value or the **measure of central tendency**. There are three types of distribution: normal distribution, skewed distribution, and bimodal distribution.

**Document-based research** The use of various kinds of documents as a source of quantitative or qualitative empirical data.

**Efficient causality** Efficient causality assumes that a known dependent variable can be causally linked back to an independent variable.

**Emergent causality** Assumes outcomes are unknowable at the outset of research. Rather, emergent causality sees causality as an emergent condition that opens up possibilities for action.

**Endnotes** A reference that appears at the end of a book or article or at the end of a section or chapter.

**Endogeneity** A situation in a statistical model where there is a correlation between an independent variable and something about your dependent variable that you have not accounted for.

**Epistemology** The study of knowledge and how knowledge is produced.

**Error** The difference between the values that are obtained through a study and the actual values.

**Experiment** See experimentation.

**Experimental research design** A controlled study in which subjects are assigned to groups and treatment is applied to only one group.

**Experimentation** Is a scientific method imported from the natural sciences that tests **hypotheses** to determine if a conjectured relationship or process will either verify or falsify these **hypotheses**.

**Explanatory variables** Variables that explain a certain outcome or **dependent variable**.

**Exploratory research** Research that helps define a concept or begin to explore a relationship.

**Extended case methodology** A research method that uses specific empirical cases to generate general principles from concrete observations.

**External validity** The degree to which the findings of a study can be applied to the population at large; it refers to whether a population is representative of a **sample**. External validity is most often ensured by attempts to minimize **selection bias**.

**Face validity** The degree to which a set of data appears valid in terms of its stated aims.

**Falsifiable** A characteristic of a good theory or hypothesis, meaning that it can be found false through experimentation or observation.

**Field experiment** A study conducted in the everyday or natural environment of the participants. This makes it hard to control extraneous variables.

**Field research** The gathering of primary data at an external research site.

**Focus groups** A form of group interview in which a facilitator leads a discussion on a specific topic in groups of six to ten participants. Generally, researchers will carry out multiple focus group discussions on a given topic.

**Footnotes** A reference printed at the bottom of a page.

**Formal models** The representation of complex reality in a stylized form, often using mathematics.

**Formalization** The translation of verbal arguments or statements into a mathematical form.

**Game theory** The application of mathematics to study strategic interactions in PIR.

**Generalizability** The degree to which one can extend findings from a study conducted on a sample population to the general population.

**Gini coefficient** A statistical measure of inequality or concentration in a country's income distribution.

**Grounded theory** Uses inductive reasoning and involves the construction of theories through the methodical gathering and analysis of data.

**Historical Comparative Research** See Historical Institutionalism.

**Historical Institutionalism** A qualitative research strategy that examines political, economic, and social change in institutions over time. Also referred to as **historical comparative research**.

**Human Development Index (HDI)** A summary measure that assesses a country's overall development based on dimensions of human development: life expectancy, education level, and income. It is published annually by the United Nations Development Programme (UNDP).

**Human subjects** Your research participants.

**Hypothesis** A statement that makes a claim as to a relationship between two or more variables, usually your independent and dependent variables.

**Hypothesis testing** The use of statistics and other tools to determine if a stated hypothesis can be accepted or not.

**Independent variable** Something that is conjectured to explain or cause the **dependent variable**.

**Inductive reasoning** The generation of theoretical propositions out of our empirical observations.

**Inferential statistics** The use of statistical tests to reach conclusions about causality.

**Informed consent** A voluntary agreement to participate in a research study. As a basic ethical obligation and a legal requirement, the participants must be made aware of the research and its risks.

**Internal validity** The extent to which results are attributable to the independent variables and not to other extraneous or confounding factors. Internal validity therefore creates confidence in the accuracy of the results of the study.

**Interpretive ethnographic research** A method for studying the ways in which a social group constructs meanings and reality.

**Interpretivism** One of two broad epistemological traditions in International Relations, the other being **positivism**. It rejects the notion that natural science methods can help to explain the world around us, and instead focuses on embedded social meanings through the interrogation of ideas, norms, beliefs, and values. This tradition has also been referred to as **constructivism**, **reflectivism**, or **post-positivism**.

**Inter-rater reliability** Also known as inter-coder reliability, this is the degree to which two or more independent raters (or coders or evaluators) agree in their implementation of a rating system.

**Intersubjective** Intersubjective understandings refer to the observation that agents are constituted through their interactions with other agents. These processes of interaction, illuminated through discourse help us understand how the social world is constituted.

**Intertextuality** An evaluative criterion for interpretive research that examines the repetition of a particular term or idea across a number of sources.

**Interval data** A level of measurement in which the order and difference between points are meaningful and standardized.

**Interview** A form of qualitative data collection whereby the researcher asks questions of a research participant. Interviews can take on many forms. The most common are **structured**, **semi-structured** and **unstructured interviews**.

**Interview consent forms** A document which is prepared for field research that allows you to secure the informed consent of interviewees.

**Introduction** The section of a research paper that presents the research questions and provides and overview of the argument and contribution.

**Keyword search** The use of key terms in database search boxes to find relevant articles and publications. The search terms represent the main concepts in the research topic.

**Laboratory experiment** A study conducted in an environment that provides a high level of control over causal variables.

**Large-N** This refers to a large number of cases, or *n*s.

**Leading question** A question that prompts or encourages a desired answer.

**Level of measurement** The relationship among the values that are assigned to a variable, important for determining which statistical tool to employ.

**Literature review** An analytical survey of published research on a topic related to the research question. It analyzes, organizes, and contextualizes the existing scholarship so as to identify gaps and other shortcomings that the writer's essay, dissertation, or thesis will address.

**Main argument** Also called a thesis statement, the overarching 'punchline' of your paper – how you answer your research question in a nutshell.

**Majority** A group that constitutes more than half of the total number.

**Margin of error** A statistical expression of the amount of random sampling error in the results of a study.

**Mean** A commonly used **measure of central tendency** that represents the average.

**Measure of central tendency** A summary statistic that describes a dataset using a single value that represents the center point. The three main measures are **mode**, **median**, and **mean**.

**Measurement** The assignment of numeric values to establish the exact properties of a concept.

**Measurement error** The difference between the measured quantity and the actual value; it consists of random error and systematic error.

**Median** A commonly used **measure of central tendency** that represents the value that falls at the center of a distribution.

**Methodological Pluralism** Refers to attentiveness and openness to different **methodologies** in PIR research.

**Methodology** The study of ways through which we acquire knowledge.

**Methods** The tools and strategies we use in research to collect or analyze data.

**Mode** A commonly used **measure of central tendency** that represents the most frequently occurring value.

**Most different systems (MDS) research design** A method involving the selection of cases that are as different as possible on potential independent variables but nevertheless have a common outcome on the dependent variable.

**Most similar systems (MSS) research design** A method involving the selection of cases that share a number of similar attributes but differ on an important outcome.

**Multimethod research** A research design that uses a combination of two or more qualitative or quantitative research methods in a single research study.

**Multivariate regression analysis** A statistical test that allows for researchers to test whether or not a relationship exists between three or more variables.

**Narratives** A qualitative research concept that focuses on how memories are constructed in the form of stories about past events, such as wars or political struggles.

**Nash equilibrium** A concept in formal models that refers to the optimal outcome or stable state in which participants have no incentive to deviate from their initial strategy.

**Naturalism** See positivism.

**Nominal data** This is the most basic level of measurement. Variables are labeled without providing any quantitative value. Nominal data are not presented in any particular order, nor do they indicate the amount of the thing being measured.

**Normal distribution** A distribution that has a peak in the middle and symmetrically distributed values on both sides. The **mean**, **median**, and **mode** are the same. It is sometimes called a 'bell curve.'

**Normative** Your beliefs or commitments to an issue, which will inevitably shape your research agenda.

**Normative arguments** Arguments based on your beliefs or commitments to an issue.

**Null hypothesis** A type of hypothesis which states that there is no relationship between the variables.

**Observational research design** A non-experimental design in which variables are not controlled or manipulated. Rather, subjects are observed and variables are measured without assigning any treatment or intervention.

**Official documents** Published documents released by a state, an organization, or a business.

**Ontological puzzle** This refers to the types of questions that can be of interest to interpretive researchers. It is contrasted with cause-and-effect puzzles of interest to positivist researchers.

**Ontology** The study of being, or the nature of social entities.

**Open-ended interview** A way of gathering information in an interview that does not entail offering a menu of possible responses.

**Operational definition** A description of a variable in specific, measurable terms.

**Operationalization** Defining concepts in such a way that they can be turned into numerical form.

**Ordinal data** A level of measurement in which data are listed in order, or ranked, and are more precise than nominal measures, although the categories remain mutually exclusive.

**Outlier** A data point or case that differs or deviates significantly from other values or cases.

**Parenthetical citation** The citation of an original source in the main text, allowing readers to immediately see where the information comes from.

**Parsimonious theory** The simplest possible explanation for the broadest possible phenomenon.

**Path dependency** The proposition that past decisions, or events, constrain the policy options available to decision-makers.

**Pearson chi-squared test** A statistical test used to evaluate the relationship between categorical data.

**Pearson correlation coefficient** A measure of the strength of the linear relationship between two variables.

**Peer review** A formal process in scientific research in which the quality and validity of an article and journal are assessed anonymously (i.e. **double-blind** review). Subject area experts carefully evaluate the manuscript before it is approved for publication.

**Per capita GDP** A measure of a country's economic output per person; it is derived by dividing the country's GDP by the size of the population.

**Philosophy of science** A field of philosophy concerned with the foundations, methods, and impact of science.

**Plagiarism** The intentional or unintentional use of someone else's words or ideas in your own work without appropriate attribution.

**Positionality** The social and political context that creates your identity according to factors such as race, class, gender, sexuality, and ability status.

**Positive theory** Theory development in the empirical tradition that focuses on explaining the relationship between variables.

**Positivism** One of two broad epistemological traditions in PIR, the other being **interpretivism**; it embraces the scientific method to explain the world around us and assumes that knowledge can be accumulated through experimentation and observation.

**Post-positivism** See intepretivism.

**Primary source documents** Original documents, authored by individuals who have had direct access to the information they are describing or who have directly experienced a particular event.

**Probability sample** A sampling technique in which all persons in the target population have a known and equal chance of being selected for the survey.

**Process-tracing** A qualitative method in which we carefully trace the story of how a change in one variable is linked to a change in another variable. For interpretivist research, process-tracing can also be used to trace the genealogy of a particular idea or concept.

**Qualitative comparative analysis** An approach to small-$n$ research design that assumes that the inherent complexity of social phenomena results in multiple causal variables interacting to produce an outcome.

**Qualitative methods** Data collection and data analysis strategies that rely upon the collection, and analysis, of non-numeric data. This does not have to be restricted to textual data and can also include speech, film, and other forms of communicative works.

**Quantitative methods** Data collection and data analysis strategies that rely upon collecting or coding data in numeric form in an attempt to determine whether or not a relationship exists between two or more variables. This entails the use of either **statistical analysis** or **formal models**.

**Question-based research** A research project in which the researcher poses a question that typically attempts to explain an uncertain relationship between two or more variables (**positivism**) or that problematizes our understanding of an existing variable (**interprevitism**).

**Random digit dialing (RDD) sampling** An example of probability sampling in which a sample of households is drawn from a set of telephone numbers.

**Random sample** A data collection method in surveying in which every potential research participant has an equal chance of being selected for participation. Random samples are sought so as to guard against **selection bias**.

**Ratio data** Similar to interval data, a level of measurement in which the difference between points is meaningful and standardized, and there is a real absolute zero. This means that it is impossible to have negative values.

**Rational choice theory** A framework to understand decision making; it assumes that an individual (or state) will act in their self-interest and make decisions among a range of options based on the maximum utility they can derive.

**Referencing** The acknowledgment of the contribution of other researchers. Not only does referencing strengthen the writer's arguments, but it also allows readers to find the original source.

**Referencing style** A set of rules and standards for acknowledging ideas, facts, and quotes by other authors or other publications and resources. Commonly used styles are APA style, MLA style, Oxford style, Harvard style, and Chicago style.

**Reflexivity** An approach to research that emphasizes self-reflection during the research process and attentiveness to your own role as a researcher.

**Reliability** The level of consistency of a test, experiment, or other measuring device; in other words, it measures the extent to which it produced the same results in repeated measurements.

**Replicability** The possibility of repeating a research study and generating similar results in order to establish its validity.

**Research** An activity in PIR in which we analyze or interpret the social world around us.

**Research design** A roadmap for how the research will go about responding to a question.

**Research notes** Short policy- or practitioner-oriented pieces or articles that focus on the presentation of new fieldwork data or reflect on fieldwork experience.

**Review essays** Essays in scholarly journals which provide an overview of the state of the PIR literature in a given area.

**Sample** The pool of potential survey or questionnaire respondents from which actual research participants are drawn.

**Sampling** The manner in which survey respondents are selected.

**Scientific method** A way of knowing that involves systematic observation and experimentation; it was first applied to making sense of the natural world, and later applied to the social sciences.

**Secondary source documents** Documents which make reference to, and analyze, primary source documents.

**Semi-structured interviews** An interview format that is commonly used because it allows the researcher not only to pose their questions, but also to ask follow-up questions that reflect the interview participant's responses.

**Simple linear regression** A statistical model that summarizes the relationship between two continuous variables by fitting a linear equation to the dataset. It is also known as the **bivariate linear regression**.

**Single case study design** A research design that examines a single case in depth, sometimes as a way to challenge a theory.

**Skewed distribution** A distribution that has a significant 'tail' on the left (**negatively skewed**) or right (**positively skewed**). For negatively skewed data, the mode is usually greater than the median, while the mean is smaller. The opposite is true for positively skewed data.

**Skewness measure** A measure of distortion from the normal distribution. Skewness can be zero, negative, or positive.

**Snowball sampling** A strategy to access human subjects during the course of **field research** in which the researcher relies on the first individuals they meet to introduce them to other potential research participants.

**Spurious relationship** This is when there appears to be a relationship between two variables but the relationship is actually produced by a third variable.

**Standard deviation** A measure of dispersion of a dataset relative to its **mean**.

**Standard error** A measure of the statistical accuracy of a sampling distribution. It is equal to the **standard deviation** of a statistical sample population.

**Statistical analysis** The analysis of large sets of numeric data either in the form of **descriptive statistics** or **inferential statistics**.

**Statistical regression** A data analysis technique used to determine how a dependent variable is affected by one or more independent variables; it is commonly used for prediction and forecasting.

**Statistical significance** The likelihood that the relationship between variables is not due to random chance.

**Straw man argumentation** A form of argumentation used to weaken or discredit an opponent's argument; it is done by presenting the opponent's argument in a distorted or misrepresented way.

**Structured interview** An interview format whereby the individual administering the interview keeps strictly to a script of questions and the respondent is asked to select from a predetermined menu of response options.

**Survey** A quantitative and qualitative research method used to collect data from a sample of respondents about their thoughts, feelings, and behaviors to draw meaningful research conclusions.

**Test-retest method** A technique that assesses the external consistency of a test. The same test is given to the same participants at different time periods and the results are then correlated.

**Theory** A set of ideas or a general proposition about how the social world works.

**Thick-description** See **thick interpretive description**.

**Thick interpretive description** A research method that is based on intensive observations and narratives; it is widely used in ethnographic research.

**Time-series design** A research design in which measurements of the same variables are taken at different points in time, often to study trends.

**Transparency** The need to be explicit and open about the methods and procedures used in research.

**Triangulation** This can either refer to a strategy for data collection, whereby the researcher relies on multiple sources of data, such as interviews, media reports, and official documents, or it can refer to a strategy for bringing together distinct research methods, such as quantitative and qualitative methods.

**Trustworthiness** Refers to the quality of our data and consists of credibility, transferability, dependability, and confirmability.

**Unit of analysis** The basic entity or subject (the who or what) of a study.

**Univariate analysis** The simplest form of quantitative analysis that focuses on a single variable.

**Unstructured interviews** An interview format that is more analogous to a conversation. The researcher will at the beginning prompt a conversation on a given topic, but then allow the conversation to evolve naturally.

**Validity** The degree to which the test, experiment, or other measuring device is truly measuring what was intended to be measured by eliminating confounding variables.

**Variable** A measurable characteristic or feature that varies.

**Visual Methods** A method that relies on the use of images, films or physical spaces as objects of analysis.

**Visual research** See **visual methods**.

**Within-case analysis** A thorough empirical study of a single case; it provides limited insights into causality by evaluating competing hypotheses against the evidence in the case.

**Works cited** A list of all sources cited and referenced in the text.

**Writer's block** An inability to continue writing; it can be brought about by a number of causes.

# REFERENCES

AAA Ethics Forum. 2012. *Principles of Professional Responsibility*. November 1. Available at: http://ethics.americananthro.org/category/statement

Achen, C. 1982. *Interpreting and Using Regression*. Thousand Oaks, CA: Sage.

Ackerly, Brooke. 2008. Feminist Methodological Reflection. In Audie Klotz and Deepa Prakash (eds.), *Qualitative Methods in International Relations*. Palgrave Macmillan, 28–42.

Ackerly, Brooke, and True, Jacqui. 2008. Reflexivity in Practice: Power and Ethics in Feminist Research on International Relations. *International Studies Review*, 10(4), 693–707.

Adcock, R., and Collier, D. 2001. Measurement Validity: A Shared Standard for Qualitative and Quantitative Research. *American Political Science Review*, 95(3), 529–546.

Allison, Graham T. 1971. *Essence of Decision: Explaining the Cuban Missile Crisis*. Boston, MA: Little, Brown.

American Anthropological Association. 2007. *American Anthropological Association's Executive Board Statement on the Human Terrain System Project*. October 31 [released on November 7]. Available at: www.aaanet.org/pdf/EB_Resolution_110807.pdf

American Anthropological Association. 2012. *Statement on Ethics: Principles of Professional Responsibility*. Arlington, VA: American Anthropological Association.

American Historical Association. 2011. *Statement on Standards of Professional Conduct* [last revised January 2011]. Available at: www.historians.org/about-aha-and-membership/governance/policies-and-documents/statement-on-standards-of-professional-conduct

American National Elections Studies. https://electionstudies.org

American Political Science Association. 2012. *Guide to Professional Ethics in Political Science*. Available at: www.apsanet.org/portals/54/Files/Publications/APSAEthicsGuide2012.pdf

Art, Robert J., and Waltz, Kenneth N. (eds.). 1993. *The Use of Force: Military Power and International Politics*. New York: University Press of America.

Ashley, Richard. 1984. The Poverty of Neorealism. *International Organization*, 38(2), 225–286.

Axinn, William G., and Pearce, Lisa D. 2006. *Mixed Method Data Collection Strategies*. Cambridge, UK: Cambridge University Press.

Ayman, S. Gulden. 2014. Turkey and Iran: Between Friendly Competition and Fierce Rivalry. *Arab Studies Quarterly*, 36(1), 6–26.

Baglione, Lisa A. 2020. *Writing a Research Paper in Political Science: A Practical Guide to Inquiry, Structure, and Methods*. Thousand Oaks, CA: Sage.

Balnaves, Mark, and Caputi, Peter. 2001. *Introduction to Quantitative Research Methods: An Investigative Approach*. London: Sage.

Barnes, Tiffany D., and Burchard, Stephanie M. 2013. 'Engendering' Politics: The Impact of Descriptive Representation on Women's Political Engagement in Sub-Saharan Africa. *Comparative Political Studies*, 46(7), 767–790.

Bates, Robert H. 1997. Comparative Politics and Rational Choice: A Review Essay. *American Political Science Review*, 91(3), 699–704.

Baylis, John, Smith, Steve, and Owens, Patricia (eds.). 2010. *The Globalization of World Politics: An Introduction to International Relations*. Oxford: Oxford University Press.

BBC News. 2014. Facebook Emotion Experiment Sparks Criticism. 30 June. Available at: https://www.bbc.com/news/technology-28051930

Bean, F. D. 2016. Changing Ethnic and Racial Diversity in the United States: A Review Essay. *Population and Development Review*, 42(1), 135–142.

Bennett, Andrew, and Checkel, Jeffrey T. (eds.). 2015. *Process Tracing*. Cambridge, UK: Cambridge University Press.

Berg, Bruce L., and Lune, Howard. 2012. *Qualitative Methods for the Social Sciences*, 8th edition. New York: Pearson.

Berg-Schlosser, Dirk. 2012. *Mixed Methods in Comparative Politics: Principles and Applications*. Basingstoke, UK: Palgrave Macmillan.

Bestor, Theodore C., Steinhoff, Patricia G., and Bestor, Victoria Lyon. 2003. *Doing Fieldwork in Japan*. Honolulu, HI: University of Hawai'i Press.

Bevir, M. 2000. *Interpretive Political Science*. Thousand Oaks, CA: Sage.

Blatter, Joachim, and Haverland, Markus. 2012. *Designing Case Studies: Explanatory Approaches in Small-N Research*. London: Palgrave Macmillan.

Blaydes, Lisa, and Chaney, Eric. 2013. The Feudal Revolution and Europe's Rise: Political Divergence of the Christian West and the Muslim World before 1500 CE. *American Political Science Review*, 107(1), 16–34.

Bleiker, Roland. 2018. *Visual Global Politics*. London: Routledge.

Blomdahl, Mikael. 2016. Bureaucratic Roles and Positions: Explaining the United States Libya Decision. *Diplomacy & Statecraft*, 27(1), 142–161.

Boduszyński, Mieczysław P. 2010. *Regime Change in the Yugoslav Successor States: Divergent Paths toward a New Europe*. Baltimore, MD: Johns Hopkins University Press.

Boduszyński, Mieczysław P. 2019. *U.S. Democracy Promotion in the Arab World: Beyond Interests vs. Ideals*. Boulder, CO: Lynne Rienner.

Boduszyński, Mieczysław P., and Christopher Lamont. 2017. The challenges of building a shared Iraqi identity. *OpenDemocracy*, November 5. Available at: www.opendemocracy.net/en/north-africa-west-asia/challenges-of-building-shared-i

Bogod, David. 2004. Nazi Hypothermia Experiments: Forbidden Data? *Anaesthesia*, 59(12), 1155–156.

Bonikowski, Bart, and Noam Gidron. 2013. Varieties of Populism: Literature Review and Research Agenda. *Weatherhead Center for International Affairs. Harvard University. Working Paper Series* 13-0004.

Bonnell, Victoria E., and Breslauer, George W. 2004. Soviet and Post-Soviet Area Studies. In David Szanton (ed.), *The Politics of Knowledge: Area Studies and the Discipline*. Los Angeles, CA: University of California Press, pp. 217–261.

Brady, Henry E., and Collier, David (eds.). 2010. *Rethinking Social Inquiry: Diverse Tools, Shared Standards*. Lanham, MD: Rowman & Littlefield.

Braumoeller, Bear F., and Sartori, Anne E. 2004. The Promise and Perils of Statistics in International Relations. In Detlef F. Sprinz and Yael Wolinsky-Nahmias (eds.), *Cases, Numbers, Models: International Relations Research Methods*. Ann Arbor, MI: University of Michigan Press, pp. 129–151.

Bryman, Alan. 2008. *Social Research Methods*, 3rd edition. Oxford: Oxford University Press.

Bunce, Valerie. 2005. The National Idea: Imperial Legacies and Post-Communist Pathways in Eastern Europe. *East European Politics and Societies*, 19(3), 406–442.

Burchill, Scott. 2001. Introduction. In Scott Burchill, Richard Devetak, Andrew Linklater, Matthew Paterson, Christian Reus-Smit and Jacqui True (eds.), *Theories of International Relations*. New York: Palgrave, pp. 1–28.

Burchill, Scott, Linklater, Andrew, Devetak, Richard, Donnelly, Jack, Nardin, Terry, Paterson, Matthew, Reus-Smit, Christian, and True, Jacqui. 2013. *Theories of International Relations*, 5th edition. New York: Palgrave Macmillan.

Cantoni, Davide, Yang, David Y., Yuchtman, Noam, and Zhang, Y. Jane. 2019. Protests as Strategic Games: Experimental Evidence from Hong Kong's Antiauthoritarian Movement. *The Quarterly Journal of Economics*, 134(2), 1021–1077.

Capoccia, Giovanni, and Kelemen, R. Daniel. 2007. The Study of Critical Junctures: Theory, Narrative and Counterfactuals in Historical Institutionalism. *World Politics*, 59(3), 341–369.

Capoccia, Giovanni, and Ziblatt, Daniel. 2010. The Historical Turn in Democratization Studies: A New Research Agenda for Europe and Beyond. *Comparative Political Studies*, 43(8/9), 931–968.

Caramani, Daniele. 2008. *Introduction to the Comparative Method with Boolean Algebra*. Thousand Oaks, CA: Sage.

Carreyrou, John. 2018. *Bad Blood: Secrets and Lies in a Silicon Valley Startup*. New York: Random House.

de Carvalho, Benjamin, Nagelhus Schia, Niels, and Guillaume, Xavier. 2019. Everyday Sovereignty: International Experts, Brokers and Local Ownership in Peacebuilding in Liberia. *European Journal of International Relations*, 25(1), 179–202.

Checkel, Jeffrey T. 2006. Tracing Causal Mechanisms. *International Studies Review*, 8(2), 362–370.

Chua, Amy. 2004. *World on Fire: How Exporting Free Market Democracy Breeds Ethnic Hatred and Global Instability*. New York, NY: Anchor.

Cohen, Dara Kay. 2013. Explaining Rape during Civil War: Cross-National Evidence (1980–2009). *American Political Science Review*, 107(3), 461–477.

Collier, David. 2011. Understanding Process Tracing. *PS: Political Science and Politics*, 44(4), 823–830.

Collier, David, and Levitsky, Steven. 1997. Democracy with Adjectives: Conceptual Innovation in Comparative Research. *World Politics*, 49(3), 430–451.

Collier, David, LaPorte, Jody, and Seawright, Jason. 2012. Putting Typologies to Work: Concept Formation, Measurement, and Analytic Rigor. *Political Research Quarterly*, 65(1), 217–232.

Collini, Stefan. 2011. Research Must Not Be Tied to Politics. The Guardian, 1 April. Available at: https://www.theguardian.com/commentisfree/2011/apr/01/research-arts-and-humanities-research-council

Connolly, William. 2004. Method, Problem, and Faith. In Ian Shapiro and Rogers M. Smith (eds.), *Problems and Methods in the Study of Politics*. Cambridge, UK: Cambridge University Press.

Connolly, William. 2005. The Evangelical-Capitalist Resonance Machine. *Political Theory*, 33(6), 869–872.

Cotton, J. 2018. A Century of Wilsonianism: A Review Essay. *Australian Journal of Political Science*, 53(3), 398–407.

Cox, Robert. 1981. Social Forces, States and World Orders: Beyond International Relations Theory. *Millennium – Journal of International Studies*, 10(2), 126–155.

David, Roman. 2011. *Lustration and Transitional Justice: Personnel Systems in the Czech Republic, Hungary, and Poland*. Philadelphia, PA: University of Pennsylvania Press.

Doyle, Michael W., and Sambanis, Nicholas. 2000. International Peacebuilding: A Theoretical and Quantitative Analysis. *American Political Science Review*, 94(4), 779–801.

Druckman, James N., Green, Donald, Kuklinski, James H., and Lupia, Arthur. 2006. The Growth and Development of Experimental Research in Political Science. *American Political Science Review*, 100(4), 627–635.

Dunning, Thad. 2012. *Natural Experiments in the Social Sciences: A Design-Based Approach*. Cambridge, UK: Cambridge University Press.

Economic and Social Research Council. 2019. *Our Core Principles*. Available at: https://esrc.ukri.org/funding/guidance-for-applicants/research-ethics/our-core-principles

Economist. 2018. *Style Guide*. London: Profile Books.

Ekiert, Grzegorz. 2015. Three Generations of Research on Post Communist Politics: A Sketch. *East European Politics and Societies*, 29(2), 323–337.

Elsevier. n.d. *Publishing with Elsevier: Step-by-Step*. Available at: www.elsevier.com/authors/journal-authors/submit-your-paper

Enloe, Cynthia. 1990. *Bananas, Beaches, and Bases: Making Feminist Sense of International Relations*. Berkeley, CA: University of California Press.

Entelis, John P. 2011. Algeria: Democracy Denied, and Revived? *The Journal of North African Studies*, 16(4), 653–678.

Eun, Yong-Soo. 2016. *Pluralism and Engagement in the Discipline of International Relations*. Basingstoke, UK: Palgrave Macmillan.

Fearon, James D. 1995. Rationalist Explanations for War. *International Organization*, 49(3), 379–414.

Fearon, James D. 2004. Why Do Some Civil Wars Last So Much Longer than Others? *Journal of Peace Research*, 41(3), 275–301.

Fearon, James D. 2017. The big problem with the North Koreans isn't that we can't trust them. It's that they can't trust us. *The Monkey Cage*, August 16. Available at: www.washingtonpost.com/news/monkey-cage/wp/2017/08/16/the-big-problem-with-north-korea-isnt-that-we-cant-trust-them-its-that-they-cant-trust-us

Feyerabend, Paul. 1993. *Against Method*, 3rd edition. London: Verso Books.

Fish, M. Steven. 2002. Islam and Authoritarianism. *World Politics*, 55(1), October, 4–37.

Friedman, Jeffrey (ed.). 1996. *The Rational Choice Controversy: Economic Models of Politics Reconsidered*, Vols 1–2. New Haven, CT: Yale University Press.

Geddes, Barbara. 1990. How the Cases You Choose Affect the Answers You Get: Selection Bias in Comparative Politics. *Political Analysis*, 2, 131–150.

Geertz, Clifford. 1973. *The Interpretation of Cultures: Selected Essays*. New York: Basic Books.

Gelman, Andrew. 2015. Fake Study on Changing Attitudes: Sometimes a Claim That is Too Good to be True, Isn't. *The Monkey Cage*, May 20. Available at: www.washingtonpost.com/news/monkey-cage/wp/2015/05/20/fake-study-on-changing-attitudes-sometimes-a-claim-that-is-too-good-to-be-true-isnt

George, Alexander L., and Bennett, Andrew. 2005. *Case Studies and Theory Development in the Social Sciences*. Cambridge, MA: The MIT Press.

Gerring, John. 2004. What is a Case Study and What is it Good for? *American Political Science Review*, 98(2), 341–354.

Gerring, John. 2007. Is There a (Viable) Crucial Case Method? *Comparative Political Studies*, 40(3), 231–253.

Gerring, John. 2012. *Social Science Methodology: A Unified Framework*, 2nd edition. Cambridge, UK: Cambridge University Press.

Gidron, Noam, and Ziblatt, Daniel. 2019. Center Right Political Parties in Advanced Democracies. *Annual Review of Political Science*, 22(1), May, 17–35.

Glaser, Barney, and Strauss, Anselm. 1967. *The Discovery of Grounded Theory*. Chicago, IL: Aldine Publishing.

Global Policy. 2019. www.globalpolicyjournal.com/contribute

*Global Times*. 2019. Traitors Seek to Separate Hong Kong and Fuel Street Violence, July 29. Available at: www.globaltimes.cn/content/1159595.shtml

Goffman, Alice. 2015. *On the Run: Fugitive Life in an American City*. New York: Picador.

Gordon, Andrew. 2003. In Theodore C. Bestor, Patricia G. Steinhoff and Victoria Lyon Bestor (eds.), *Doing Fieldwork in Japan*. Honolulu, HI: University of Hawai'i Press, pp. 261–276.

Grewal, Sharan, M., Kilavuz, Tahir, and Kubinec, Robert. 2019. *Algeria's Uprising: A Survey of Protesters and the Military*. Washington, DC: The Brookings Institution, July. Available at: www.brookings.edu/research/algerias-uprising-a-survey-of-protesters-and-the-military

Guo, S. 2018. Political Science and Chinese Political Studies – Where is Chinese Political Science Headed? *Journal of Chinese Political Science*, 23(2), 287–295.

Gustafsson, Karl. 2014. Memory Politics and Ontological Security in Sino-Japanese Relations. *Asian Studies Review*, 38(1), 71–86.

Harding, Sandra, and Norberg, Kathryn. 2005. New Feminist Approaches to Social Science Methodologies: An Introduction. *Signs*, 30(4), 2009–2015.

Hardy, Cynthia, Harley, Bill, and Phillips, Nelson. 2004. Discourse Analysis and Content Analysis: Two Solitudes? *Qualitative Methods*, 2(1), 19–22.

Harrison, Lisa, and Callan, Theresa. 2013. *Key Research Concepts in Politics & International Relations*. London: Sage.

Harvard Kennedy School Communications Program. n.d. *How to Write an OpEd or Column*. Available at: https://projects.iq.harvard.edu/files/hks-communications-program/files/new_seglin_how_to_write_an_oped_1_25_17_7.pdf

Harvey, William S. 2011. Strategies for Conducting Elite Interviews. *Qualitative Research*, 11(4), 431–441.

Hay, Colin and Wincott, Daniel. 1998. Structure, Agency, and Historical Institutionalism. *Political Studies*, 46, 951–957.

Hellyer, Hisham A. 2017. *A Revolution Undone: Egypt's Road Beyond Revolt*. Oxford: Oxford University Press.

Hollis, Martin, and Smith, Steve. 1990. *Explaining and Understanding International Relations*. Oxford: Clarendon Press.

Horiuchi, Yusaku, Imai, Kosuke, and Taniguchi, Naoko. 2007. Designing and Analyzing Randomized Experiments: Application to a Japanese Election Survey Experiment. *American Journal of Political Science*, 51(3), 669–687.

Horowitz, Michael C., and Stam, Allan C. 2014. How Prior Military Experience Influences the Future Militarized Behavior of Leaders. *International Organization*, 68(3), 527–559.

Houghton, David Patrick. 2013. *The Decision Point: Six Cases in US Foreign Policy Decision Making*. Oxford: Oxford University Press.

Howard, Christopher. 2017. *Thinking Like a Political Scientist: A Practical Guide to Research Methods*. Chicago: University of Chicago Press.

Howard, Marc Morjé. 2003. *The Weakness of Civil Society in Post-Communist Europe*. Cambridge, UK: Cambridge University Press.

Imai, Kosuke, et al. 2011. Unpacking the Black Box of Causality: Learning about Causal Mechanisms from Experimental and Observational Studies. *American Political Science Review*, 105(4), 765–789.

Inglehart, Ronald, and Welzel, Christian. 2010. Changing Mass Priorities: The Link between Modernization and Democracy. *Perspectives on Politics*, 8(2), June, 551–567.

Jackson, Patrick Thaddeus. 2006. *Civilizing the Enemy: German Reconstruction and the Invention of the West*. Ann Arbor, MI: The University of Michigan Press.

Jackson, Patrick Thaddeus. 2010. *The Conduct of Inquiry in International Relations*. New York: Routledge.

Jacobsen, Karen, and Landau, Lauren B. 2003. The Dual Imperative of Refugee Research: Some Methodological and Ethical Considerations in Social Science Research and Forced Migration. *Disasters*, 23(3), 185–206.

Jacobson, Gary C. 2015. It's Nothing Personal: The Decline of the Incumbency Advantage in US House Elections. *Journal of Politics*, 77(3), July, 861–873.

Japan Society for the Promotion of Science. n.d. *For the Sound Development of Science*. Available at: www.jsps.go.jp/j-kousei/data/rinri_e.pdf

Johnson, James. 2019. Formal Models in Political Science: Conceptual, Not Empirical. *The Journal of Politics*, 81(1), e6–e10.

Jowitt, Ken. 1992. *New World Disorder: The Leninist Extinction*. Berkeley: University of California Press.

Kahler, Miles. 1998. Rationality in International Relations. *International Organization*, 52(4), 919–941.

Kellstedt, Paul M., and Whitten, Guy D. 2009. *The Fundamentals of Political Science Research*. Cambridge, UK: Cambridge University Press.

Keohane, Raobert O. 1988. International Institutions: Two Approaches. *International Studies Quarterly*, 32(4): 379–396.

King, Gary, Keohane, Robert O., and Verba, Sydney. 1994. *Scientific Inference in Qualitative Research*. Princeton, NJ: Princeton University Press.

Kinsella, David. 2005. No Rest for the Democratic Peace. *American Political Science Review*, 99(3), 453–457.

Klotz, Audie, and Prakash, Deepa (eds.). 2008. *Qualitative Methods in International Relations: A Pluralist Guide*. New York: Palgrave.

Kramer, Adam D. I., Guillory, Jamie E., and Hancock, Jeffrey T. 2014. Experimental Evidence of Massive Scale Emotional Contagion through Social Networks. *Proceedings of the National Academy of Sciences of the United States of America (PNAS)*, 111(24), 8788–8790.

Krook, Mona Lena. 2010. Women's Representation in Parliament: A Qualitative Comparative Analysis. *Political Studies*, 58(5), 886–908.

Lai, Daniela, and Roccu, Roberto. 2019. Case Study Research and Critical IR: The Case for the Extended Case Methodology. *International Relations*, 33(1), 67–87.

Lamont, Christopher K. 2010. International Criminal Justice and the Politics of Compliance. Farnham, UK: Ashgate.

Lamont, Christopher. 2015. Research Methods in International Relations. London: Sage.

Lees, Charles. 2018. The 'Alternative for Germany': The Rise of Right-wing Populism at the Heart of Europe. *Politics*, 38(3), 295–310.

Levitsky, Steven and Ziblatt, Daniel. 2018. *How Democracies Die*. New York: Broadway Books.

Levy, Jack S. 2002. Qualitative Methods in International Relations. In Frank P. Harvey and Michael Brecher (eds.), *Evaluating Methodology in International Studies*. Ann Arbor, MI: University of Michigan Press, pp. 131–160.

Lewis-Beck, Michael S. 1986. Comparative Economic Voting: Britain, France, Germany, and Italy. *American Journal of Political Science*, 30(2), 315–346.

Lewis-Beck, Michael S., and Stegmaier, Mary. 2000. Economic Determinants of Electoral Outcomes. *Annual Review of Political Science*, 3, 183–219.

Linklater, Andrew. 1992. The Question of the Next Stage in International Relations Theory: A Critical-Theoretical Point of View. *Millennium*, 21(1), 77–98.

Lipset, Seymour Martin. (ed.). 1969. *Politics and the Social Sciences*. Oxford: Oxford University Press.

Lipset, Seymour M., and Rokkan, Stein. 1967. *Party Systems and Voter Alignments: Cross-National Perspectives*. New York: Free Press.

Lipson, Charles. 2005. *How to Write a BA Thesis: A Practical Guide from Your First Ideas to Your Finished Paper*. Chicago, IL: University of Chicago Press.

Lipson, Charles. 2018. Chapter 5: How to Build a Reading List. In *How to Write a BA Thesis: A Practical Guide from your First Ideas to your Finished Paper*, 2nd edition. Chicago, IL: University of Chicago Press, pp. 70–75.

Lipton, Eric, Williams, Brooke, and Confessore, Nicholas. 2014. Foreign Powers buy Influence at Think Tanks. *New York Times*, September 6. Available at: www.nytimes.com/2014/09/07/us/politics/foreign-powers-buy-influence-at-think-tanks.html

Lobo-Guerrero, Luis. 2013. Wondering as Research Attitude. In Mark B. Salter and Can E. Mutlu (eds.), *Research Methods in Critical Security Studies: An Introduction*. Abingdon, UK: Routledge, pp. 25–28.

Lowe, Will. 2004. Content Analysis and Its Place in the (Methodological) Scheme of Things. *Qualitative Methods*, 2(1), 25–27.

Mahoney, James. 2007. Qualitative Methodology and Comparative Politics. *Comparative Political Studies*, 40(2), 122–144.

Mahoney, James, and Goertz, Gary. 2006. A Tale of Two Cultures: Contrasting Quantitative and Qualitative Research. *Political Analysis*, 14(3), 227–249.

Mansfield, Edward D., Mutz, Diana C., and Silver, Laura R. 2015. Men, Women, Trade, and Free Markets. *International Studies Quarterly*, 59(2), June, 303–315.

Margalit, Yotam. 2013. Explaining Social Policy Preferences: Evidence from the Great Recession. *American Political Science Review*, 107(1), 80–103.

McCarthy, Nolan, and Mierowitz, Adam. 2007. *Political Game Theory: An Introduction.* Cambridge, UK: Cambridge University Press.

McLaren, Lauren. 2012. Immigration and Trust in Politics in Britain. *British Journal of Political Science*, 42(1), 163–185.

Mearsheimer, John J. 1990. Back to the Future: Instability in Europe After the Cold War. *International Security*, 15(1), 5–56.

Merritt, Richard L., and Rokkan, Stein. 1968. Comparing Nations: The Use of Quantitative Data in Cross-National Research. In *International Conference on the Use of Quantitative Political, Social, and Cultural Data in Cross-National Comparison*. New Haven, CT: Yale University Press.

Milgram, Stanley. 1963. Behavioral Study of Obedience. *The Journal of Abnormal and Social Psychology*, 67(4), 371–378.

Miragliotta, N. L. 2017. Elections and Electoral Politics: A Review Essay. *Australian Journal of Political Science*, 52(4), 615–625.

Moaz, Zeev. 2002. Case Study Methodology in International Studies: From Storytelling to Hypothesis Testing. In Frank P. Harvey and Michael Brecher (eds.), *Evaluating Methodology in International Studies*. Ann Arbor, MI: University of Michigan Press, pp. 161–186.

Moe, Kristine. 1984. Should the Nazi Research Data Be Cited? *The Hastings Center Report*, 14(6), 5–7.

Monroe, Burt L., et al. 2015. No! Formal Theory, Causal Inference, and Big Data are not Contradictory Trends in Political Science. *PS: Political Science & Politics*, 48(1), 71–74.

Moravcsik, Andrew. 2014. Transparency: The Revolution in Qualitative Research. *PS: Political Science & Politics*, 47(1), 48–53.

Morgan, Kimberly J. 2018. Gender, Right-wing Populism, and Immigrant Integration Policies in France, 1989–2012. *West European Politics*, 40(4), 887–906.

Morgenthau, Hans (revised by Kenneth W. Thompson and W. David Clinton). 2005. *Politics among Nations: The Struggle for Power and Peace*, 7th edition. New York: McGraw-Hill.

Moses, Jonathon, W. and Knutsen, Torbjorn L. 2012. *Ways of Knowing: Competing Methodologies in Social and Political Research*, 2nd edition. Basingstoke, UK: Palgrave Macmillan.

Neal, Andrew W. 2013. Empiricism without Positivism. In Mark B. Salter and Can E. Mutlu (eds.), *Research Methods in Critical Security Studies: An Introduction*. Abingdon, UK: Routledge.

Netherlands Organization for Scientific Research. 2018. *Netherlands Code of Conduct for Research Integrity*. Available at: www.nwo.nl/en/documents/nwo/policy/netherlands-code-of-conduct-for-research-integrity

Norman, Julie M. 2009. Got Trust? The Challenges of Gaining Access in Conflict Zones. In Chandra Lekha Sriram, John C. King, Julie A. Mertus, Olga Martin-Ortega and Johanna Herman (eds.), *Surviving Field Research: Working in Violent and Difficult Situations*. New York: Routledge, pp. 71–90.

Nye Jr, Joseph S. 2004. *Soft Power: The Means to Success in World Politics*. New York: Public Affairs.

Osborne, Martin J. 2004. *An Introduction to Game Theory*. New York: Oxford University Press.

Pavlaković, Vjeran. 2014. Blowing Up Brotherhood and Unity: The Fate of World War Two Cultural Heritage in Lika. In *The Politics of Heritage and Memory*. Zagreb: Sveučilište u Zagrebu.

Pavlaković, Vjeran and Perak, Benedikt. 2017. How Does This Monument Make You Feel? Measuring Emotional Responses to War Memorials in Croatia. In Tea Sindaek Andersen and Barbara Törnquist-Plewa (eds.), *The Twentieth Century in European Memory: Transcultural Mediation and Reception*. Amsterdam: Brill, pp. 268–304.

Pearl, Judea. 2009. Causal inference in Statistics: An Overview. *Statistics Surveys*, 3, 96–146.

Pepinsky, Thomas B. 2019. The Return of the Single Country Case Study. *Annual Review of Political Science*, 22(1), May, 187–203.

Persily, Nathaniel. 2017. The 2016 U.S. Election: Can Democracy Survive the Internet? *Journal of Democracy*, 28(2), 63–76.

Peterson, Erik. 2016. The Rich are Different: The Effect of Wealth Partisanship. *Political Behavior*, 38(1), 33–54.

Petrović, Vladimir. 2015. Power(lessness) of Atrocity Images: Bijeljina Photos between Perpetration and Prosecution of War Crimes in the Former Yugoslavia. *International Journal of Transitional Justice*, 9(3), 367–385.

Pole, Christopher J., and Lampard, Richard. 2002. *Practical Social Investigation: Qualitative and Quantitative Methods in Social Research*. Harlow, UK: Pearson Education.

Porter, Geoff D. 2019. Survey Distorts Political Attitudes of Algeria's Military. *NARCO Analysis*, July. Available at http://northafricarisk.com/analysis/2019-07-23

Pratt, Nicola. 2007. *Democracy & Authoritarianism in the Arab World*. Boulder, CO: Lynne Rienner.

Ragin, Charles C. 2008. What is Qualitative Comparative Analysis? Available at: http://eprints. ncrm.ac.uk/250/1/What_is_QCA.pdf

Ragin, Charles C., and Becker, Howard Saul (eds.). 1992. *What is a Case? Exploring the Foundations of Social Inquiry*. Cambridge, UK: Cambridge University Press.

Research Ethics Framework (REF), updated January 2015. 2015. Economic and Social Research Council. London: Economic and Social Research Council. Available at: https://esrc.ukri.org/ files/funding/guidance-for-applicants/esrc-framework-for-research-ethics-2015

Risse, Thomas, Ropp, Stephen C., and Sikkink, Kathryn (eds.). 1999. *The Power of Human Rights: International Norms and Domestic Change*. Cambridge, UK: Cambridge University Press.

Roselle, Laura, and Spray, Sharon. 2012. *Research and Writing in International Relations*. New York: Pearson.

Rossi, Peter H., Wright, James D., and Anderson, Andy B. (eds.). 2013. *Handbook of Survey Research*. London: Academic Press.

Salter, Mark B. 2013. The Ethnographic Turn: Introduction. In Mark B. Salter and Can E. Mutlu (eds.), *Research Methods in Critical Security Studies*. London: Routledge, pp. 51–58.

Salter, Mark B., and Mutlu, Can E. (eds.). 2013. *Research Methods in Critical Studies*. London: Routledge.

Sarsons, Heather. 2015. Rainfall and Conflict: A Cautionary Tale. *Journal of Development Economics*, 115, 62–72.

Schwartz-Shea, Peregrine. 2015. Judging Quality: Evaluative Criteria and Epistemic Communities. In Dvora Yanow and Peregrine Schwartz-Shea (eds.), *Interpretation and Method: Empirical Research Methods and the Interpretive Turn*. New York: Routledge.

Schwartz-Shea, Peregrine, and Yanow, Dvora. 2013. *Interpretive Research: Concepts and Processes*. London: Routledge.

Scott, Greg, and Garner, Roberta. 2013. *Doing Qualitative Research: Design, Methods, and Techniques*. Boston, MA: Pearson.

Seale, Clive. 2011. *Researching Society and Culture*. London: Sage.

Shapiro, Ian, and Smith, Rogers M. 2004. *Problems and Methods in the Study of Politics*. Cambridge, UK: Cambridge University Press.

Shim, David. 2013. *Visual Politics & North Korea: Seeing is Believing*. New York: Routledge.

Shively, W. Phillips. 2013. *The Craft of Political Science Research*, 9th edition. New York: Pearson.

Shuster, Evelyne. 1997. Fifty Years Later: The Significance of the Nuremberg Code. *The New England Journal of Medicine*, 337(20), 1436–1440.

Sides, John, Tesler, Michael, and Vavreck, Lynn. 2017. The 2016 U.S. Election: How Trump Lost and Won. *The Journal of Democracy*, 28(2), 34–44.

Sims, Christopher. 2015. *The Human Terrain System: Operationally Relevant Social Science Research in Iraq and Afghanistan*. Carlisle, PA: US Army War College Press.

Skocpol, Theda. 1979. *States and Social Revolutions: A Comparative Analysis of France, Russia and China*. Cambridge, UK: Cambridge University Press.

Small, Mario Luis. 2011. How to Conduct a Mixed Methods Study: Recent Trends in a Rapidly Growing Literature. *Annual Review of Sociology*, 37, 57–86.

Smith, Linda Tuhiwai. 2012. *Decolonizing Methodologies: Research and Indigenous Peoples*, 2nd edition. London: Zed Books.

Smith, Steve. 2002. The United States and the Discipline of International Relations: 'Hegemoni Country, Hegemonic Discipline'. *International Studies Review*, 4(2), 67–85.

Sriram, Chandra Lekha, King, John C., Mertus, Julia A., Martin-Ortega, Olga, and Herman, Johanna (eds.). 2009. *Surviving Field Research: Working in Violent and Difficult Situations*. London: Routledge.

Stebbins, Robert A. 2001. *Exploratory Research in the Social Sciences*. London: Sage.

Stewart, Heather, and Mason, Rowena. 2016. Nigel Farage's Anti-migrant Poster Reported to Police. *The Guardian*, June 16.

Subotic, Jelena. 2013. Stories States Tell: Identity, Narrative and Human Rights in the Balkans. *Slavic Review*, 72(2), 306–326.

Tavris, Carol A. 2014. Teaching Contentious Classics. *The Observer*, September 30. Available at: www.psychologicalscience.org/observer/teaching-contentious-classics

Tickner, J. Ann. 2005. What is Your Research Program? Some Feminist Answers to International Relations Methodological Questions. *International Studies Quarterly*, 49(1), 1–22.

Tilly, Charles. 1984. *Big Structures, Large Processes, Huge Comparisons*. New York: Russell Sage Foundation.

Tilly, Charles. 2001. Mechanisms in Political Processes. *Annual Review of Political Science*, 4, 21–41.

UNDP (United Nations Development Program). *Human Development Index*. Available at: http://hdr.undp.org/en/content/human-development-index-hdi

Van Evera, Stephen. 1997. *Guide to Methods for Students of Political Science*. Ithaca, NY: Cornell University Press.

Varieties of Democracy. 2019. Democracy Facing Global Challenges. Available at: www.v-dem.net

Vaus, David de. 2001. *Research Design in Social Research*. London: Sage.

Wall Street Journal. 2002. Investigating Ms. Goodwin. Available at: www.wsj.com/articles/SB1018483437272436400

Walt, Stephen M. 1999. Rigor or Rigor Mortis? Rational Choice and Security Studies. *International Security*, 23(4), 5–48.

Walt, Stephen M. 2005. The Relationship between Theory and Policy in International Relations. *Annual Review of Political Science*, 8, 23–48.

Walt, Stephen M. 2011. How to Do Social Science. *Foreign Policy*, September 29. Available at: www.foreignpolicy.com/posts/2011/09/28/how_to_do_social_science

Walter, Barbara F. 2002. *Committing to Peace: The Successful Settlement of Civil Wars*. Princeton, NJ: Princeton University Press.

Waltz, Kenneth N. 1979. *Theory of International Politics*. New York: McGraw-Hill.

Weldes, Jutta. 1996. Constructing National Interests. *European Journal of International Relations* 2(3), 275–318.

Weldon, S. L. 2019. Power, Exclusion and Empowerment: Feminist Innovation in Political Science. *Women's Studies International Forum*, 72, 127–136.

Wesley, Michael. 2008. The State of the Art on the Art of State Building. *Global Governance*, 14(3), 369–385.

Williams, John H. P., and Zeager, Lester A. 2004. Macedonian Border Closings in the Kosovo Refugee Crisis: A Game-Theoretic Perspective. *Conflict Management and Peace Science*, 21(4), 233–254.

Willis, Derek. 2014. Professors' Research Project Stirs Political Outrage in Montana. *The New York Times*, October 28.

Wood, M. 2014. Bridging the Relevance Gap in Political Science. *Politics*, 34(3), 275–286.

Yanow, Dvora, and Schwartz-Shea, Peregrine. 2015. Introduction. In Dvora Yanow and Peregrine Schwartz-Shea (eds.), *Interpretation and Method: Empirical Research Methods and the Interpretive Turn*. New York: Routledge.

Yashar, Deborah. 1997. *Demanding Democracy: Reform and Reaction in Costa Rica and Guatemala, 1870s–1950s*. Stanford, CA: Stanford University Press.

Yin, Robert K. 2017. *Case Study Research and Applications: Design and Methods*. Thousand Oaks, CA: Sage.

# INDEX

Figures and Tables are indicated by page numbers in bold print. The letter "*b*" after a page number refers to bibliographical information in a Suggested Further Reading section.

Made in the USA
Middletown, DE
26 January 2024

48501875R00139